Routledge Revivals

I0130581

Homes Fit For Heroes

Homes Fit for Heroes looks at the pledge made 100 years ago by the Lloyd George government to build half a million 'homes fit for heroes' – the pledge which made council housing a major part of the housing system in the UK. Originally published in 1981, the book is the only full-scale study of the provision and design of state housing in the period following the 1918 Armistice and remains the standard work on the subject. It looks at the municipal garden suburbs of the 1920s, which were completely different from traditional working-class housing, inside and out. Instead of being packed onto the ground in long terraces, the houses were set in spacious gardens surrounded by trees and open spaces and often they contained luxuries, like upstairs bathrooms, unheard-of in the working-class houses of the past. The book shows that, in the turbulent period following the First World War, the British government launched the housing campaign as a way of persuading the troops and the people that their aspirations would be met under the existing system, without any need for revolution. The design of the houses, based on the famous Tudor Walters Report of 1918, was a central element in this strategy: the large and comfortable houses provided by the state were intended as visible evidence of the arrival of a 'new era for the working classes of this country'.

Homes Fit For Heroes

The Politics and Architecture of Early State Housing in Britain

Mark Swenarton

Routledge
Taylor & Francis Group

First published in 1981
by Heinemann Educational Books

This edition first published in 2018 by Routledge
2 Park Square, Milton Park, Abingdon, Oxon, OX14 4RN
and by Routledge
711 Third Avenue, New York, NY 10017

Routledge is an imprint of the Taylor & Francis Group, an informa business

© 1981 Mark Swenarton

Publisher's Note
The publisher has gone to great lengths to ensure the quality of this reprint but
points out that some imperfections in the original copies may be apparent.

Disclaimer
The publisher has made every effort to trace copyright holders and welcomes
correspondence from those they have been unable to contact.

A Library of Congress record exists under LCCN: 81154098

ISBN 13: 978-1-138-36022-8 (hbk)
ISBN 13: 978-0-429-42700-8 (ebk)
ISBN 13: 978-1-138-36027-3 (pbk)

Author's Biography, 2018

Mark Swenarton is an architectural historian, critic and educator, with a career spanning four decades. *Homes fit for Heroes* (1981) was the first of the ground-breaking works that he has published on architecture and housing, followed by *Artisans and Architects* (1989), *Architecture and the Welfare State* (2015) and *Cook's Camden* (2017). In 1981 with Adrian Forty he set up the first architectural history masters degree in architectural history in the UK, at the Bartlett (University College London); and in 1989 he co-founded the independent monthly review *Architecture Today*, which he edited until 2005. He was professor and head of the School of Architecture at Oxford Brookes University from 2005 to 2010, when he was appointed the first James Stirling Chair of Architecture at Liverpool University, where he is now Emeritus Professor of Architecture.

HOMES
—fit for—
HEROES

MARK SWENARTON

HOMES FIT
FOR HEROES

The Politics and Architecture
of Early State Housing in Britain

MARK SWENARTON

Heinemann Educational Books

Heinemann Educational Books Ltd

22 Bedford Square, London WC1B 3HH
LONDON EDINBURGH MELBOURNE AUCKLAND
HONG KONG SINGAPORE KUALA LUMPUR NEW DELHI
IBADAN NAIROBI JOHANNESBURG
EXETER (NH) KINGSTON PORT OF SPAIN

British Library Cataloguing in Publication Data

Swenarton, Mark
  Homes fit for heroes.
  1. Housing policy – Great Britain – History
  I. Title
  301.5′4′0941   HD7333.A3
  ISBN 0-435-32994-4

Filmset by Northumberland Press Ltd
Gateshead, Tyne and Wear
Printed in Great Britain by Richard Clay (The Chaucer Press) Ltd
Bungay, Suffolk

Contents

List of Illustrations and Tables

Introduction

At the end of the First World War, the slogan 'homes fit for heroes' was coined to describe the great house-building campaign promised by Lloyd George's coalition government. Half a million houses worthy of the 'heroes' who had won the war was the government's pledge, and to realise it a Housing Act was introduced in 1919 which, for the first time, made local authorities into major suppliers of housing. Today, a little more than sixty years later, the slogan is also the title of this book, the aim of which is to explain how these houses came into being and what they represented in political, ideological and architectural terms. As an introduction, it may be useful to give a brief explanation of how I became interested in the subject and how the book evolved.

The cottage estates built by local authorities in the 1920s form a distinctive element in the British townscape and an important part of our housing stock. Two-storey cottages, built in groups of four or six, with medium or low-pitched roofs and little exterior decoration, set amongst gardens, trees, privet hedges and grass verges, and often laid out in cul-de-sacs or around greens: estates such as these are to be seen in every town and rural district in Britain and they have such a distinct character that it is hard to mistake them for anything else (see Figure 1). In all, local authorities in England and Wales built about three-quarters of a million houses of this kind between the two world wars, which means that even today they provide the home of nearly one family in twenty. How did they come to be built?

This was the question with which I began five years ago. On the facts and figures of housing policy after the First World War there was a good deal of information, although most of it was based on published sources and therefore did not get to the hidden factors and secret deliberations that lay behind the public statements. But on the architecture of these houses there was virtually nothing written at all. This was remarkable, since further investigation revealed that the physical form of these 'homes fit for heroes' was, in fact, extremely interesting. The manner in which they were laid out represented a marked departure from ordinary working-class housing of the time. There was a similar contrast in relation to the internal arrangement

Figure 1   A high quality council estate of the 1920s: Camberwell Borough Council's Casino estate, London

of the house, for the houses built by the state provided not just the basic necessities, but also included luxuries that previously had been found only in the houses of the well-to-do.

In the books that dealt with the history of housing, however, none of this received more than a passing mention. Of the many historians who have looked at public housing, hardly any have given serious attention to the physical form of the houses, or regarded this as a matter that they are required to explain or take into account. This seemed to me to be a serious omission, not just because the form of the houses was of interest to me personally but because most of the people who wrote about housing policy at the time treated design as one of the most important aspects of the housing question. As the slogan 'homes *fit* for heroes' itself suggested, housing quality was seen by the government as being at least as important a part of its new policy as mere numbers. It seemed to me, therefore, that a satisfactory account of the 'homes fit for heroes' campaign would have to explain the change it entailed in the design, as well as the provision, of public housing. This is what I have attempted to do in this book.

In a sense, the way in which the housing of this period has been treated by historians is a particular instance of a general division, both of labour and of subject-matter, that seems to arise over design. Historians and sociologists deal with politics and society but leave out design; art or design historians look at design and ignore everything else – or at best relegate it to what is called 'the social background' which, by its name, implies that design and society are not involved in a single process but are separate and distinct. In this book a very different view is taken. Design is treated not as a question divorced from politics and housing policy but – as it was seen by the government at the time – as a central part of politics and policy. In particular, it is shown that the government looked to design to carry out the ideological function that lay at the heart of the 'homes fit for heroes' campaign. While dealing with a particular period of history, therefore, the book is also intended to contribute to our understanding of design in general and especially of its relationship to ideology and the state.

The contents of the book fall into three parts. The first part (Chapters 1 to 3) covers the pre-history of 'homes fit for heroes': the first chapter deals with the innovations in housing design pioneered by the garden city movement before the First World War; Chapter 2 looks at the development of housing policy and the design of public housing in the same period; and Chapter 3 examines the adoption by the government of the garden city model for wartime housing requirements. The second part (Chapters 4 and 5) looks at the development of the thinking in Whitehall and Westminster that led to the housing campaign, and reveals the political considerations to which deliberations on both policy and design (including the famous Tudor Walters Report) were subject. The last part (Chapters 6 to 8) deals with the housing campaign itself and shows what happened when the government had to translate the promise of 'homes fit for heroes' into reality. Chapter 6 follows the Cabinet decisions that determined the course, and eventually brought about the premature termination, of the campaign. Chapter 7 deals with the administration of the campaign and examines the instructions on design issued to local authorities by Whitehall, while Chapter 8 shows how all these factors worked out on the ground, in the houses built by two municipalities (York and the London County Council). Finally, the Conclusion draws together the strands of the argument and suggests some of its more general implications.

This book is based on a doctoral thesis submitted to the University of London. In this connection I would like to record my debt to my supervisors, Reyner Banham and Peter Cowan, as well as to my examiner, F. M. L. Thompson. I have also been fortunate in the advice and criticism received from friends and colleagues, especially Peter Clarke, Ed Cooney, Peter Dickens, the late Ruth Issacharoff, Ellen Leopold, Stephen Merrett, Stefan Muthesius, Robert Thorne and Bridget Wilkins. I must record a special debt to Simon Pepper: the material presented in Chapter 3 was jointly researched and the account draws heavily on conclusions jointly arrived at. Above all I am obliged to Adrian Forty for intellectual encouragement and painstaking criticism and to Christopher Renshaw for personal support throughout the period involved in researching and writing this book. Now that it has finally appeared, needless to say, I alone must bear responsibility for the ideas and arguments that it contains. I should also like to record my gratitude to my typist, Gitta Lunt, and to the staff of the various archives and libraries who gave their assistance in tracking down the material on which this study is based: the Public Record Office, the Greater London Council Record Office, York City Archives, the Rowntree archive at the University of York, the House of Lords Record Office, the British Library, the British Architectural Library, and the libraries of the Department of the Environment, the Town and Country Planning Association, the Royal Town Planning Institute, the TUC, Middlesex Polytechnic, the University of London and University College London.

My thanks are also due to the following for permission to reproduce photographs: the British Architectural Library, the GLC Photograph Library, York City Archives and the Guildhall Library.

1 The Legacy of the Garden City Movement

At the end of the First World War the government promised to build half a million houses of a kind completely different from that to which the majority of the population was accustomed. In making this pledge the government took its model from the garden city movement which, in the years before 1914, had developed a format for residential development and design that was strikingly unlike that found in existing towns. This chapter looks at this transformation in house and environment provided by the garden city movement, and deals both with the considerations that lay behind it and with the innovations in residential design that followed. In relation to the latter it focuses in particular on the writings and designs of Raymond Unwin, for Unwin was not only the leading architect of the garden city movement before the war (involved with Letchworth Garden City, Hampstead Garden Suburb and numerous other schemes) but after 1914 became the central figure in the design of state housing.

The Garden City Movement

The garden city movement was not, as the term might seem to imply, a homogeneous group with a single ideology, but was rather a heterogeneous collection of different groups and interests, linked only by a common commitment to bringing about a transformation in what was referred to as 'the housing and surroundings of the people'. At least three distinct strands can be detected within the movement. In chronological sequence, these were: the model villages built by the industrialists Lever and Cadbury; the garden city itself, expounded in theory by Ebenezer Howard in 1898 and founded at Letchworth in 1903; and the garden suburbs, the most famous being Hampstead Garden Suburb, started in 1906.

Since the early days of the Industrial Revolution, factory owners had known that their power over their workforce could be greatly increased if they controlled, not just the jobs, but also the houses of their employees. For instance, in building his factory-village at Copley, outside Halifax, Colonel Akroyd's motive was primarily to make his mills 'secure against the sudden withdrawal of work-people'.[1] Towards the end of the nineteenth century a small group of industrialists developed a rather different approach that was to lead them to build model villages of a more ambitious nature. The underlying idea was that, by making a dramatic improvement in the housing conditions of his employees, the employer could make them more contented and therefore more productive. In 1887 Lever Brothers moved their soap factory from Warrington to an open site on the Mersey and, in the following year, started construction of a factory-village of a most spectacular kind. This, they insisted, was not out of philanthropic motives but purely from self-interest: the annual outlay on the village made from the profits of the firm was outweighed by the high productivity and good industrial relations it created. Some years later, in 1895, the Cadbury brothers decided to establish a similar model village adjacent to their cocoa factory at Bournville, near Birmingham. As a Quaker family, the Cadbury's were a good deal more explicitly humanitarian than the Levers, but their venture in village building was informed by a comparable business sense. As Edward Cadbury stated in 1914, 'we have always believed that business efficiency and the welfare of employees are but different sides of the same problem'.[2] It was this belief that, applied to housing and the physical environment, provided at Port Sunlight and Bournville the beginning of the garden city movement.

The relationship between housing and production was most conspicuous in the factory-villages but it was also implicit in the other two strands of the garden city movement, the garden city and the garden suburbs. Both in Howard's writings and in practice at Letchworth, the one element that was taken over unchanged from the orthodox town to the garden city was the factory. The garden suburbs were, by definition, intended to be solely residential; by excluding employment and production, they necessarily left the basic economic activities unchanged. Common to all three strands of the movement was the belief that life could be improved in a significant way by a transformation that left the place of work untouched. It was the political ambiguity of this belief that won for the garden city movement the simultaneous adherence of both socialists and capitalists. For socialists such as Raymond Unwin, the garden city movement was the way to make an unparalleled improvement in the lives of the people; for capitalists such as Lever, it offered a way of making the workforce more contented (and thereby more productive) without affecting the basic relationships of capitalist production. It was this latter aspect that, at the end of the First World War, was to make the doctrines of the garden city movement so attractive to the state: for these doctrines implied that, by improving conditions of housing and the physical environment, it was possible to make the people contented with a status quo that was, in other respects, unchanged.

What defined the garden city movement in its own eyes, however, were not political considerations of this sort but the physical changes that resulted: the rejection of the built form of contemporary towns and the search for an alternative based on the village and the countryside (see Figures 2 and 3). At Hampstead Garden Suburb, for instance, it was said that they 'were getting back something of the old English village life'.[3] At Port Sunlight the escape from the contemporary city took a predominantly visual form: 'a singularly vivid impression of rusticity was created', it was noted; 'nothing seems to have been neglected which may produce in the town-dweller the illusion that he has indeed gone back to the land'.[4] At Port Sunlight Lever drew on the traditions of the estate village of the country landowner and produced a spectacular re-creation of an old English village, complete with the picturesque trappings of half-timbered elevations, village green and old English inn. When the

Figure 2   Typical housing built at the turn of the century: speculative builders' terraced cottages in Tottenham, London

Figure 3   Hampstead Garden Suburb: a cul-de-sac in the early part of the suburb, built by Hampstead Tenants (1908)

tenants failed to maintain their front gardens and cottage creepers in conformity with the image desired, responsibility for their maintenance was taken over by the estate office. At Bournville it was the more serious moral aspect of the rural or quasi-rural life that inspired the founder. George Cadbury wrote:

> I know the Birmingham housing question by visiting men in their houses in the city, and I have had the great privilege of reforming many hundreds of drunkards there. The question that came to me was, 'What have you to offer the working-man in the evening except the public house?', and this was the answer I arrived at: 'The most legitimate occupation is for them to come back to the land'. . . .
>
> I can see no other way of saving England, for if a man works in the factory by day and sits in the public houses by night, what can you expect but a poor emaciated creature without physical or moral strength?[5]

Accordingly at Bournville each cottage was supplied with a garden of an average size of one-eighth of an acre: 'nearly every householder spends his leisure in gardening', it was stated, 'and there is not a single licensed-house in the village'.[6]

Bournville also differed from Port Sunlight in the relationship between village and factory. Whereas the buildings at Port Sunlight were directly owned by the firm, the Bournville village was managed by an independent trust and tenancy was not confined to Cadbury employees. Cadbury believed that model houses with substantial gardens would prove profitable in their own right and that – once the initial capital had been provided by a benefactor – the model village could expand on the basis of ploughed-back profits, in the manner of an ordinary business. Accordingly, Cadbury provided the initial capital in the trust deed of 1900 and required that the houses be let at rentals calculated to give a 4 per cent return, so that the accumulated profits could eventually be used to establish further villages. The same idea was written into a similar scheme founded by another cocoa manufacturer, Joseph Rowntree, in 1901. This was the New Earswick village, near York, which in concept was modelled directly on Bournville, although in terms of house design (as will be seen below) it was considerably more innovatory.

The concepts of an economic return and indefinite expansion inherent in the trust deeds of the Cadbury and Rowntree schemes were also implicit in Ebenezer Howard's idea of the garden city. Here, however, capital growth was to take place on the increase in land values brought about by city development, rather than on the accumulation of profits from house rents. Howard's proposals had the elegance of simplicity. To start with, a public company paying a limited dividend would be formed and would buy a suitable site consisting of agricultural land, part of which it would develop and let out in plots to companies and individuals for industries and housing. While the agents of the building of the new town would thus be ordinary firms operating in the normal manner, the increase in land value brought about by the development would, thanks to the leasehold system, remain in the hands of the company, to be put to public use. As the first chairman of the Garden City Company said, 'the automatic rise in the value of the land which will take place as soon as you attract people to your city ... is the real basis of the thing'.[7] The increment in value would be enjoyed by the community in the form of public amenities (parks, open spaces, public buildings) and in relief of local rates. At the same time the company would retain control of development, ensuring among other things the preservation of an 'agricultural belt' surrounding the entire city. When the garden city reached its population target (Howard suggested 32 000), development would continue not by encroaching on the agricultural belt but by establishing 'another city some little distance beyond its own zone of country'.[8] In this way all the advantages of town and country would be combined without the disadvantages of either. More garden cities would be founded as their unique advantages were recognised and existing cities, faced with the exodus of their inhabitants, would be compelled to remould themselves in the new pattern in order to avoid depopulation.

Howard thus envisaged a gradual revolution effected through the agency of the garden city. Capitalism would survive, but shorn of its defects by the social and environmental transformation of what he called 'Town-Country'. Compared with this grand ideal the progress of the First Garden City founded at Letchworth in 1903 was less than impressive for, despite the interest aroused by Howard's book, the practical problems of building a new town in the agricultural wastes of Hertfordshire were enormous. It was hard to persuade firms that there was any commercial gain in moving to a site with neither raw materials, energy supplies nor local market. Above all, there was the difficulty of raising capital. By 1914 the town supported a population of 9000 but, according to C. B. Purdom, it was the First World War that brought prosperity and 'real stability'.[9]

The garden city took the idea of the transformed environment to its fullest extent by attaching it to an entirely new town; and for this reason, the problems it faced were enormous. In contrast the third strand in the garden city movement applied the environmental improvements of Letchworth or Bournville – low-density housing, quasi-rural surroundings, better housing standards – to the ordinary processes of suburban growth. For this it was not necessary to attract industry; the inhabitants would continue to work in the city but at the end of the day would travel out to the 'garden suburb'. The first and largest venture of this sort was Hampstead Garden Suburb, founded in 1906 by Henrietta Barnett on a site overlooking the Hampstead Heath Extension, in the preservation of which she herself had played a leading part. Mrs Barnett was interested not just in preserving rural beauty but also in improving society. She aimed both to provide a new home for the slum dwellers from the East End (where, at Toynbee Hall, she and her husband had been working for twenty years) and to reverse what she regarded as the potentially explosive trend towards the geographical separation of classes. Modelled on the English village of the past, Hampstead Garden Suburb was intended to be a socially mixed and harmonious community.

Like the Garden City Company at Letchworth, the Hampstead Garden Suburb Trust did not build houses itself, but only developed the site and leased plots for building. There was little difficulty in attracting would-be occupants from the upper end of the market, but house-building for lower income groups was much more problematic, since it was difficult to raise the capital for an enterprise that was never likely to be very profitable. Under the Industrial and Provident Societies Act of 1893, a housing company could register as a public utility society if it undertook to limit its annual dividend to a maximum of 5 per cent. This enabled it to borrow up to one-half (increased in 1909 to two-thirds) of its initial capital from the Public Works Loan Board, but the remainder still had to be found. To meet this difficulty, both the Garden City Company and the Hampstead Garden Suburb Trust turned to a new sort of house-building agency – the co-partnership society – that sought to raise at least part of its capital from the tenants themselves. The idea of co-partnership housing had been successfully adopted for the first time at Henry Vivian's scheme at Ealing, started in 1901, and it was to these societies that both Letchworth and Hampstead looked for the erection of low-cost housing. Co-partnership groups were also responsible for many of the much smaller schemes 'on garden city lines' inspired by the example of Hampstead Garden Suburb.[10] In view of the garden city movement's reliance on these societies for low-cost housing, it is important to note that the cost of this form of ownership was, nonetheless, beyond the means of the majority of the population. In the pioneer scheme at Ealing, each prospective tenant had to buy shares to the value of £50 – a sum equivalent to the entire annual earnings of an unskilled labourer.[11] In fact, the societies stated quite openly that they were not attempting to cater for ordinary labourers. As one contemporary observed, co-partnership housing was only 'successful in helping those in a position to help themselves' – a verdict that was equally applicable to the garden city movement as a whole.[12]

Layout

The various strands comprising the garden city movement shared in common one central belief: a rejection of the city as it then existed and a search for some kind of better alternative based on the countryside and the village. Howard sought to destroy contemporary urbanism through the union of town and country in the garden city; Cadbury and Rowntree and the co-partnership societies sought the creation of model village communities. While patrons of the movement agreed on the desirability of providing quasi-rural surroundings for industrial workers, it is not clear how far this conviction was shared by the beneficiaries of this concern. A survey carried out by the magazine *The Garden City* in 1909 to establish whether the town worker really liked living in the country revealed a decidedly lukewarm attitude. Lever, with characteristic bluntness, stated that the average working man 'finds the solitude of the country irksome, except as an occasional break, or for a holiday', and would accept quasi-rural conditions only if they could be obtained near a town. As for the rural solitude of Letchworth, one of the first firms to be established in the new city, the Garden City Press, reported somewhat dolefully: 'We think that slowly the working class population are beginning to get more contented with their surroundings here, as one hears less grumbling about the lack of town pleasures than say twelve months ago.'[13]

The architects took a much more enthusiastic view of the joys of country and village life. To architects such as Unwin, reared on the teachings of Ruskin and Morris, the industrial town was the product of the greed of capitalists who, in their search for profit, had destroyed the village communities of pre-industrial Britain. 'Our towns and suburbs express by their ugliness the passion for gain which so largely dominates their creation',[14] wrote Unwin. The architect should, he insisted, reject the legacy of contemporary towns, formed by the speculative builder's pursuit of profit, and instead seek to meet the needs of the people who were to inhabit his buildings. In this he should take the old English village for his inspiration.

In the eyes of Unwin and the garden city movement the physical character of contemporary towns derived from the combination of the greed of the speculative builder and the building controls operated by the bylaw system. From the middle of the nineteenth century, bylaws had been adopted on an individual basis by many of the large municipalities (Liverpool, Bradford, Sheffield, etc.), and in 1875 the Public Health Act gave the power to adopt bylaws to local authorities in general. The aim was to check the worst features of contemporary building (particularly the dense packing of dwellings around small courts) by regulating not only standards of construction, but also the width of streets and the provision of open spaces. Under the bylaws commonly in force in the early 1900s, every street over 100 feet in length had to be at least 36 feet wide, with a carriageway 24 feet wide, two footways, channels and kerbs.[15] Similar minima governed the provision of space between the backs of buildings. While these regulations prevented the gross overcrowding of houses that Engels had described in Manchester in the 1840s, they also created a form of development which, by the

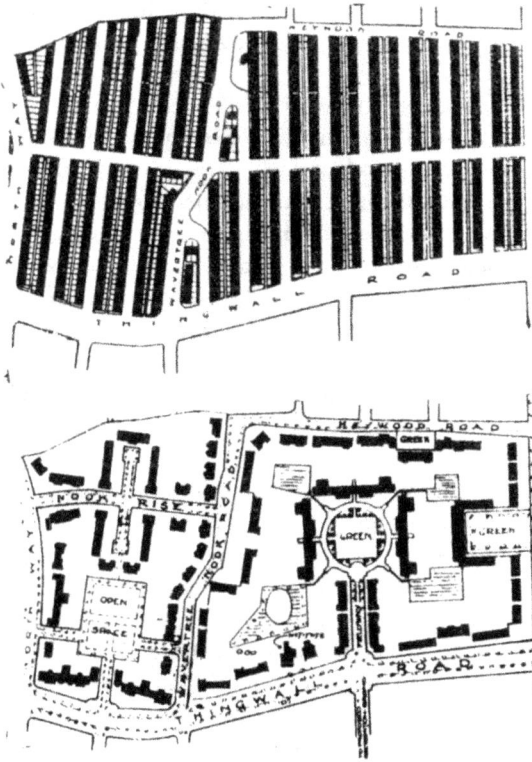

Figure 4 Conventional versus garden city layout: a 20-acre site in Liverpool, (above) as it might have been, laid out to meet bylaw requirements, at 41 houses per acre; (below) as it was, laid out as a garden suburb at 11 houses per acre

early twentieth century, seemed to housing reformers only marginally less objectionable (see Figure 4). Houses were built in long terraces, separated from one another at the front by a street of the prescribed width and, at the rear, by backyards and rear-access alleys. Given the restrictions imposed by the bylaws, parallel rows of houses gave the highest densities. The number of houses per acre was limited by the width of frontage allowed to each house in the terrace: under the Liverpool bylaws in force in 1912, for example, a frontage of 18 feet meant a density of 31 houses to the acre, but by decreasing the frontage to 15 feet, the density could be increased to 41. Roads followed a grid pattern corresponding to the parallel lines of the terraces. The result was, as the garden city advocates complained, that most of the ground was covered with buildings and tarmacadam with only the smallest of gardens provided between the front of the house and the street.

The basic difference between garden city layouts and those of standard speculative housing was density. In place of the high densities and 'pocket-handkerchief' gardens of speculative development, the garden city movement adopted low densities and large gardens. At New Earswick the overall density was eight to the acre and the average garden was 350 square yards, 'a size determined upon after careful consideration of the amount a man can easily and profitably work by spade cultivation in his leisure time'.[16] In general eight houses to the acre in rural areas and twelve to the acre in urban areas was recommended by Unwin and his partner Barry Parker, and it was this yardstick that was followed by most developments 'on garden city lines'.

The economic rationale for low-density development was set out by Unwin in a famous pamphlet published in 1912, entitled *Nothing Gained by Overcrowding!* Unwin attempted to show that, although it cost rather more, low-density layout offered much better value for money than the conventional layout of the speculative builder. The argument turned on the relationship between the cost of land and the cost of road construction and development: high-density layout economised on land but was costly in terms of the amount of road frontage wasted at intersections (see Figure 4); conversely, low-density layout was costly in terms of land but did not waste so much road frontage in this way. In urban areas, high land costs obviously dictated high density; but in suburban areas, where land was relatively cheap, Unwin claimed that the householder would get much better value from low-density layout. In a typical suburban site, he stated, a density of thirty-four houses to the acre would give each house a plot of 83 square yards for a ground rent of 8d per week: but a density of fifteen houses to the acre would increase plot size by more than 200 per cent (to 261 square yards) but would increase the ground rent by less than 50 per cent, to 11¾d. 'Suppose there were two village shops, and one offered to supply 83 common marbles for 8d, and the other offered 261 marbles ... for 11¾d, can it be supposed that there would be any village boy who would not know which shop to patronise?'[17] This was, of course, to assume not just that marbles and garden size were analogous commodities but also that the householder was able to pay the 50 per cent increase in ground rent. This was perhaps not a matter of general concern so long as garden suburbs were confined to various forms of private enterprise. Once the possibility arose of garden suburbs being built by the state, however, the question of cost became of considerable political importance.

In Unwin's presentation the economic viability of garden city development rested on the reduction of road costs made possible by the reduction of density. A wasted piece of frontage, an unnecessary intersection or an excessive width to the carriageway, and the low-density scheme would lose the saving in road costs by which it sought to compensate for the additional cost in land. The first requirement, therefore, was freedom from bylaw regulations. Unwin conceded that bylaws had performed a useful function in checking the worst evils of overcrowding and jerry-building, but their rigid insistence on minimum widths and types of roadway made impossible a type of development that relied on economising on road construction. Both New Earswick and Letchworth were in rural areas free from bylaw restrictions, but Hampstead Garden Suburb was subject to the bylaws of Hendon UDC. To circumvent these a local Act of Parliament was secured in 1906 which, in return for certain undertakings by the Trust (including an overall maximum density of eight houses to the acre), the Suburb was exempted from bylaw regulations on the width and construction of roads. This enabled Unwin in planning the layout to match the width and construction of the roads to the amount of traffic that they would carry; as he stated, in some places 'a well-made track, with a grass margin on each side, and in some cases a simple gravel or paved footway of narrow width for use in wet weather, is all that need be demanded'.[18] In 1914 a committee, of which Unwin was a member, was appointed to review the bylaw question; and following its report in 1918, exemption from bylaw requirements (which had been enjoyed by government housing schemes built during the war) was extended to schemes built by local authorities under the Housing Act of 1919.[19]

Economy in low-density development depended on more than just exemption from bylaws: the adoption of specific layout techniques was also required. As the Tudor Walters Report put it in 1918, 'Economy in development is only secured when areas are specially planned to suit the particular number of houses to the acre'.[20] Well before 1914, the main elements of the planning expertise required for successful low-density layout had been demonstrated by Unwin, both on the ground, at Hampstead Garden Suburb and elsewhere, and in print, primarily in his book *Town Planning in Practice* (1909). The basic technique involved the creation of large blocks of land with the houses built around the perimeter. The backland, instead of being taken up by the unsightly backyards and rear-access alleys of speculative housing, was filled with individual gardens and, in some cases, communal facilities such as tennis-courts or bowling-greens. Unwin emphasised that it was important to locate these within the block rather than adjacent to the road, where they would occupy expensive frontage. Rear access to the houses (required primarily for the delivery of coal and collection of refuse) was provided without resort to back alleys. The houses were built, not in long terraces, but in short groups of four or six units. For end houses rear access posed no problem; for middle houses, access to the rear was via a 'tunnel', 'an open archway through the ground floor storey ... giving access by a joint path to two gardens behind'.[21] This, Unwin claimed, was not only visually preferable to a backroad but was also cheaper.

Where the backland was sufficiently extensive it could be opened up by means of a technique that was to become all too common in the inter-war period: the cul-de-sac. This type of road, built to a reduced specification, provided extensive frontage in relation to the cost of its construction and, since it did not connect with another road at its far end, economised on frontage that would otherwise have been lost by intersection (see Figure 20). Cul-de-sacs of various shapes and forms were used extensively by Unwin at Hampstead Garden Suburb (see Figure 3). Another related idea also used at Hampstead was the location adjacent to the road of a green with houses built along three sides; this again created an extensive frontage for building at a relatively small cost in road development.

In his discussion of roads Unwin was as much concerned with visual effect as with economy. The job of the architect was, he stated, to create beautiful surroundings, and the overall effect deriving from the placing of buildings was always to be borne in mind.[22] His writings show a constant concern for what he called the 'street picture' (see Figure 5). In a straight road, he said, definition in the centre of the street picture should be supplied by a building placed at right angles to the road. On a curving road, similarly, visual emphasis should be supplied in some way, such as by the use of a set-back or some other definite feature (see Figure 22).

On the aesthetics of town planning there were at the time, as Unwin noted, two opposing schools of thought. On the one hand there was the picturesque approach which corresponded with the romantic aspirations of many of the people who actually went to live on garden city schemes. Protagonists of this approach looked to the works of Camillo Sitte, in which town planning was treated in

Figure 5   Creating the street picture: drawing from Unwin's Town Planning in Practice, *showing on the right the 'uninteresting vanishing perspective' of conventional terrace housing, and, on the left, the more interesting picture created by breaks in the building line*

terms of the creation of a succession of enclosed spaces and changing street pictures.[23] Unwin stated in 1909 that the importance of creating a sense of enclosure was something he learned directly from Sitte, although this was only after the plan of Letchworth (which he considered defective in this respect) had been prepared. The influence of Sitte was also to be seen at the London County Council's Old Oak estate (started in 1911) and even more strikingly at the Well Hall estate described in Chapter 3 (see Figures 12 and 14).

In direct opposition to the picturesque approach was the formal school of urban design associated with the American City Beautiful movement, which revived the Beaux Arts tradition of straight roads, formal approaches and symmetrical layout (see Figure 19). In Britain, the influence of City Beautiful attitudes to town planning was greatly reinforced by the establishment of the Department of Civic Design at Liverpool University in 1909. Financed by Lever, the department was staffed by architects who were, like the Professor of Architecture, C. H. Reilly, sympathetic to formal design. From 1910, through the *Town Planning Review*, members of the Department at Liverpool – led by Stanley Adshead and Patrick Abercrombie – mounted an onslaught on romanticism in architecture and urban design which, as will be seen later, was to have a considerable effect on the design of state housing.

In face of this polemic between the formal and the picturesque, Unwin's advice in *Town Planning in Practice* was clear. Instead of dogmatising about theories and insisting on certain canons of beauty, designers should, he stated, 'keep very closely in touch with actual requirements, and be content if we can give comely form and expression in the most simple and practical manner to the obvious needs of those who are to dwell in the towns or suburbs we plan.'[24] Unwin argued that beauty did not lie exclusively in either the formal or the picturesque, but arose from what he called 'rightness of form'. Instead of imposing preconceived forms on *a priori* grounds, the job of the planner was to find the forms appropriate to the site, to the needs of the inhabitants and to the function of the town. As such, the plan should represent, not the imposition of the will of the planner, but the 'artistic expression for the requirements and tendencies of the town'.[25] Unwin believed that in order to create desirable alternatives to contemporary towns, all inflexible formulae – whether the standard format of the speculative builder or the aesthetic dogma of civic design – had to be replaced by the individual skill of the architect-planner. It was a view that he was to reiterate in the Tudor Walters Report and that was to shape the design of state housing after the First World War.

House Types

It has been seen that the main characteristics of garden city layout resulted from a rejection of the example of the contemporary town: in place of long rows of terraced houses, small groups of four or six houses; in place of high densities and grid-iron layout of roads and houses, densities of eight or twelve to the acre and a flexible approach to planning permitting the matching of layout to site; and so on. What was true of the surroundings applied equally to the house itself. In the internal planning and design of the house it was the search for an alternative to what were regarded as the objectionable practices of the speculative builder that constituted the main direction of garden city architecture.

The type of working-class housing erected by the speculative builder under bylaw regulations had a distinct and easily recognisable character: a 'very objectionable type of house with long projections running out behind' and a narrow frontage was how Unwin described it (see Figure 6).[26] The house was much deeper than it was wide,

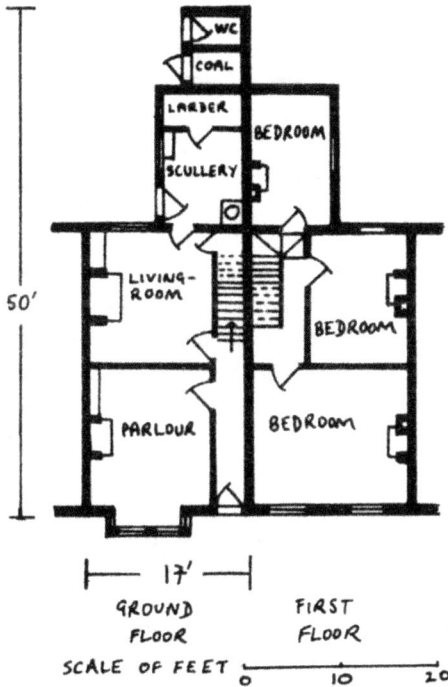

Figure 6 Speculative builders' housing: plans of typical terraced cottages built around the turn of the century. This example comes from York; the houses illustrated in Figure 2, from London, follow an identical arrangement

with the scullery and third bedroom located in a projecting wing at the rear. Internally, the planning showed no variation in accordance with either aspect or outlook; houses on opposite sides of the street had the same internal layout. Typically this consisted, on the ground floor, of a front room (parlour) and back room (living-room) with a projecting scullery and WC at the rear and the entrance lobby and staircase adjacent to the party wall. The first floor contained three bedrooms but there was no bathroom, usually only a tub that could be filled from the water-heater or 'copper' in the scullery. The cooking-range, the main piece of equipment built into the house, was located in the living-room.

At neither Port Sunlight nor Bournville was the reform of the internal layout of the house a major goal. Lever was primarily concerned with the appearance of the houses and Cadbury with the working of the gardens. It was Parker and Unwin who formulated a clear alternative to the house types of the speculative builder, both in practice, with the first houses at New Earswick in 1902–3, and in print with the publication by the Fabian Society of Unwin's pamphlet *Cottage Plans and Common Sense* in 1902. In this Unwin argued for a type of cottage which in its design and planning entirely rejected the legacy of the speculative builder. In place of a standard plan, Unwin insisted that the plan of each cottage should be adapted to suit its aspect: since sunlight was known to be essential for health, he demanded that 'no house be built with a sunless living-room'. The conventional plan followed by speculative builders he entirely condemned, on the ground that its narrow frontage, considerable depth and back projections conspired to obstruct the free entry of sunlight into the house.

> These projections effectually shade the rooms from such sunshine as they might otherwise get, and impede the free access of fresh air.... Every house in a row should contain all its rooms and offices [i.e. WC and coal-store] under the main roof, and present an open and fair surface to sun and air on both its free sides.[27]

What the improved type of house might be in practice was demonstrated by Parker and Unwin in the first cottages at New Earswick (Figure 7). Instead of being deep and narrow, the plan was square, with only a bay window projecting from the main walls. The houses had a north-west aspect and the offices (coal-store, earth-closet and larder) were therefore moved from their traditional place at the back of the house to the front, to leave the south frontage free for living-room and scullery. This meant that a visit to the toilet was open to view from the road – something which not surprisingly was said to have 'provoked a good deal of criticism'[28] at the time. The greater part of the ground floor was given over to a single living-room which extended the full depth of the house; in the case of the end houses, the living-room was lit from three sides and, in the case of the middle houses, from two – an arrangement giving the maximum light and ventilation. This room also served for circulation, with stairs, entrance-porch and scullery opening off it. The wide frontage permitted natural lighting of the staircase and landing (from a window on the north-west side) and also enabled two of the three bedrooms to open onto the south aspect.

The incident over the location of the toilet revealed a somewhat zealous rationalism on the part of Parker and Unwin which was to involve them in a much more prolonged conflict with popular opinion on another issue. This arose from their desire to eliminate

N · W · ELEVATION

LIVING · RM.

SCULLERY

COAL

GROUND · FLOOR · PLAN

BED RM. Nº 1

BED · RM Nº 3

BED · RM · Nº 2

FIRST · FLOOR · PLAN

COTTAGES · BUILT · NEAR · YORK
FOR · MESSRS · ROWNTREE · & · Cº

BARRY · PARKER · &
RAYMOND · UNWIN
ARCHITECTS · BUXTON
& BALDOCK · HERTS.

Figure 7   Cottages at New Earswick designed by Parker and Unwin
(1902–3)

the parlour in favour of a single large living-room. Everyone agreed that where the tenant could not afford it the parlour had to be omitted and only a living-room and scullery be provided; but Parker and Unwin appeared to regard the elimination of the parlour less as an economic necessity than as a desirable goal. On this point Fabian rationalism and medievalising romanticism, combined with hostility to the practices of the speculative builder, led Parker and Unwin into direct conflict with popular taste. In their eyes the parlour had no justification since it was put to only infrequent use. How much better, they believed, to use the space to create one large room for family living, as in the 'old days', rather than to allow the tenants to imitate their social superiors by the proliferation of superfluous reception rooms. Unwin wrote:

When mankind first took to living in houses these consisted of one room; perhaps the most important fact to be remembered in designing cottages is that the cottager still lives during the day-time in one room. . . .
However desirable a parlour may be, it cannot be said to be

necessary to health or family life.... There can be no possible
doubt that until any cottage has been provided with a living-room
large enough to be healthy, comfortable and convenient, it is worse
than folly to take space from that living-room, where it will be
used every day and every hour to form a parlour, where it will
be used only once or twice a week.[29]

The tenants, however, did not agree. The extent to which the
parlour, as a best room reserved for guests and formal occasions,
symbolised the aspirations of the 'respectable working class' was
something that Parker and Unwin found extremely hard to compre-
hend. It was nonetheless something to which they were compelled
to concede. At Letchworth in 1906 a number of cottages were built
by Garden City Tenants to designs by Parker and Unwin; in the
magazine *The Garden City* it was reported that the tenants were
strongly dissatisfied with the 'replacement of the conventional sub-
division of the ground floor' by the non-parlour arrangement.

> The workmen and their wives ... do not take kindly to this
> innovation; they like the parlour and they mean to have it.... It
> is therefore evident that a considerable number of the conventional
> type of cottage will have to be erected.[30]

Accordingly, whatever the reservations of the architects, parlour
houses had to be designed and built. Apart from the conventional
speculative builder's type (which continued to be used at Port Sunlight up to 1914), a number of type-plans for parlour houses were
developed that attempted to eliminate the cramped frontages and
rear projections disliked by housing reformers. One plan widely used
at garden city suburbs was essentially a development of the conventional type, in which the frontage was increased to permit the scullery
and third bedroom to be brought into the main body of the house, and
the staircase to be tucked into the corresponding corner at the front
of the house. This type was used by Unwin both before the war and
at his munitions housing scheme at Gretna. Alternatively, while
keeping the same general arrangement, the bathroom could be
located on the first floor, although this involved considerable expense.
In this form the plan was used at Bournville by Harvey. The
arrangement was endorsed by the Tudor Walters Report in 1918
(Figure 21, Type Plan C) and later, in the 1930s, was to become
the standard plan for speculative builders.

This type-plan involved a wide frontage – some 25 feet in Harvey's
Bournville version. An even wider frontage was involved in the other
main type-plan for parlour houses used by the garden city movement.

This followed the double-fronted arrangement generally reserved by speculative builders for up-market villas. In the form used by the garden city movement, the centrally placed entrance lobby and staircase bisected the house, with the living-room to one side and the parlour and scullery to the other. This type was endorsed by the Tudor Walters Committee in 1918 and adopted by many local authorities thereafter (see Figure 21, Type Plan D).

Before 1914 the advantages of a double frontage had been extended to an even smaller class of house. The architect associated with this was Percy Houfton, whose double-fronted design for a non-parlour house won first prize at two important competitions, the Sheffield Corporation competition of 1903 and the Letchworth Cheap Cot-

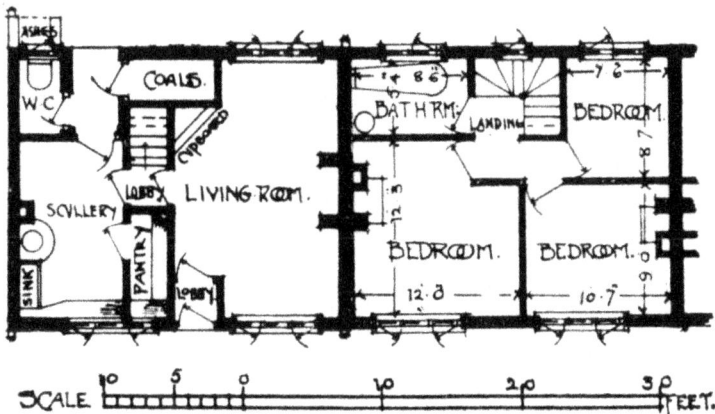

Figure 8   Plans of double-fronted cottages designed by Percy Houfton (1903) and built by Sheffield Corporation at Wincobank

tages Exhibition of 1905 (Figure 8). In its original form, it provided on the ground floor a living-room on one side and scullery and offices on the other, and a bathroom and either two or three bedrooms on the first floor. With its wide frontage, absence of projections, through living-room, natural lighting of the staircase, and upstairs bathroom, it seemed to offer in a house of modest size everything that critics of conventional housing desired.

The Design of Low-Cost Housing
Before the outbreak of the First World War moie than fifty schemes 'on garden city lines' had been started in Britain and some 11 000

houses completed. The contrast, in terms of both environment and house-design, that these schemes offered with the housing generally available elsewhere attracted immediate attention and widespread admiration. Visitors from the continent and the USA flocked to Bournville, Letchworth and Hampstead and set up Garden City Associations in their own countries. At home, reformers and public figures from most shades of the political spectrum were impressed by the garden city example and sought to attach its 'lessons' to their own particular causes. As early as 1907, for instance, the Local Government Board (as will be seen in the next chapter) decided to confer general powers of town planning on local authorities, based on the Hampstead Garden Suburb Act of the previous year. Before 1914, the garden city movement had, it seemed, shown how housing conditions and the physical environment could be totally transformed.

The problem with all this, however, was that whatever its architectural achievements, the type of house and layout developed by the garden city movement was too expensive for the majority of the population. As *The Garden City* journal put it, 'the standard of comfort aimed at is beyond the reach of the labourer'.[31] At Letchworth, for instance, it was recognised that 'for this class the problem of housing remains unsolved';[32] even the special 'cheap cottages' built for the exhibition of 1905 were for the most part taken not by 'what may be properly termed the "labouring classes" but by people of small means'.[33] Later, at the end of the First World War, it was precisely the fact that garden city housing had thitherto been beyond the reach of most working-men that made it so attractive to the government as a political device. Nonetheless, before 1914 the problem of building to a minimum cost was not altogether ignored by garden city architects. In 1906 both Alexander Harvey (the Bournville architect) and Raymond Unwin published their views on the subject. Eschewing as they did most of the picturesque individuality central to the appeal of garden city living, the answers that they provided had relatively little impact on garden city schemes before 1914: but when the state adopted the garden city model after the war, official policy on design was to follow much the same lines as those recommended by Harvey and Unwin in 1906.

Harvey and Unwin agreed that for the erection of the most economical form of cottage there were two absolutely fundamental elements: the simplification of design and the standardisation of building components. In this emphasis they directly foreshadowed the recommendations of the Tudor Walters Report of 1918. Unwin wrote that 'a thoroughly economical plan with great simplicity of design must be adopted'. Harvey noted of his design for a £135 cottage that

> The roof runs uninterruptedly from end to end, by which unnecessary roof complications are avoided ... the eaves run uninterruptedly.... In cottages of this class, compactness and regularity should always be aimed at in planning and the wall lines ... should be as long and unbroken as possible.[34]

Such simplicity, both insisted, was not incompatible with beauty. Beauty, wrote Harvey, consisted not of 'useless and sometimes costly decoration' nor of 'shoddy and meaningless display'; 'the soul of beauty is harmony, which may co-exist with the veriest simplicity'. In such cases Harvey and Unwin agreed that good effect would depend on proportion and arrangement, and in this context Unwin recommended the arrangement of the buildings around a green or square, as in a quadrangle. As Unwin stated, 'where groups of cottages must be kept absolutely simple, good result will depend largely on the arrangements of them'.

The two architects also agreed on the importance of the standardisation of components, such as doors, windows, fire-grates and mantels. Harvey stated that economy would be secured by the architect specifying 'worthy stock articles of building', which could then be ordered on a large scale. Unwin particularly emphasised the importance of securing economies of scale, both by building on a large scale in the first place and by then reaping the benefit by purchasing all materials 'in sufficiently large quantities to get the best terms'. Although neither architect commented on the fact, the large-scale use of standard components was, of course, an economic necessity of low-cost housing with which speculative builders were already familiar.

In elevational treatment both the Harvey and Unwin designs were severely simple with unbroken eaves-lines and with projections from the cube reduced to a minimum. The plan in both cases was a compromise between the ambitions of housing reform and the economic realities of low-cost building. Unwin's plan for the Garden City Tenants retained the square form of his New Earswick design and provided a front living-room with rear scullery and offices, with the staircase lit from a window in the rear wall and three bedrooms above (see Figure 9). Harvey's design followed a similar arrangement although the shape was narrow and deep rather than square. In both cases services were of the most economical kind. Plumbing was kept to a minimum by putting the bath in the scullery where hot water

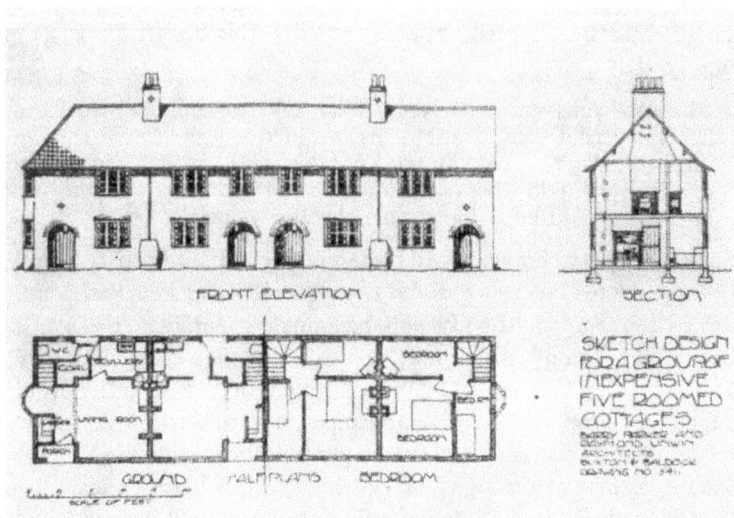

Figure 9   Design for minimum-cost cottages by Parker and Unwin (1906)

could be fed direct from the copper. Outlet flues from the copper, the living-room range and the grates in the two larger bedrooms were grouped together, with a single chimney-stack for each pair of houses.

Thus as early as 1906 architects from the garden city movement formulated definite views on the design and construction of minimum-cost housing. With the emphasis on simplicity of design and standardisation of components, these views implied a very different kind of architecture from the romantic, gable-ridden elevations generally associated with the garden city movement. The significance of this consensus was not immediately apparent, but when a decade later the government adopted the garden city model for its housing programme, it was to have a major effect. In the intervening years, the emphasis on simplification was reinforced and elaborated as an aesthetic doctrine by the Liverpool school of Reilly, Adshead and others. But the basis of the design policy had already been provided: the formulations on low-cost design which in 1906 appeared in *The Garden City* were, little more than a decade later, to reappear as the official doctrines of state housing.

2 Housing and the State before 1914

The 'homes fit for heroes' campaign marked a turning point both in the importance attached to housing as an instrument of social policy and in the scale of housing provision by the state. It was not, however, by any means the beginning of state involvement in the housing question or even of state provision of houses. Subsumed at first under other concepts related to the problems created by urbanisation (notably that of public health), housing had by the late nineteenth century emerged as a subject in its own right to which parliamentary enquiries and legislation were specifically devoted. By 1914 housing had become a recognised political issue from which both of the major parties attempted to extract electoral advantage.

This chapter looks at some of the main developments that took place in housing policy in the years before the First World War and, in particular, examines the state's response to the environmental critique made by the garden city movement. It will be seen that although by 1914 the government had been largely persuaded by the arguments of the garden city lobby, housing initiatives envisaged before the outbreak of war, nonetheless, were very limited in both scale and purpose, when compared with that actually adopted by the government after the Armistice in 1918.

Politics and Legislation

Until the end of the nineteenth century the active involvement of the state in the housing question derived almost entirely from its concern at the part played by the slums in the generation and diffusion of disease and crime. 'Society must do something to protect itself against disease and vice', said the Lord Provost of Edinburgh in 1866, launching an 'improvement scheme' that involved major slum clearance and rehousing.[1] In particular, as Engels noted, once it had been shown that the poor districts of the towns were the source of diseases and epidemics that affected the rich as well as the poor, public opinion was aroused and legislation followed.[2] The supposed remedy for the problem involved the demolition of the insanitary buildings and their replacement by new and salubrious housing, and during the third quarter of the century local authorities were given powers enabling them to undertake these activities. Under the Artisans' and Labourers' Dwellings Act of 1868 (the Torrens Act) local authorities were empowered to deal with insanitary houses on an individual basis by requiring owners to improve their property or else to have it demolished. Subsequently, under the Artisans' and Labourers' Dwellings Improvement Act of 1875 (the Cross Act), local authorities were empowered to clear entire areas but were required, in so doing, to provide new housing in replacement. To meet this requirement most local authorities tried to get outside bodies such as the Peabody Trust to undertake the rebuilding, but in some cases – notably the London County Council's first major slum clearance and rehousing venture, the Boundary Street scheme in Shoreditch – the local authority preferred to build itself.[3]

The clearance of slum areas and the provision of new housing in replacement remained a major concern of local authorities until 1914 and after. Indeed, the years immediately prior to the First World War saw major clearance and rebuilding schemes launched by the London County Council, Liverpool and other municipalities. From the last decade of the nineteenth century, however, there emerged in addition a new type of local authority housing provision, designed not to replace unhealthy houses lost through clearance but to constitute a net addition to the housing stock. The statutory basis for this new kind of activity was the famous Part III of the Housing of the Working Classes Act of 1890. The first two parts of this measure consolidated and amended legislation deriving from the Cross and Torrens Acts; but Part III gave local authorities effective powers for the first time to deal not just with the qualitative aspect of the housing problem (the threat to public health) but with the quantitative aspect – in other words, with the housing shortage. The outcome was the emergence of a significant new area of state housing activity. Between 1890 and 1913 the London County Council, for instance, provided housing for some 25 000 people under Part III of the 1890 Act, slightly more than the 22 000 catered for by the council under Parts I and II of the Act in the same period.

Although in retrospect it seems to mark a new phase in the history of state housing, at the time it was largely by reference to traditional arguments of public health that this innovation was justified. Where the shortage of housing prevented the closure of unhealthy houses, local medical officers of health advised their councils that their duty to protect public health required that steps be taken to relieve the housing shortage. As early as 1891 the Medical Officer of Health for Coventry reported that the housing shortage was preventing action on insanitary dwellings and urged the council to consider building houses itself.[4] In York the local MOH made a similar recommendation in 1913:

> There is no doubt that ... the City has become faced by something of a house famine....
>
> We have Closing Orders upon 373 houses and tenements.... [But] we are having to be very lenient in requiring occupiers to quit houses, because they find great difficulty in obtaining houses fit for human habitation. Yet it is unthinkable that we should not continue the work of improvement or demolition of existing unhealthy dwellings....
>
> It appears evident, therefore, that the municipality will soon have to provide a large number of dwellings.[5]

There were, however, political factors involved. It was the skilled working class that was most directly affected by the cyclical slumps in speculative house-building and it was this class that had the most direct interest in persuading a local authority to act. At both Coventry and Lincoln, for instance, much of the pressure exerted on the council to build came from organised labour, operating through trades councils and *ad hoc* bodies. Likewise in London, in the late 1890s a number of working-men's organisations were set up on a local basis to press for municipal action to relieve the housing shortage. To co-ordinate this campaign the Workmen's Housing Council (later the Workmen's National Housing Council) was established in 1898.[6] In accordance with this, housing policy often followed party–political lines. In Sheffield, for instance, the corporation purchased the 60-acre Wincobank site for Part III building in 1900 but in 1908 the Conservatives took control of the council and proposed to lease the site to speculative builders. It was not until control returned to the Liberals in 1910 that building resumed.[7]

The most spectacular example both of Part III building and of the political considerations to which such building was subject was provided by the London County Council (LCC). In December 1898, following the electoral victory of the Progressives (the London equivalent of the alliance of Liberal and Labour), the LCC agreed to a report from its housing committee recommending the commencement of building operations independent of any rehousing obligation incurred through slum clearance. The strategy was to meet overcrowding in the different sectors of the metropolis by creating large cottage estates in the suburbs that would attract population from the inner areas. In the south a 39-acre site near Tooting (Totterdown Fields) was acquired in 1900, followed by a 30-acre site at Norbury, near Croydon, the following year; in the north-east the White Hart Lane estate of more than 200 acres at Tottenham was purchased in 1901; and eventually in 1906 a fourth estate was purchased in the western sector, the 54-acre Old Oak estate at Hammersmith. But in 1907 the election victory of the Moderate (that is, Conservative) group on the council brought into question the entire policy of house-building on suburban estates. The initial impulse of the Finance Committee, it was reported, was to end all suburban building by leasing the remaining undeveloped 13 acres at Norbury and selling both the remaining 200 acres at White Hart Lane and the entire Old Oak estate. In May 1909, however, the Housing Committee secured the agreement of the council to a somewhat less extreme policy. This still involved the sale of all the remaining portions of Norbury and White Hart Lane but also provided for the immediate development of Old Oak and the remaining 12 acres of Totterdown Fields. But the major part of the council's budget was directed towards slum clearance: for the Conservatives who controlled the LCC regarded ordinary housing as the preserve of private enterprise and believed that local authorities should deal only with those aspects of the housing problem that affected everyone – in other words, the threat to health from the slums. Accordingly, in 1910 the council adopted a major improvement scheme for the Tabard Street area of Southwark, involving the clearance of 18.5 acres of slums and the rehousing of 2580 people on site. At £389 000 the estimate for clearance alone, excluding rebuilding, was greater than the proposed expenditure on the whole of the Old Oak estate.[8]

Local authorities were generally under greatest pressure to build under Part III when the market shortage of housing was at its most acute. Accordingly Part III building in aggregate tended to follow a cyclical pattern related to the building cycle. In the years 1900 to 1905 the Local Government Board (LGB) sanctioned borrowing by urban district councils under Part III for a total of £1.2 million but for the period 1906 to 1912 the figure was little more than half that amount (£670 000).[9] Then as the market surplus left by the building boom of 1898–1904 was taken up, local authorities came under renewed pressure to build, and from 1910 the number and value of loan sanctions showed a marked increase. In 1910 the LGB sanctioned loans for only 78 houses to be built by two local authorities, but over the next four years the number of loan sanctions increased steadily, so that in 1914 loans were sanctioned for 2465 houses to be built by 79 local authorities.[10]

In the towns, some aspects of the housing problem were related to the cyclical pattern of speculative house-building and were susceptible to amelioration by market forces. In the countryside, however, this was not the case, for speculative builders had long since ceased to build for agricultural workers. The problem of rural housing presented in transparent form the economic disparities at the root of the housing question: the wages of the chronically underpaid agricultural labourers were simply far too low to meet the economic rent on a new cottage. Speculative builders thus had no interest in an undertaking that could never be profitable and landowners (who were traditionally responsible for housing farm workers) showed an increasing aversion towards this unremunerative investment. With nobody prepared to meet the growing shortage of rural workers' cottages, pressure was exerted on the state to step in. Under Part III of the 1890 Act rural district councils had powers to build in relief of housing shortage, but by 1905, as observers never failed to point out, only four such councils in the whole country had carried out housing schemes under this provision.[11]

Housing politics at Westminster from the 1890s until the outbreak of the First World War was largely a response to these 'ground roots' issues, with the localities rather than central government providing the impetus for fresh legislation. The two main issues were the rural housing shortage and the escalation in costs faced by local authorities when they attempted to build. The rural problem stood at the fore-front of debate up to 1914, attracting, in the words of a Conservative and Unionist publication of 1913, 'more interest than the evil in the towns'.[12] The major piece of legislation from this period, the Housing and Town Planning Act of 1909, originated, as the President of the LGB, John Burns, stated, in an attempt 'to meet the rural difficulties':[13] a rural housing Bill was introduced by a private member in 1906, to which Burns responded with the appointment of a Select Committee and the drafting of an 'improved' Bill by the LGB. The second major issue, the rise in the cost of building, emerged in the late 1890s as the rate of interest began to rise; the problem was basically a costs/income squeeze, for between 1895 and 1914, while the amount that the tenant could afford (measured by real income) remained stagnant, building costs rose by 20 per cent and the rate of interest, measured by the bank rate, doubled.[14] At first local authorities such as the LCC sought a solution by an im-provement in the terms under which they could borrow money from the Public Works Loans Board (PWLB), but by about 1906 there were many – including the Select Committee appointed in that year

– who felt that the difficulty could be met only by a direct Treasury subsidy. Thus the Select Committee of 1906 called for the PWLB to make advances to local authorities at rates of interest below those at which the Treasury itself could borrow. This, however, the Treasury would not accept. The Chancellor of the Exchequer, H. H. Asquith, told the President of the LGB in 1907, 'the policy of doles – direct or indirect – is, as you recognise, objectionable and dangerous, and, if we adopt it, I confess I do not see where we shall be able to stop.'[15] The Treasury would agree only to extend the period and improve the terms of PWLB loans; and it was this change, not the explicit subsidy demanded by the Select Committee, that was introduced by the Act of 1909.

The housing section of the Housing and Town Planning Act of 1909 was, in fact, a more or less minimal response by the LGB to the demands for housing reform. Instead of transferring responsibility for rural housing from rural district councils (RDCs) to county councils as the 1906 Select Committee had recommended, the Act only simplified the procedure for action by RDCs and provided, in cases of default, for action by county councils or the LGB. On housing finance, as noted above, the Act fell short of radical demands. The most substantial changes made by the Act were to simplify the procedure for the compulsory purchase of land for Part III building, to require county councils to appoint medical officers of health, and to increase (from half to two-thirds) the proportion of the initial capital that the PWLB could loan to public utility societies, such as the co-partnership societies at Letchworth or Hampstead Garden Suburb. The LGB itself was conscious of the poverty of the reforms it proposed. As a departmental memorandum noted of the eight-clause draft Bill prepared in March 1907, its 'slender dimensions' suggested a 'rather inadequate treatment of a subject which, in popular estimation, has become important'.[16] To distract attention from this, the board adopted two diversionary tactics. First, it added a mass of amendments to existing legislation; as an LGB official noted towards the end of 1907, 'the President wants to amplify the Housing Bill, and at his instance we have been through the Housing Acts with a view to considering further amendments'.[17] This operation resulted in the much-criticised delay in the introduction of the Bill but on its own terms was successful, accounting for no less than thirty-six of the fifty-three clauses in the housing section of the eventual 1909 Act. The other remedy for the 'slender dimensions' of the draft Bill came from the advocates of town planning, led by Councillor Nettlefold of Birmingham, who in February 1907 sent

Burns the draft of a Town Planning Bill.[18] Here was an opportunity to distract attention from the housing clauses while giving the measure the semblance of a coherent policy on housing and urban development. The outcome was the addition of a town planning section to the housing clauses, making what became the Housing and Town Planning Act of 1909.

The failure of the 1909 Act to tackle effectively the perceived problems of housing meant that housing remained an open political issue, to which both major parties returned before 1914. In December 1911 the Conservative opposition introduced a Housing Bill to provide a Treasury grant of £1 million per annum towards the cost of local authority housing schemes.[19] It subsequently emerged that the £1 million was to be divided equally between Part III building in rural areas and slum clearance projects in towns, with Part III building in towns excluded altogether. For it was claimed by the promoter of the Bill, Sir Arthur Griffith-Boscawen, that whereas 'the chief difficulty in the rural districts is the shortage of houses ... the chief difficulty in the towns is not the shortage of houses; it is the continual existence of foul, festering slums and the difficulty of cleaning them out'.[20] The Conservatives stated that the Bill had been specially drafted to meet the requirements of the large urban authorities which, under Conservative control, were at that time involved in major slum clearance schemes. What they were proposing was that part of the enormous cost of these clearance schemes should fall to the tax-payer: 'I know it will be said that State aid towards housing and building ... is simply subsidising rents out of public money. But that is done now out of the rates to a large extent – and must be. All that we propose is to come to the assistance of the ratepayers.'[21]

Before the outbreak of the First World War, the Liberal government had responded to this challenge, admitted the inadequacies of the 1909 Act and launched its own counter-offensive. Housing was included as one item in a wide-ranging programme of social reform announced by Lloyd George in the autumn of 1913 as the prelude to the general election due to be held in 1914 or 1915. The proposals made in the 'Land Campaign' involved not just housing, but also far-reaching changes in land-tenure, wages and taxation. The laws of tenure were to be reformed to the benefit of the user rather than the owner of land, with a Ministry of Lands or Land Commission established to control contracts between landlord and tenant. For the agricultural labourer, the government promised, first, legislation to guarantee a 'living wage'; secondly, an acceleration of the small holdings programme to free him from dependence on the farmer for employment; and, thirdly, a house-building programme run by the Board of Agriculture to provide the labourer with an alternative to the tied cottage.[22] For the towns, the government proposals were much less clearly formulated. Lloyd George's budget of May 1914 proposed a fundamental reform of local and national taxation, with a separate rating of land and buildings and a new system of Exchequer grants in aid of the latter alone.[23] It was stated that a public health grant of £4 million per annum would be available towards the cost of hospitals, tuberculosis sanatoria and small holdings, as well as housing, and that this grant would be conditional on the satisfactory performance of their duties by local authorities. The new President of the LGB, Herbert Samuel (who replaced Burns in February 1914) specified that these would include a 'statutory duty ... to see that the population of their districts are adequately housed', as well as a duty to control future development through town planning.[24] But these declarations of intent had not been finalised, let alone translated into a legislative draft, before the outbreak of war in August 1914; although, as will be seen below, a Housing Bill dealing with rural areas alone was introduced to Parliament by the government in July 1914.

State Housing and the Garden City Movement

At this point something should be said about the design of state housing, especially in relation to the ideas developed by the garden city movement. Had local authorities confined themselves to building on central sites cleared of slums, where high land values necessitated high-density forms of housing, the question of adopting garden city ideas for state housing could never have arisen. But the introduction of a new type of housing activity under Part III of the 1890 Act took local authorities into the suburbs in search of cheap land and made the adoption of low-density layout on the garden city model at least a possibility. So complete was the appeal of the low-density, quasi-rural format of the garden city movement that its desirability was not questioned; what was at issue was the extent to which its adoption by local authorities was practicable. For, as has been shown, garden city development was successful for the more affluent but had not been successfully applied to the housing needs of the ordinary worker; whereas it was generally held that the function of local authority housing was precisely to provide for those who could not afford the houses of the speculative builder.

It was the cost of low-density development that constituted the obstacle to the adoption of the garden city model by local authorities. The cost of land fell ultimately on the occupants of the houses built on it and, as even Unwin did not attempt to deny, the fewer the houses, the greater the land charge borne by each house. Thus it was said of the LCC's suburban estates that the 'price of land prohibits the number of houses to the acre being limited as at Bournville and Port Sunlight'; the result was a density of over twenty-five houses to the acre, as against the eight to twelve houses per acre of garden city developments.[25] Similarly a much smaller local authority, Chelmsford UDC, building under Part III in 1911, found itself 'unable to keep the number of houses lower than 22 to the acre' for its suburban scheme.[26] With densities of this order, the wide-fronted house – with all it meant in terms of internal arrangement, lighting and ventilation – was an impossibility. House-plans therefore remained in the narrow-fronted tradition of the speculative builder.

These points can be illustrated by two of the schemes undertaken by the largest of municipal housebuilders, the LCC. For the design of its White Hart Lane estate (purchased in 1901) the LCC turned to the example provided by one of the 'philanthropic' housing trusts, the Artisans', Labourers' and General Dwellings Company, at its nearby Noel Park estate. Noel Park had been developed from the 1880s at a density of twenty-seven houses to the acre, following the familiar grid layout of the speculative builder: the houses, as Alderman Thompson noted, were of the type 'which seems to have been universally adopted in all town and suburban terrace dwellings'.[27] The same was true of the LCC's White Hart Lane estate, where house-plans were firmly in the 'narrow and deep' tradition; the house types from White Hart Lane published in 1909 had frontages of 12 ft, 15 ft and 18 ft 9 in (see Figure 10).[28] For the Old Oak estate (developed from 1911) the LCC followed a similar formula, with the slightly lower overall density of 24.5 houses to the acre but with house-plans again of the 'narrow and deep' variety. The accommodation provided at Old Oak was, however, decidedly inferior to that at White Hart Lane; for, as part of its reassessment of housing policy, the ruling Conservative group on the LCC decided to concentrate on smaller cottages for those whose needs were 'not supplied by other agencies',[29] rather than infringe on the territory of the speculative builder with larger houses. Accordingly the majority of houses at Old Oak were of the smaller type, with only three or four rooms plus scullery and offices.[30]

With housing densities and house-types of this kind, any application

GROUND PLAN

1ST FLOOR PLAN

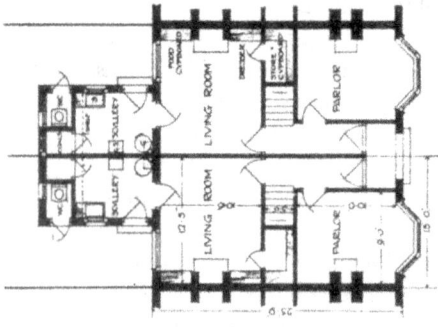

GROUND PLAN

1ST FLOOR PLAN

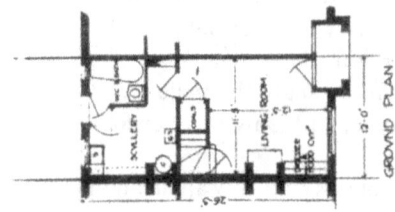

TYPES OF THREE-ROOM COTTAGES.

A.

B.

GROUND FLOOR PLAN.

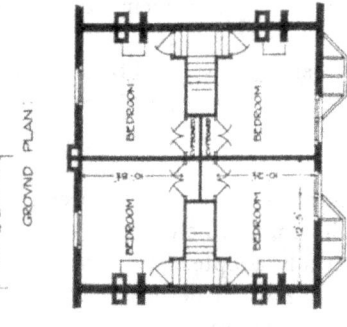

FIRST FLOOR PLAN

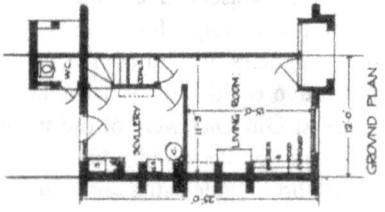

PARISIAN COTTAGES.

DWELLING COTTAGES.

FIGURE 10. London County Council White Hart Lane cottage plans for three-, four-, and six-bedroom

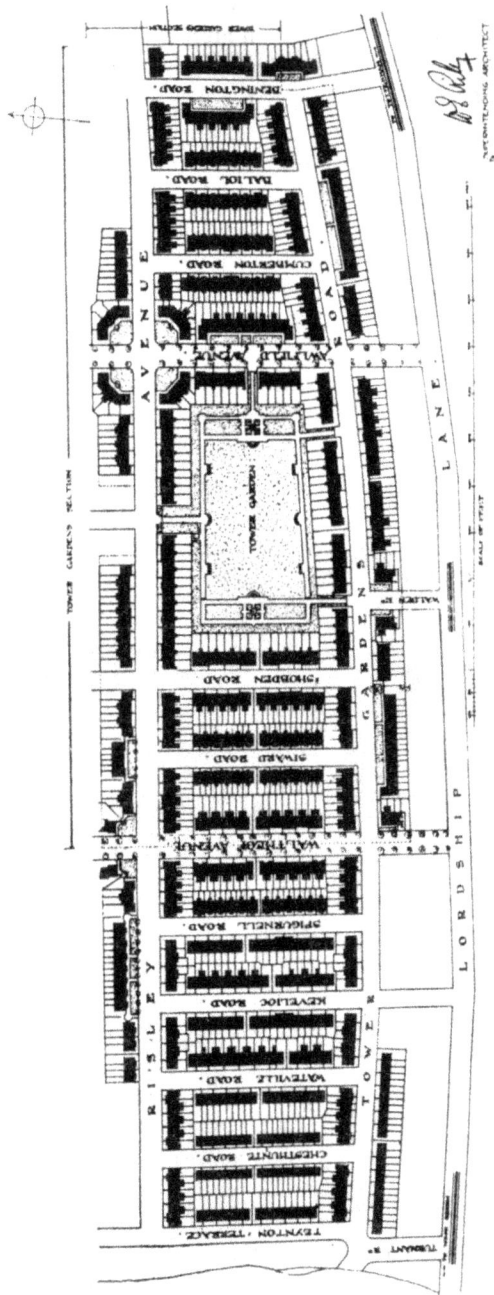

Figure 11   London County Council, White Hart Lane estate: portion developed before 1913

of garden city ideas had to be largely cosmetic. At White Hart
Lane some points of layout (notably the set-back of houses around
the major road intersection) showed an affinity to garden city practice (see Figure 11). At Old Oak, which was regarded as a prestige
estate by the LCC, there was a stronger architectural intention at
work. The buildings themselves were of high-quality material and
workmanship, with steep tiled roofs and inventive detailing reminiscent of the romantic country houses of Lutyens and others. The
siting of the buildings, employing set-backs and greens, showed the
clear influence of Hampstead Garden Suburb and of Unwin's con-

Figure 12   London County Council, Old Oak estate: prewar portion
(1911–14)

cept of the 'street picture', although the blocks were much longer
than those used by Unwin and the overall effect rather more enclosed, in the manner of Camillo Sitte (see Figure 12).

Among prewar cottage estates, the high quality of the Old Oak
architecture was unique; and even at Old Oak the houses were small
and the densities high in comparison to garden city practice. In
general, as the LGB's 1913 *Memorandum* with its low space standards
and narrow-fronted plans made evident, the conclusion was that
garden city forms were not viable for state housing (see Figure 13).[31]
There was, however, another way in which the state could extend

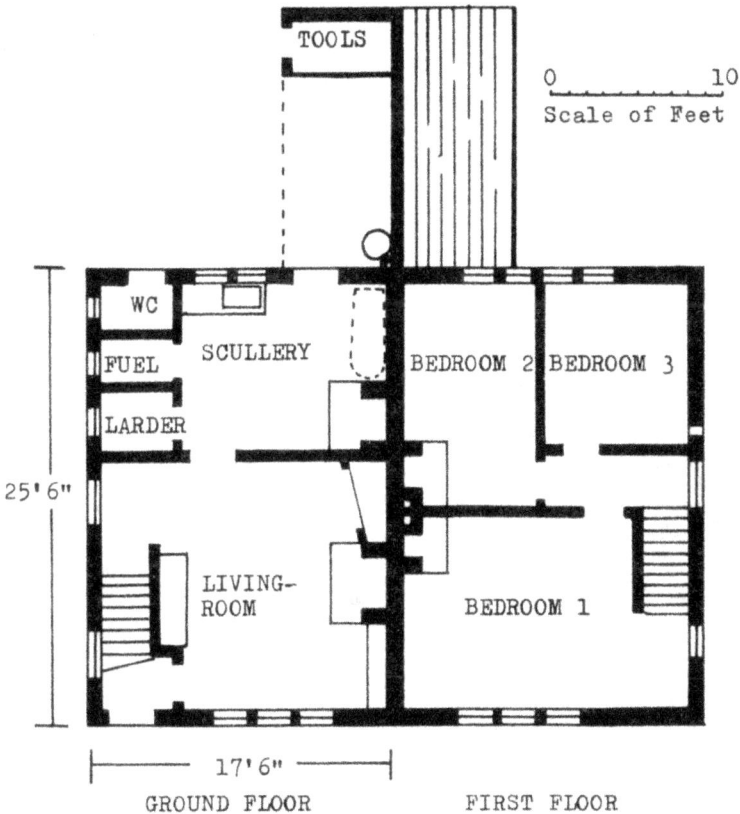

*Figure 13   The largest cottage plan recommended in the Local Government
Board's* Memorandum *of 1913*

the application of the garden city example. This was through town
planning. By town planning, it appeared, the ordinary processes of
speculative building could be remodelled to garden city standards,
while local authorities were left to deal with the housing of those
ignored by private enterprise. Town planning had another advantage: the national application of garden city environmental
standards that it offered would be achieved at little or no cost to the
state. Introducing his Housing and Town Planning Bill in May
1908, John Burns said that town planning would enable local
authorities to reproduce the Bournville experiment 'a hundred or a
thousand times all over the kingdom'. He continued:

> No-one could go to Port Sunlight, or Earswick, ... without seeing
> the enormous schemes which had, during the last ten years, been

undertaken ... nearly all of which were, in plan and execution, superior to anything which he had seen in any country in the world....

What a few public-spirited owners, companies and corporations had done, without loss to themselves ... the Bill would enable a number of other people and associations to accomplish....

They could see at Ealing, at Hampstead Garden Suburb, and at a number of other places, examples of what prescience, outlook and the development of estates according to a coherent and progressive plan were capable of doing.[32]

Accordingly, the Act of 1909 empowered local authorities to prepare town planning schemes, subject to the authorisation of the LGB. But this prospect of getting something for nothing – garden suburbs nationwide at no cost to the state – proved to be largely delusory and by 1914 only two town planning schemes (both in Birmingham) had secured LGB approval.

During Burns' period of office (from 1906 to February 1914), the LGB thus envisaged a two-tier system in which it was hoped that private enterprise, reformed by town planning, would build for the better-off and local authorities would cater for the remainder. The objection to this in practice was that, with house-building in recession after about 1906, very little was being built at all, and the market shortage that was emerging in many towns in the years immediately prior to the war was affecting the better-off as much as the poor. In this situation the argument for local authorities confining their attention to the poor lost much of its force. At a similar point of cyclical depression in house-building, in the 1890s, some local authorities had built for a much wider social spectrum, since, as they had said, the 'house famine' hit 'not merely the poorest poor, but ... all grades of workmen, skilled and unskilled'.[33] This was the case with the first council to build under Part III, Richmond Town Council, in 1894–5. In addition, in the prewar years, the escalation in the cost of new housing in relation to incomes gave local authorities a financial inducement for aiming somewhat higher up the market. For instance, when Chelmsford council built the first houses on their suburban site in 1911, they found that the parlour houses proved much easier to let than the non-parlour types, despite the higher rent of some 30 per cent involved. Accordingly, the council decided that 'no further cottages should be erected lacking parlour accommodation'.[34]

If garden city housing was to be built by the state, the prerequisite – short of a massive subsidy of rents – was that the houses be built for the better-off rather than the poor. It was this change, corresponding with developments in the housing market, that was suggested by the Land Enquiry Committee of 1913–14 and adopted in the government's Land Campaign proposals of the same period. The Land Enquiry Committee was largely the work of Seebohm Rowntree (of York and New Earswick) and its reports reflected his belief that the housing problem was basically a problem of wages and costs. 'The present unsatisfactory housing conditions', it said, 'are largely due to the presence ... of a considerable proportion of persons unable to pay an economic rent for a sanitary dwelling'.[35] But to introduce a housing subsidy, the committee argued, would only make things worse, for it would eliminate the opportunity for the builder to make a profit and therefore delay the solution of the problem by ordinary market forces. In the long term, the real answer was to ensure that everyone could afford an economic rent through minimum wage legislation; in the short term, the housing shortage could be alleviated by state provision of houses, so long as they were built and let at strictly economic rents.

This analysis formed the basis of the government proposals unveiled in the autumn of 1913. As part of his rural land programme, the President of the Board of Agriculture, Walter Runciman, proposed a major cottage-building programme to be conducted under the auspices of his department.[36] These rural cottages were to be let on an economic basis, even if this at first put them beyond the means of agricultural labourers. In the long term Runciman looked to the government's proposed minimum wage legislation to solve this problem; in the short term, to the 'housing flow'. It was not to the poor but to the better paid members of the village community – 'railwaymen, carpenters, policemen, postmen' – that the new cottages would be let: 'they vacate their old house, and the agricultural labourer is enabled to leave his insanitary dwelling, which ... is then closed, and takes the house which has been vacated by a man who belongs to a social order slightly above him'.[37] Although his proposals for urban housing were less clearly formulated, the new President of the LGB, Herbert Samuel, also accepted this principle of building on economic lines for the better-off as the basis for future municipal action in the towns.

The implications of this policy change for housing form were clear: it left the way open for the adoption of the garden city model for state housing. With Seebohm Rowntree, both through his role in the Land Enquiry and through his close personal contacts with Lloyd George, providing most of the intellectual thrust of the Land Campaign, it was not going to be long before these implications were brought home to the government.[38] By 1914, as will be seen below, the garden city lobby, in the persons of both Cecil Harmsworth, the chairman of the Garden Cities and Town Planning Association, and Raymond Unwin, was well established as adviser to the Cabinet on housing questions. This new status for garden city ideas was clearly demonstrated in March 1913 when the Board of Agriculture published the report of a departmental committee on buildings for small holdings. The committee, which included both Unwin and Harmsworth, had been appointed by Runciman in February 1912, and its report (described by the Prime Minister as 'very interesting and comprehensive') dealt with labourers' cottages as well as small holdings.[39] On general questions of design, the report largely reiterated views already expressed by Unwin. Thus, on the internal arrangement of the house, the report emphasised the importance of aspect, ventilation and attention to practical details and the shape of rooms and the placing of windows and doors, as Unwin had in his earlier writings. On the controversial question of the parlour, the report repeated the argument of Unwin's 1902 Fabian pamphlet that although the tenants' desire for a parlour was undeniable, it should be provided only where 'economy is a less urgent consideration'. As to aesthetics, the report stated:

> Breadth and simplicity of design ... should be aimed at, and the introduction of useless features for the sake of effect should be avoided. Orderly arrangement of the buildings, the observance of good proportion in the spacing and form of doors and window openings, the maintenance of some relation between windows of different sizes by means of a common unit, and other simple elements of good design which are costly only in thought and care, can and should be secured even where the cost of the building must be kept within strict limits.[40]

This passage both reflected recommendations previously made by Unwin (notably in his 1906 article) and foreshadowed the arguments of the Tudor Walters Report of 1918. The same was true of the most important section of the report, that dealing with housing standards. As Unwin had proposed in an article published in 1905, the report called for a minimum standard of three bedrooms, living-room, scullery, larder, fuel-store and closet. Two sets of minima for room sizes were provided (see Table 1): the first was described as the absolute minimum for a small holder's house and the desirable minimum for a labourer's cottage, while the second was termed the absolute minimum for a labourer's cottage. The first set was based on figures previously given in Unwin's article of 1905 and was later, in 1918, to be taken by the Tudor Walters Report as the 'minimum size of rooms which it is desirable to build'.

Table 1 Minimum room sizes recommended by the Departmental Committee on Buildings for Small Holdings (1913) (square feet)

| | Minimum for smallholder's house Desirable minimum for rural labourer's cottage | | Absolute minimum for rural labourer's cottage |
	When parlour is not provided	When parlour is provided	
Parlour	—	120*	—
Living-room	180*	(180)*	165
Scullery	80*	(80)*	65
Larder	24*	(24)*	18
Fuel-store	35	(35)	—
Bedroom 1	150*	160*	144
Bedroom 2	100*	120*	—
Bedroom 3	65*	110*	65

Brackets indicate that figures were not given in the original tables but can be inferred from the text.

Dashes indicate that figures are not applicable or cannot be inferred from the text.

Asterisks indicate figures repeated in the Tudor Walters Report of 1918 as the 'desirable minimum size of rooms'.

Several plans for rural labourers' cottages were published with the report. These included plans for single-storey and three-storey dwellings, but these were housing types that the committee considered desirable only in special circumstances. For the normal cottage on two storeys, equipped in the manner considered desirable by the committee, three plans were given. Of these, two were definitely the work of Parker and Unwin, one being the plan for 'minimum cost cottages at Letchworth' published in 1906 (see Figure 9) and the other being a design used at New Earswick. In the 1913 Report of the Departmental Committee, in other words, not only the higher standards, but also the actual house-plans, of the garden city movement were officially recommended for state housing for the first time.

It was clearly Runciman's intention to build cottages of the type suggested by the committee. During 1913 the Board of Agriculture urged the report onto the attention of county councils, a number of which responded by adopting the plans contained in it. In November 1913, having obtained Cabinet approval for his rural housing proposals, Runciman appointed a small advisory committee to make detailed recommendations on plans, specifications and building methods. The membership of this committee again included Unwin and Harmsworth, and it was generally and correctly assumed that its deliberations would continue on the lines established by its predecessor.[41]

Housing Policy on the Eve of the First World War

By 1914 the government was committed by the speeches and literature of the Land Campaign to the active promotion of housing on garden city lines. The President of the Board of Agriculture had outlined plans for a major house-building programme in rural areas; the President of the LGB had said that housing was to be made a duty of local authorities in the towns. What is the significance of these developments in relation to the subsequent history of housing? Do they mean that the innovations normally associated with the postwar period had already been introduced before the war? This is an interpretation that has sometimes been advanced, albeit based on somewhat slender evidence.[42] New material, however, has come to light at the Public Record Office which offers a more secure foundation for some general conclusions.[43] It consists of interdepartmental correspondence dating from the spring and early summer of 1914, which led in July to the introduction of a government Housing Bill and the passage of the Housing Act of 1914, and it offers the clearest available view of government housing policy on the eve of the war.

The Housing Act of 1914 was a belated response to a crisis that had emerged out of the naval building programme – an early sign of the way in which military requirements were to affect housing policy over the next few years. In 1909 work had begun on the construction of a new naval base at Rosyth, on the Firth of Forth, and despite (or, rather, largely as a result of) much talk about developing the area as a 'town planning scheme on garden city lines' (for which the Admiralty engaged Unwin as consultant),[44] five years later the building of permanent housing for civilian employees at the dockyard had still not started. According to an Admiralty estimate in 1914, 3000 houses were required over a period of two to three years. Neither the Admiralty nor the local authority, Dunfermline Borough Council, wanted to build the houses; and although both a public utility society and a commercial syndicate had offered to do so, both insisted on massive financial assistance from the government. This would require parliamentary sanction: as the Admiralty stated at the beginning of June 1914, 'if a Bill ... is not introduced this session, it will be impossible to provide in time for the housing of the men to be employed at Rosyth'.[45] There were problems of similar urgency, although not similar scale, at the Admiralty's base at Crombie and the War Office's aircraft factory at Farnborough; and political considerations made it imperative that the 'serious scandals' that threatened to blow up over the government's failure to house its own employees should be averted.[46]

It was recognised by all the departments involved that these questions could not be dealt with in isolation from the general housing policy of the government. The Admiralty stated in April that 'the situation at Rosyth and Crombie imposes on His Majesty's Government the obligation of adopting the principles of a housing policy and presents an admirable opportunity for applying those principles'.[47] The President of the Board of Agriculture agreed with the Treasury's view that 'the whole question is tied up with the general housing policy of the Government and it is important to lay down a general and consistent policy at the outset'.[48] What then *was* the general housing policy of the government? It was, first, as the Admiralty put it, 'the recognition by the State of the duty of seeing that a relative standard of comfort and convenience is secured in the housing of the working classes'. They had therefore to ensure at Crombie and Rosyth that the 'new townships may be developed from the outset in a manner that shall secure to the future community at reasonable rentals the model standards of health and comfort which it has been their aim to provide.'[49] How was this to be done? Here was the second element in the government's policy: state aid to public utility societies. The Admiralty cited a letter from the President of the Board of Agriculture, which stated that

> Far and away the most valuable housing experiments and undertakings have been done by these societies.... Neither private owners nor corporations nor district councils nor the Crown have combined so completely efficient design with economy of construction.[50]

The societies to which Runciman was referring were public utility societies run on co-partnership lines: he sent the Admiralty a paper by Cecil Harmsworth, incorporating additional notes by Unwin and Henry Vivian, which explained the workings and advantages of

co-partnership housing. The Treasury agreed to the proposal: aid to
public utility societies involved no departures in principle and was
considered preferable on political grounds both to building by
central departments and to financial assistance to private builders.

A small inter-departmental committee, with representatives of the
Treasury, Admiralty, War Office and the Local Government Boards,
was set up in May 1914 to resolve the scheme. Previous attempts
to form a public utility society at Rosyth had failed to raise the one-
third of the initial capital of £1 million needed in order to qualify
for state assistance under the terms of the 1909 Act. If a public
utility society was to build at Rosyth, the state contribution would
have to be increased from two-thirds to nine-tenths; this the Treasury
reluctantly accepted. But, equally, some provision had to be made
in case the public utility society scheme fell through. In this case,
the committee decided, the Scottish LGB rather than the Admiralty
should be the department responsible. By the end of May, a Bill on
these lines had been drafted, enabling the Scottish LGB to make
advances to public utility societies for the housing of government
employees of up to nine tenths of the cost, or in lieu to build itself.[51]

Scarcely by coincidence, this proposal was markedly similar in
form to that now favoured by Runciman for rural areas. The Board
of Agriculture was still to be responsible for the cottage-building
programme but where possible it was to lend to public utility societies
rather than build itself; and if the Treasury was now prepared to
increase to nine-tenths the proportion of initial capital that could be
lent to the societies, it was reasonable to believe that their operations
would be greatly increased. Since the schemes for rural areas and
for government employees ran parallel, there was no objection to
combining them, and in the Housing Bill introduced at the beginning
of July 1914 clauses dealing with rural housing had been appended
to those dealing with Rosyth.[52] The Board of Agriculture was empowered by the Bill to 'acquire and dispose of land and buildings
with the consent of the Treasury and to do all other things which
appear to them necessary or desirable' for the provision of houses
for the working classes in agricultural districts, 'including the making
of any arrangements for that purpose' with public utility societies;
and the Treasury was empowered to advance up to £3 million for
capital expenditure on this account. The Local Government Boards
were given similar powers in respect of housing for government
employees; £2 million was allocated for this. Loans to public utility
societies were to be for a maximum of nine-tenths of capital expenditure, repayable over 40–60 years, and all expenditure under the Bill

was to be in the nature of an investment, not a subsidy, with strictly economic rents charged for the houses.

Whether it was ever hoped to secure parliamentary approval for the rural clauses so late in the session appears highly doubtful; it seems more likely that they were intended as a distraction from the difficulties into which the government had run over the budget and as a token of future intentions on housing. At any rate, Runciman showed no particular reluctance in announcing, in the second reading debate on 20 July, his willingness to jettison the rural clauses in order to secure the passage into law of those dealing with Rosyth. This excision was carried out in committee stage and on 10 August the remaining clauses, dealing with the housing of government employees, reached the statute book as the Housing Act of 1914.[53]

The discussions in Whitehall that led to the Act show the extent to which the government saw the improvement of housing conditions on garden city lines as a primary goal of its housing policy: the extension of the environmental improvements made by the garden city movement which in 1909 had been the goal of town planning was now accepted as part of housing policy. But they also show that the government hoped to achieve this goal by increasing the financial assistance given to public utility societies rather than by expanding the house-building activities of the state itself. It was the First World War that was to create the conditions for a different kind of policy: a housing programme on a really large scale (a planned 500 000 houses in 1919 as against the planned 25 000 in 1914) to be built not by state-aided public utility societies but by the state itself.

3 The Wartime Housing Programme

The First World War had a dramatic effect on housing in Britain: it drove up the cost of building, brought house-building to a standstill and eventually led in 1919 to the 'homes fit for heroes' campaign. But even more immediately, the war affected the housing responsibilities of the state in a more limited field. Between 1915 and 1918 the need for a massive supply of arms and armaments propelled the government into an unprecedented programme of house-building for workers engaged on the production of munitions. This involved not just temporary, but in some cases permanent, accommodation; and here the opportunity was taken to realise those plans for state-promoted housing on garden city lines frustrated by the outbreak of war in 1914. Before turning to the 'homes fit for heroes' campaign, something must be said about this building programme: for, when it came to launch the far larger housing campaign that followed the end of the war, the government was to draw heavily on this wartime experience for ideas and personnel.

The Housing (no. 2) Act of 1914

Before dealing with munitions housing, however, brief mention must be made of a measure significant not for anything that it achieved but for the thinking that it revealed. This was the Housing (no. 2) Act of 1914, which entered the statute book on 10 August, less than a week after the declaration of war. The Act originated with MPs on both sides of the House who feared that the outbreak of war would lead to a suspension of building and therefore to widespread unemployment in the building trades. It empowered the LGB and Board of Agriculture to spend up to a total of £4 million on housing for the relief of unemployment, either by making arrangements with local authorities and public utility societies or by building themselves. These powers were, however, to last for only one year and their exercise was conditional on the agreement of the Treasury. For the government, Herbert Samuel emphasised that the new measure did not involve a housing subsidy and that economic rents would be charged for the houses: expenditure under the Act was an 'investment rather than a charitable grant'.[1] He did, nonetheless, concede that if houses were to be built under the peculiar financial conditions created by the war, some allowance might have to be made for the exceptional costs involved. This idea was explicitly formulated by the Treasury in November 1914. 'In view of the exceptional monetary conditions and the high cost of building materials', stated the Treasury, 10 per cent of the capital cost of building under the Act would be covered by a Treasury grant.[2] This was the first appearance of a general principle that was to be adopted both for the housing schemes built for munitions workers and, on a much larger scale, for the housing programme of 1919.

It seems that Samuel regarded the Housing (no. 2) Act as an opportunity for a major housing initiative. In August 1914 he issued a circular to local authorities stating that the Act was intended not just for meeting unemployment but also for 'providing and improving the housing accommodation of the working classes': local authorities were urged to submit proposals to the LGB 'without delay', and even councils in areas where unemployment was not anticipated were invited to act, provided that their areas were accessible to those in which unemployment was likely to arise.[3] But this prospect of large and, in its view, needless capital expenditure did not appeal to the Treasury. At the same time as announcing the 10 per cent grant, the Treasury warned that the conditions under which the Act could be implemented had not been, and probably never would be, fulfilled. Advances under the Act would be made only 'in cases where unemployment in the building trade consequent on the War is exceptional and insistent. . . . Unemployment in the building trade is so low at present that there is no prospect of any houses being built'.[4] Since the anticipated unemployment in the building trade never materialised, the Act remained inoperative.

Housing for Munitions Workers

Although the Housing (no. 2) Act came to nothing, by the middle of 1915 the state had become involved in a housing programme arising directly from the needs of war, in which some of the elements of the aborted Act were to be realised. For obvious reasons, the production of munitions was of vital importance to the war effort; as Lloyd George said in June 1915, 'ultimate victory or defeat depends on the supply of munitions'.[5] It was failure in this area, and particularly the scandal caused by alleged shell shortages on the western front, that had brought about the fall of Asquith's government and the formation of the coalition in May 1915, in which Lloyd George took the new post of Minister of Munitions. In order to increase output Lloyd George imposed a number of controls that, while falling short of industrial conscription, severely limited the rights of munitions workers: strikes and stoppages were made illegal, the unions were compelled to accept dilution of skilled trades, and workers were effectively tied to their places of employment by the system of 'leaving certificates'. These and other less draconian measures – notably the work of the famous welfare section of the ministry headed by Seebohm Rowntree – dealt with conditions inside the factories, but conditions outside the factories also affected production and could not, therefore, be ignored. Chief among these was the problem of housing. At Woolwich, where already in 1914 it was reported that all the surplus accommodation had been taken up, the numbers employed by the Royal Arsenal rose from 10 866 on the outbreak of war to 74 467 in 1917. At Gretna in 1915 the ministry planned an explosives factory to employ between 10 000 and 15 000 workers in a district capable of accommodating, within a radius of 25 miles, only an estimated 4500 people. This scale and rate of increase presented problems of accommodation that could hardly be left to market forces to solve, particularly in view of the state to which the building industry had been reduced by the war. As the War Office stated in December 1914 in relation to the Arsenal, the increase in the size of the workforce 'has made the question of accommodation one of ... vital importance and urgency in the interests not merely of the workmen but of the work itself'.[6] As employers producing vital goods, the War Office and the Ministry of Munitions had no alternative but to look to the housing of their employees.

Nonetheless, while involvement in housing was to that extent involuntary, the attitude taken by the government departments was not exclusively utilitarian. Lloyd George and the others were, as ministers of state, responsible for the efficient management of munitions supply; but they were also politicians who, only a year earlier, had been making sweeping promises about social reform. Christopher Addison, who was appointed by Lloyd George as Under Secretary responsible for labour affairs, later recalled:

> The Ministry of Munitions as a manufacturing and employment agency was in a unique position. Never before had the State assumed such extensive responsibilities for directing and originating production.... It provided a new kind of opportunity.... Lloyd George and I agreed ... that ... use ought to be made of the exceptional situation to secure a better and more humane standard of working conditions. [7]

The extent to which this ambition could be realised in an improvement of housing conditions was limited by the control over expenditure exercised by the Treasury. It was only under the most extreme pressure from the War Office that the Treasury consented, at the beginning of 1915, to the erection of a permanent housing scheme at Woolwich; and by the middle of 1915, as the extraordinarily high cost of building at Well Hall became apparent, the Treasury was regretting its decision. A letter to the new Ministry of Munitions in June 1915 laid down the Treasury's rules on housing expenditure: housing schemes would be permitted only where they could be shown to be necessary for war production; and all schemes were to be temporary, except where this could be shown to be impossible. Furthermore, it was stated, 'in view of the supreme importance of restricting capital expenditure at the present moment ... the erection of houses ... on Garden City lines must be abandoned'.[8]

In all some £4.3 million was allocated to housing by the Ministry of Munitions between 1915 and 1918. Following the Treasury's instructions, most of the housing was in the form of temporary buildings: the ministry provided temporary hostels for 20 000 workers (mainly women) as well as 2800 temporary cottages. But not all the cost advantages were on the side of temporary structures. The cost of building constituted only a part of the total capital cost of providing housing: the substantial costs of site development (roads, drains and mains services) had to be borne whether permanent or temporary buildings were erected, and for this reason it was at least arguable that in the long term temporary building was more expensive than permanent, particularly since even temporary buildings had a life of twenty-five years. Moreover, as timber stocks were used up and prices rose, even the initial cost advantage of temporary building became doubtful.[9]

For these reasons, where there was a proven demand for houses that would outlast the war, the Treasury agreed to the erection of permanent houses. Altogether some 10 000 permanent houses were built in connection with munitions factories on thirty-eight different estates in various parts of the country. And, despite the Treasury, this permanent housing was on best 'garden city lines'. Here the Ministry of Munitions followed the precept established by Samuel and the LGB for the Well Hall scheme at Woolwich in 1915: whatever permanent housing was built had to be of the improved garden city type. On this point the commitment of politicians, housing experts and designers proved too strong even for the Treasury.

Various expedients were adopted to get the houses built. At first the

Ministry of Munitions tried to work through local authorities, by offering to meet a portion of the cost of building; but disagreements between the Treasury and the local authorities limited the scope of this arrangement to four schemes agreed in 1915. Many more schemes were undertaken by the munitions manufacturers themselves, with financial aid from the government. This was the case with the Crayford and Barrow schemes built by Vickers in 1915 with a grant from the War Office, and with a number of schemes sponsored by the Ministry of Munitions in 1916–17; in all, twenty or so schemes were built in this way. Often, however, the central departments found that they had to undertake the building themselves. This was the position with the Woolwich scheme for the Royal Arsenal in 1915; with the schemes undertaken in connection with explosives factories by the Ministry of Munitions, most notably at Gretna; and with many of the smaller schemes undertaken in the latter part of the war. In all, thirteen schemes were undertaken by the central government departments.

Between 1914 and 1918 the cost of building doubled and the rate of interest rose by about one-third: it was evident therefore that the rents obtainable for the houses would not match their cost and that some kind of government subsidy was unavoidable. Where the central government departments built and owned the houses, it was possible for the subsidy to be settled on a more or less *ad hoc* basis. But where it was a case of persuading firms or local authorities to build, a clear definition of the terms of financial assistance had to be provided. At first the Ministry of Munitions followed the lines established by the Treasury in November 1914 and offered a grant to cover the excess of actual over notional prewar cost. As the war continued and costs continued to rise, however, the Treasury adopted a different principle: the grant was to cover the difference between actual cost and not prewar cost, but postwar value. This principle was adopted in a number of schemes agreed in 1917, in which the Ministry of Munitions built the houses but the local authorities or firms undertook to buy them at a value to be determined at a certain date (usually three or seven years) after the end of the war. As will be seen below, it was this principle, of a grant to cover the difference between actual cost and postwar value as established after seven years, that the Treasury was to adopt for the postwar housing campaign.

One result of the diverse organisation of munitions housing was the involvement of a number of different architectural practices. Three departments of state contributed the services of their architects. The Office of Works provided design groups led by two of its principal architects, Frank Baines and R. J. Allison. At the Ministry of Munitions, the Department of Explosives Supply set up its own housing branch under Raymond Unwin, who had been appointed by Samuel as Chief Town Planning Inspector at the LGB in the autumn of 1914 but who was seconded to the Ministry of Munitions in 1915. Unwin's team included S. B. Russell and several architects from Hampstead Garden Suburb, notably Courtenay Crickmer and Geoffrey Lucas. Staff from the LGB were also involved in munitions housing, principally George Pepler who was, in Unwin's absence, the board's chief town planning adviser. In addition, the schemes undertaken by armaments manufacturers offered scope for the employment of non-official architects: for instance, Vickers' Crayford scheme was designed by Gordon Allen and the Dorman Long scheme (near Redcar) by Abercrombie, Adshead and Ramsey. By one means or another, many of the architects who had been involved in the design of low-cost housing before the war contributed to the munitions housing programme.

Well Hall

Of the government wartime housing schemes it was the first, Well Hall, that was the most celebrated. 'A community which ... is, from the architectural standpoint, without equal in the world', wrote the Secretary of the International Garden Cities and Town Planning Association, E. G. Culpin: 'there is not a colony in the world which approaches to the general excellence of this Woolwich scheme'.[10]

It was the Royal Arsenal at Woolwich that bore the brunt of the initial programme of increased munitions output during the first months of the war. By the beginning of 1915 the workforce at the Arsenal, which in August 1914 had stood at just under 11 000, had more than doubled, and the Director anticipated that a further 3000 to 4000 employees would have to be taken on in 'the next few months'.[11] Accordingly, on 30 December 1914 the War Office asked the LGB, in conjunction with the Office of Works, to take immediate action under the 1914 Housing Act to provide at least 1000 houses for employees at the Woolwich Arsenal. The urgency of the need, the War Office stated, was such as to exclude action through a public utility society or through the local authority, which otherwise would have been regarded as preferable. The President of the LGB, Herbert Samuel, concurred in the proposal. The Treasury was not convinced and saw a number of objections, but the War Office insisted: the proposal, the Treasury was told on 8 January, 'affords the only practicable solution of a difficulty which threatens seriously to affect the efficiency of the Arsenal at a very critical period'. Four days later a conference was held between representatives of the War Office, Treasury, LGB and Office of Works:

> The War Office stated that it was of the most cardinal importance for war purposes that more cottages should be immediately provided at Woolwich. . . . As time was of the essence of the matter and the War Office was so insistent on the necessity and the urgency, Mr Montagu [the Financial Secretary to the Treasury] regretfully agreed that the work must be entrusted to the Office of Works.

The decision that a housing scheme was to be built by the Office of Works immediately raised the question of the form that it should take. The first Housing Act of 1914 (dealing with housing for government employees) was the only statute covering the situation and under this the responsible department was the LGB. The Treasury was informed that: 'Mr Herbert Samuel hopes that care will be taken to ensure that any site is laid out with due regard to the best practice in connection with the planning of estates'; and the Office of Works was instructed by the LGB that the estate was to follow 'best town-planning lines', with twelve houses to the acre, and that the 'opportunity should be taken to show what a scheme of this nature should be under Government auspices'.[12]

How had this come about? Once the decision had been made to build a permanent scheme, the project was no longer just an emergency expedient but became a part of the government's response to the housing question in general: if the Woolwich scheme was to be of 'permanent assistance in the housing problem',[13] it could not simply reproduce the form of the existing housing of the locality. Only a few weeks earlier Samuel had emphasised his commitment to 'housing on garden city lines' by announcing the appointment of Raymond Unwin as Town Planning Inspector at the board.[14] Frustrated first by the outbreak of war and then by the Treasury's embargo on the Housing (no. 2) Act of 1914, it seems that Samuel was determined to take the opportunity offered by the Woolwich housing crisis to implement those promises of a fundamental improvement in housing conditions so frequently made only a few months earlier, before the outbreak of the war.

But although the scheme was to be of the highest standard, speed in the provision of the housing accommodation was essential, and the entire estate of 1298 dwellings was completed before the end of 1915. The result of this speed, however, was an enormous escalation of cost. The average cost per dwelling at Well Hall finally worked out at £622, more than double the estimate given by the Office of Works in January 1915.[15] It was also almost double the figure claimed for the Crayford scheme built in the same year along much simpler lines – a point that was not to be lost in the subsequent debate on housing design.

The standards of the housing provided at Well Hall were decided in consultation with the Director of the Arsenal. There were four general types. Class I consisted of parlour, living-room, scullery, WC, four bedrooms and bathroom, the fourth bedroom generally being on the ground floor; 116 houses of this type were built. Class II provided similar accommodation but with only three bedrooms; there were 357 of this type. Nearly half of the total number of dwellings (613 out of 1298) were of Class III: these also had three bedrooms, but neither parlour nor separate bathroom, a bath being provided in the scullery. Unlike the first two classes, houses of Class III did not generally have a through living-room (one with windows at both ends) or a double frontage; they were in fact similar to the typical prewar designs of the LGB, with the scullery opening off the back of the living-room and the staircase running up the side. The fourth class of dwelling at Well Hall was introduced in an attempt to counter the soaring cost of the scheme: it was a 'cottage flat' – a single-storey flat built in a two-storey block resembling an ordinary cottage in appearance. At Well Hall the flat contained only two bedrooms, living-room, scullery and offices. The design economised on circulation space inside the flats by opening the bedrooms and scullery directly off the living-room, and on staircases by providing only one staircase for each group of four flats. The architect at Well Hall, Frank Baines, claimed that the cottage flats were 'found to be strikingly popular'; at a later scheme, the Roe Green estate (built by the Office of Works for the Aircraft Manufacturing Company at Hendon between 1917 and 1919), Baines increased the proportion of cottage flats to 40 per cent of the total dwellings.[16] The use of cottage flats was one of the issues on which Baines and Unwin were to disagree in the discussions of the Tudor Walters Committee.

At Well Hall these dwelling types were provided by Baines in an architectural ensemble that for sheer versatility in the use of the picturesque elements of the 'old English Village' far exceeded anything ever attempted by Unwin (see Figure 14). Baines argued that the answer to the problems of building in wartime conditions of dislocation was to make use of each and every material that came to hand. At Well Hall the wide range of materials was put to dramatic visual effect and emphasised by the variety of finishes: brick, stone, roughcast, half-timbering, tile-hanging, slate-hanging and weatherboarding. Diversity of finishes was matched by complexity of shape and

Figure 14   Well Hall estate (1915)

silhouette, achieved not only through the usual gables and dormers but also through overhangs, tunnels, assorted projections and recessions and careful adjustments of the building line. The layout of the scheme followed the precedents for low-density development established by the garden city movement. Baines departed from Unwin's example, however, in using long blocks of cottages of anything up to sixteen units, and in making the street into a single spatial unit that was bounded on either side by a carefully staggered range of buildings and closed off at the end by a deflection in the course of the road (see Figure 15). All this showed a marked affinity to the ideas of Camillo Sitte, who had written:

> The ideal street must form a completely enclosed unit! The more one's impressions are confined within it, the more perfect will be its tableau: one feels at ease in a space where the gaze cannot be lost in infinity.... The winding character of the ancient streets kept sealing off perspective views in them while offering the eye a new aspect at each succeeding turn.[17]

Responsibility for the design of Well Hall lay with Frank Baines, one of the three principal architects of the Office of Works. Like Unwin, Baines came from an Arts and Crafts background, having served his architectural apprenticeship in the 1890s with C. R. Ashbee, the

Figure 15   Well Hall estate: layout of eastern portion

founder of the Guild and School of Handicraft. Until 1911 Baines had been a Temporary Draughtsman at the Office of Works, involved mainly with the restoration of historic buildings, but after that date his ascent through the grades of the civil service had been little short of meteoric, culminating in his appointment in January 1914 as principal architect, at the comparatively young age of 37.[18]

As an essay in picturesque design, based on intricacy and complexity of form (broken roof-lines, projecting gables, overhanging floors), Well Hall stood in direct opposition to the demand for the simplification of design that had been made by the Report of the Departmental Committee on Small Holdings in 1913. Indeed the advocates of simplification might well have taken some of the elements at Well Hall as examples of the 'useless features' which they wished to avoid. Likewise the variety of materials at Well Hall was totally at odds with the growing demand for standardisation of materials and fittings. But not long after the completion of Well Hall another munitions housing scheme showed what an entire town, designed on the theory of simplification, would be like. This was the township built to accommodate workers at the explosives factory at Gretna, designed by the Department of Explosives Supply under the direction of Raymond Unwin.

Gretna

In June 1915 the newly established Ministry of Munitions decided to build a huge explosives factory on a remote site between the small villages of Gretna and Eastriggs, in Dumfries. The site offered good rail and road connections, would be served by coastal barges and, being on the west coast, was safe from German naval bombardment. It was clear from the start that, given the remoteness of the site, accommodation would have to be provided for most of the construction and factory workforce. To undertake this the Department of Explosives Supply set up a housing branch which, as already noted, was headed by Unwin. Courtenay Crickmer was appointed resident architect for the Gretna site.[19]

It was estimated by the ministry that accommodation for some 13 500 people was required. At first, following Treasury directives, it was intended that this should be met almost entirely by temporary structures, of three kinds: 'cottages' (four-room huts for married workers, built in pairs), 'hostels' (larger huts accommodating nine workers each) and 'barracks' (accommodating 70 workers). But in May 1916, following a visit to the site, Addison decided that there should be 'a permanent housing scheme at Dornoch [Eastriggs] and a small amount of permanent housing at the village near the Gretna side'.[20] Underlying this decision was the rise in the price of timber which, at the same time, led at Gretna to the substitution of concrete for timber in temporary buildings:

> It was found that the cost of temporary buildings ... was, after taking into account the necessary expenditures for water-supply, drainage and road-work, so little less than that for permanent buildings that it was poor economy to erect temporary houses except only where urgence of the short time available demanded it.[21]

The permanent housing was to follow the three types already established, with the hostels and barracks designed so as to convert to self-contained cottages after the war.

Excluding these converted units, 310 permanent cottages were built at Gretna and Eastriggs, six plans for which were published in 1917 in the *Journal of the American Institute of Architects*.[22] Three of the plans were of the non-parlour type, two had parlours and one was of an intermediate type. Of the non-parlour houses, one was a double-fronted plan similar to Houfton's Sheffield design (see Figure 8); the other two were narrow-fronted plans that had been designed by Parker and Unwin before 1914 for New Earswick and that had already been published in the Reports of the Departmental and Advisory Committees of 1913 and 1915. The internal arrangement of these two plans followed the traditional front living-room/back scullery arrangement, with the stairs running up the party wall (see Figure 21, Type Plan A); unlike the double-fronted plan, neither of these included a separate bathroom. Of the two plans for parlour houses, one was designed for a south aspect: the parlour and living-room were placed at the front of the house and the entrance at the side – an arrangement which, as will be seen in Chapter 5, was endorsed by the Tudor Walters Report (Figure 21, Type Plan E). This was the more luxurious of the two, with a frontage of nearly 28 feet and an upstairs bathroom. The other parlour type followed normal Ministry of Munitions policy in putting the bath in the scullery; it was recognisable externally by its bay window, cut-brick arch over the front door and the external 'link' building housing the offices. This plan, modified to provide a separate bathroom, was also reproduced in the Tudor Walters Report (Figure 21, Type Plan C). The final published design, the 'intermediate' type, provided, in addition to the living-room, a small scullery and a separate kitchen housing the cooking-range; this evidently was an experiment in the distribution of the functions of cooking and heating between the different rooms which, as the Tudor Walters Report stated, was one of the basic questions in cottage design.

Well Hall had been criticised by garden city enthusiasts for its lack of communal facilities. By contrast, the provision of public buildings at Gretna was lavish. As well as shops there was a laundry, central kitchen, post office, cinema, hall, dental clinic, institute and school. There were no pubs, but spiritual refreshment was provided by no less than five new churches. The provision of so many communal facilities at Gretna attracted considerable attention but it was claimed that their rationale was entirely utilitarian. The official history of the Ministry of Munitions stated:

> In the early days of the factory it was found that there was an increasing tendency for workers to remain at Gretna for comparatively short periods. A special investigation was held, resulting in the conclusion that the leakage of labour was almost entirely due to the absence of any regular means of recreation for either men or women in their leisure hours.... In order to alleviate these conditions the Ministry proceeded without delay to erect various places of entertainment.[23]

The Gretna housing was acclaimed as the first large-scale demonstration of simplification of design (Figure 16). Gone were the

Figure 16   Gretna: semi-detached houses for foremen (1916–17)

broken roof-lines, complex shapes and variety of materials of Well Hall. Unwin and Crickmer used simple hipped roofs, eliminated dormers and other breaks in the eaves-line, and restricted finishes to brick or roughcast. In general, the only relief to the 'brick box' effect came from the inventive treatment of porches and lintels and from the neo-Georgian elements (sash-windows and brick quoins) which were widely used and were particularly noticeable in the public buildings. The layout of the residential buildings had a staccato quality very different from the enclosed, sinuous effect of Well Hall: the houses were either semi-detached or grouped in short blocks of four to six units, with some visual continuity supplied by brick outhouses and screen walls placed between otherwise isolated buildings (see Figure 17). While the use of these links and the other techniques of low-density layout (cul-de-sacs, set-backs and closes) at Gretna could be traced back to Unwin's prewar work for the garden city movement, the effect

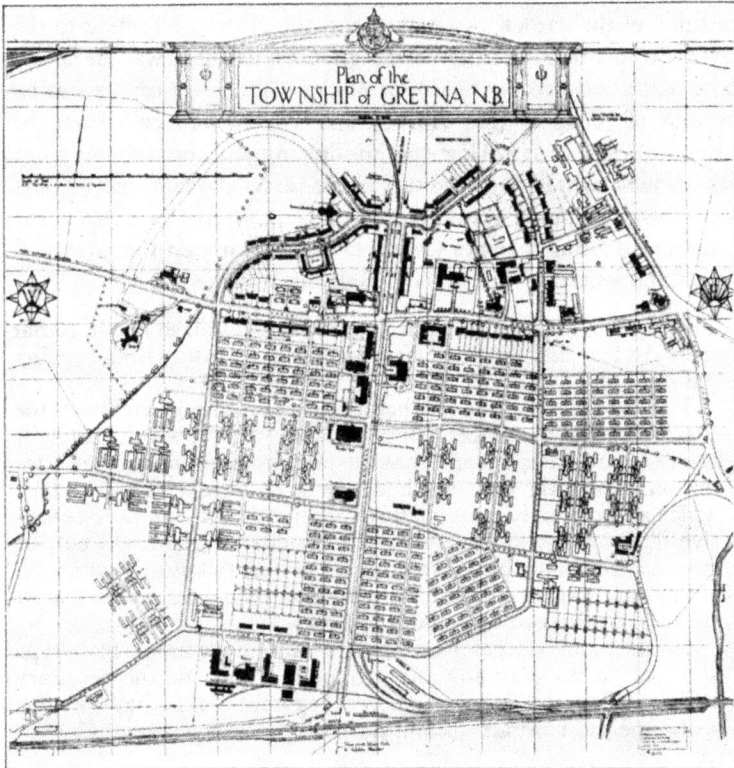

Figure 17   Gretna: layout. Permanent buildings (dark ink) in northern part

was a good deal less sumptuous on the flat terrain of Dumfries than it had been on the slopes of Hampstead Garden Suburb. In 1918 Mrs Alwyn Lloyd, a friend of Unwin, inspected the site on behalf of the Women's Housing Sub-Committee and concluded that the 'whole effect of severely simply designed red brick and slate-roofed houses is depressing', although she added that 'the accommodation in the houses is the best that I have seen in wartime building'. The scheme did, however, look rather better in photographs than it did on the ground – a factor of some importance, given the inaccessibility of the site: Gordon Allen, for instance, was able to write of the photographs of Gretna reproduced in his book (1919) that 'a pleasant Georgian character is the external note'.[24]

Lessons for the Design of State Housing

Well Hall and Gretna offered alternative models for the architecture of state housing: the one continuing and elaborating the picturesque tradition of the garden city movement, the other conforming to the new doctrine of simplification of design. On what basis was the choice to be made between the two? One obvious factor was cost: it was on grounds of economy that Harvey and Unwin had called for the simplification of design of low-cost housing in 1906, and the same point was made in 1917 by the Secretary of the International Garden Cities and Town Planning Association, E. G. Culpin. Reviewing the munitions housing schemes Culpin lavished praise on the quality of design and workmanship at Well Hall but stated:

> The expense on the Well Hall Estate was colossal, so much so that there is a fear that the extravagance may deter others from copying the example....
> The logic of circumstances has forced upon cottage architects the conclusion that the simple type of cottage is the one which must now be concentrated upon, and that the plain roof is much superior for this purpose to the type which was formerly so much used – a type which was certainly more picturesque but which was more expensive, did not contain so much accommodation, and was not, by reason of the many breaks in the roof, so impervious to weather....
> Building has become, I fear, permanently dearer, and we must cut our coat according to our cloth....
> For the moment, therefore, I pin my faith to the simple plain type and look to site-planning and grouping to provide the necessary variety. When things become normal again, then, perhaps, we can add some more ornament and have more freedom in design.[25]

There were however more positive grounds for espousing simplicity of design. To arts and crafts designers of a certain persuasion it was to be preferred on aesthetic grounds as well. Faced with the harsh realities of low-cost housing, the picturesque and ornamental could be seen as a 'sham', a 'pretence' reminiscent of the speculative builder; 'rightness of form' could be obtained only by a simple type of house without any false pretensions. This was the argument suggested by Unwin in 1902 and it was repeated in 1906 by – ironically – Baines' former mentor, C. R. Ashbee. In designing a dwelling that the working man could afford, Ashbee wrote, the designer must 'eliminate all aesthetic superfluities, all hand work, and above all every pretence at it ... [making it] as simple, severe and economical as it can be made'.[26]

But at Gretna there was more than just simplicity of design: there was the simplicity of design of a recognisable historical period – the eighteenth century. There can be little doubt that this derived from the arguments emanating from the University of Liverpool. In the ten or so years before 1918, the Liverpool group, under the aegis of Professor Reilly, had mounted a formidable attack on romanticism in architecture, particularly as represented by the garden city movement. Writing in the first volume of the *Town Planning Review* in 1910, Reilly asked of the houses built in the garden suburbs:

> Is it entirely appropriate that they should in the main be based upon the early medieval type of cottage, with high pitched roof and gables ... rather than on the later Georgian types, with flatter roofs and sash windows, which are found so sedately set round many an English green ... contributing so largely to its restful character?[27]

The theme was taken up in rather less measured prose by other members of the faculty, with articles in the *Town Planning Review* by Abercrombie in 1913 and by Adshead, Budden and Ramsey in 1916.[28] Letchworth was depicted as a 'haunt of cranks', of 'little coteries of romantic enthusiasts', who attempted to live out a 'bucolic fantasy' through an architecture of gables, oak beams, inglenooks, and bob-and-string latches. In place of all this the Liverpool group called for a sober style of design which relied for its effect, not on picturesque detail and idiosyncratic individuality, but on proportion, repetition and similarity. Inspiration, they said, should be sought from the Georgian period, when a restful and satisfying overall effect had been obtained by the repetition of simple blocks with carefully placed and pro-portioned doors and windows. By taking this for its model, architecture would express the realities of the day which, according to these writers, were collectivism and standardisation, not individualism and craftsmanship. Adshead wrote in 1916:

> The standard cottage will depend for any attraction that it may possess, not upon the toolmarks of the workman, nor upon its

peculiarity or idiosyncrasy, nor in a word upon its individuality, but upon more general characteristics such as suitability to purpose and excellence of design. It will not be the home of an individual, of an anarchist; but the home of a member of a certain class, of a communist.

And thus with the well-designed standard cottage we will get, not a village where each dwelling expresses the foibles of its tenant, or what in practice usually happens, the expression of these as understood by an architect; but instead a thoughtfully composed collection of similar units, each of which contributes to the making of a composite design, and each of which bears the impress of being part of a carefully considered scheme.[29]

Adshead and Abercrombie saw their 'standard cottage' in heavily neo-Georgian guise. At the 'Dormanstown' scheme, designed in 1917, they provided not only sash windows but also six-panelled doors, cornices and triangular pediments, and laid out the roads and buildings in a highly formal, symmetrical manner (see Figures 18 and 19). While Unwin and his colleagues did not go quite so far, it was evident that the neo-Georgian overlay that they applied to simplified design at Gretna owed much to the ideas of the Liverpool school.

During the war the architectural arguments in favour of simplicity of design received powerful reinforcement from a trend of opinion only loosely related to questions of building. This was the movement for

Figure 18   Dormanstown: houses built on the 'Dorlonco' steel-frame system

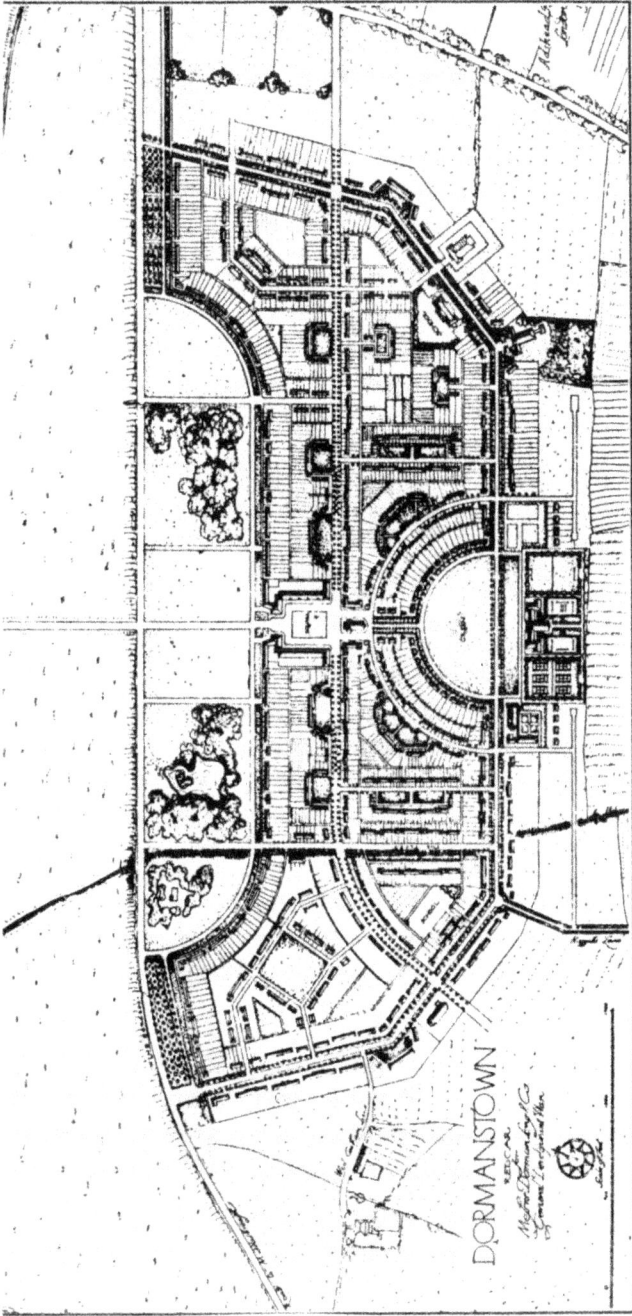

Figure 19   Dormanstown: layout plan, by Adshead, Ramsey and Abercrombie (1918)

industrial standardisation which, it appeared, had proved so beneficial when applied to aircraft construction and naval shipbuilding. By 1918 'simplification and standardisation' had become a catch-all slogan: every problem was to be solved in the way in which Henry Ford had 'solved' the problem of motor-car manufacture – by the mass-production of a limited range of standardised components of simple design. The result was that by 1919 MPs were citing the example of the Ford car in relation to the housing problem.[30] It was in vain that Baines pointed to the limitations of the theory when applied to housing. Most building materials, he insisted, were not produced in a factory, and to standardise one type for each component – for instance, one length of timber for joists – could only lead to a scarcity of the type selected and a surplus of all the others. A sympathetic review of the Roe Green estate reproduced Baines' argument:

> Standardisation, as advocated by many enthusiasts, is likely to become an unmeaning and depressing fetish. The economy to be attained by repetition in building is limited, and cannot be compared to that which can be effected in turning out machines or domestic implements. It is as easy and cheap to make 3 or 4 types of doors or windows in a large scheme as one, as easy and cheap to build a dozen types of houses as one, and in this scheme [Roe Green] no practical economy has been lost by the adoption of a design marked by a careful and well-considered variety of type.[31]

But by the time of the Armistice 'simplification and standardisation' had acquired all the force of popular orthodoxy, and Baines was more or less an isolated figure.

It was not only on questions of architecture that Gretna, Well Hall and the other schemes were seen as potential prototypes for any future state housing. Equally important was the question of housing standards. This is explored in some detail in Chapter 5 but at this point the wide range of standards bequeathed by the wartime programme should be noted. At the one extreme, there were (as at Gretna) houses with three bedrooms, a parlour, and an upstairs bathroom; but at the other, there were the small cottage flats at Roe Green and Well Hall with only two bedrooms and neither parlour nor separate bathroom; and only in a very few cases had the space standards recommended by the Departmental Committee of 1913 (see Table 1) been met. The wartime housing schemes provided examples of both relatively high and relatively low standards of accommodation: it still had to be settled to which any postwar state housing would incline.

4 The Drift of Policy 1916–19

In 1919 the government was pledged to secure the building of 500 000 houses on garden city lines and on 31 July of that year a Housing Act was passed to implement this promise. The purpose of this chapter and the one that follows is to show how this commitment came into being by examining in detail the development of official thinking on housing during and immediately after the First World War. This chapter looks at the discussions that took place on the general nature and goals of the proposed housing campaign while Chapter 5 looks at questions of design and housing standards. It is shown that in both cases government action was determined less by questions of housing *per se*, than by the uses to which housing could be put for wider political and ideological ends. During the war announcements of housing policy were used by the government as a pawn in its complex relationship with labour. In the wake of the Armistice, the 'homes fit for heroes' campaign was adopted as the major weapon of the state in the 'battle of opinion' on which, it was believed, the future of the entire social order depended.

First Thoughts

For the first two years of the war, government thinking on housing was dominated by immediate problems: the Housing Acts of 1914, the housing of munitions workers and the rent strikes and legislation of 1915. During 1916, however, and particularly after the establishment of the Reconstruction Committee in March of that year, attention turned to the question of housing after the war. Here a general consensus gradually emerged as to both the seriousness and the nature of the material problem. With the resources of capital, labour and materials taken up by the war effort, general residential building (which had produced an average of about 75 000 houses a year before the war) had, by the end of 1916, ground to a halt. The result was that long before the Armistice most parts of the country were faced with a severe housing shortage. The problem that this presented was compounded by the fact that the cost of house-building increased enormously during the war (by at least 100 per cent) and there was a general expectation that it would eventually fall when normal conditions had been restored. A Ministry of Reconstruction document of 1917 put the problem succinctly:

> In the years immediately following the war, prices must be expected to remain at a higher level than that to which they will eventually fall when normal conditions are restored.... Anyone building in the first years after the war will consequently be faced with a reasonable certainty of a loss in the capital value of their property within a few years.[1]

In a housing system that depended on the profit motive both for the initial construction and for the subsequent letting of the houses, this meant, in effect, that no houses would be built unless the government intervened in some way to write off the loss. Landlords, builders and tenants all agreed that state aid of some sort was the only answer.

The problem was first outlined in a memorandum prepared by the LGB in June 1916 at the request of the Reconstruction Committee. The board noted that, in view of the high costs of building, there would be little hope of private enterprise meeting the housing shortage that would have accumulated by the end of the war. State aid to private enterprise was politically contentious: 'few will ... suggest that ... State assistance should be given to private individuals'.[2] The capabilities of the public utility societies (to which the government had looked in the first 1914 Housing Act) were too limited to deal with a shortage of the extent anticipated. This left only the local authorities, but in postwar conditions they could not be expected to build unaided and so some sort of Treasury assistance would have to be provided. The LGB suggested that the line of action developed to deal with the problem of the housing of munitions workers should be adopted for the postwar problem: the Treasury should provide local authorities with a capital grant to cover the increase in building costs brought about by the war.

In government thinking about postwar housing the experiences of the Ministry of Munitions formed one obvious point of reference. The National Housing and Town Planning Council, for instance, in May 1917 'assumed that the assistance by the State ... will be on the lines of the housing that had been done for munitions workers'.[3] This implied that the leading role in housing provision would be taken by the central government – something that was, however, by no means universally acceptable. Such an explicit and open-ended acceptance by the state of responsibility for housing was not welcome to the markedly conservative thinking that dominated the LGB during the presidency of W. Hayes Fisher, from mid-1917 to October 1918. On the other hand – as will be seen below – the government programme for munitions workers provided a precedent that radicals were anxious to see extended.

Housing expertise from the Ministry of Munitions was brought to bear directly on the problem of postwar housing early in 1917, when Seebohm Rowntree left the Welfare Section of the Ministry and joined the reconstituted Reconstruction Committee formed by Lloyd George. The membership of this body was dominated by radicals, including the Fabians Beatrice Webb and Thomas Jones as well as Rowntree himself, but it lacked powers other than those of enquiry and exhortation. Beatrice Webb commented that the Reconstruction Committee 'is the maddest bit of machinery ... if there be neither open revolt nor silent obstruction in Whitehall, I shall be agreeably surprised ... We shall be marooned in one way or another by an enraged Whitehall'.[4]

In May 1917 Rowntree produced for the Housing Panel of the Reconstruction Committee a memorandum on *Housing in England and Wales*. This 'most useful document', as Beatrice Webb described it, provided the basis of much subsequent radical thinking on the postwar problem. Rowntree estimated the housing shortage at 300 000 units, more than double the estimate of 120 000 made by the LGB. His argument followed the familiar lines.

> The cost of building at present is abnormally high, and ... will still be high at the end of the war. Until it becomes normal ... no appreciable number [of houses] will be built unless action is taken by the Government. Aid to private enterprise would be politically unacceptable, the capacity of public utility societies was inadequate for the problem. Therefore housing must be provided by local authorities or by the State [i.e. central government] direct.[5]

In some of the munitions schemes, house-building had been undertaken by the central departments, but for the postwar programme Rowntree considered that this would be both undesirable and impracticable. It should, he said, be the local authorities that undertook the building, with a grant from the Treasury (as in some of the Ministry of Munitions schemes) to cover the 'difference between the cost of building during the period under consideration and its future normal cost' as established by valuation three years after the end of the war. It would then be the responsibility of the local authorities to obtain rents based on the normal cost of building or else to face a reduction in the Treasury subsidy. Reiterating the argument of the Land Enquiry Reports, Rowntree emphasised that economic rents were essential, for otherwise the state would be left with permanent responsibility for the provision of new houses.

The purpose of the housing programme was to secure the building of houses at a time of temporarily high costs when all the normal incentives would tend towards delaying building until costs had fallen. Rowntree therefore proposed that the government should impose definite time limits for the submission and implementation of local authority proposals. The positive rather than merely permissive role for central government that this suggested was reinforced by the Housing Panel to which Rowntree submitted his memorandum. In accepting Rowntree's proposals, one significant alteration was made, at the suggestion of the Chairman, Lord Salisbury: that where local authorities proved dilatory, central government should have powers to deal with recalcitrant authorities and undertake building of the houses itself.

Meanwhile the LGB had not been inactive. Under its energetic President, Lord Rhondda – one of the businessmen appointed to his new government by Lloyd George in December 1916 – the board undertook a series of interviews in May 1917 with the major interested parties of the 'housing world', including the National Housing and Town Planning Council (7 May), the Garden Cities and Town Planning Association (14 May), representatives of private enterprise (22 May) and the Workmen's National Housing Council (12 June). From these it emerged that private enterprise would not, on its own admission, be able to deal unaided with the housing shortage that would face the country at the end of the war and that some sort of aid by the central government to local authorities appeared unavoidable. Before the details of this could be settled, however, Rhondda considered it necessary to find out more about the extent of the housing shortage. Accordingly, in a minute to the War Cabinet of 14 June 1917 he sought authority to issue a circular informing local authorities of the government's intention to provide financial assistance for housing and requesting them to provide details of the housing requirements of their respective areas. Only by making an announcement of this sort, Rhondda stated, would the local authorities be induced to provide an accurate and realistic estimate of their housing needs.[6]

'Announcements should be made'
It was at this point that the deliberations of the housing mandarins in Whitehall came into contact with the hurly-burly of the political

world. Two days prior to Rhondda's Cabinet paper, on 12 June 1917, Lloyd George had set up a commission of enquiry to report on the industrial unrest affecting the country. The 'May strikes' of the engineering workers, together with more general evidence of discontent and war-weariness amongst the working class, appeared to amount to a major crisis for the state and a direct threat to the prosecution of the war. On 12 July the commissioners' reports were complete; on 17 July Lloyd George received a summary made by Barnes. Believing that 'for the vigorous prosecution of the war a contented working-class was indispensable',[7] the War Cabinet responded immediately and directly to the recommendations of the commission. The main conclusion of the enquiry was that the 'most important of all causes of industrial unrest'[8] lay in the soaring price and inequitable distribution of food. The government had to some extent anticipated this by announcing at the end of June the appointment of a Food Controller; this post was given to Rhondda, who was succeeded as President of the LGB by the former Parliamentary Secretary, W. Hayes Fisher. But the reports of the Industrial Unrest Commission also referred to housing. The commissioners stated that a cause of unrest that was 'acute in some districts' was the 'want of sufficient housing accommodation', and they recommended that even if the government was not prepared to meet the shortage by building, 'announcements should be made of policy as regards housing'.[9] While unwilling to commit resources on any large scale to house-building, the Cabinet responded swiftly to the call for announcements on housing policy. On 24 July the Cabinet discussed the question of housing and, after minimal debate, authorised the President of the LGB to issue the circular to local authorities. Four days later he did so. Stating that 'private enterprise will be quite unable to grapple successfully and speedily' with the housing shortage, the circular informed local authorities that the

> Government recognises that it will be necessary to afford substantial financial assistance from public funds to those local authorities who are prepared to carry through, without delay at the conclusion of the war, a programme of housing for the working classes approved by the LGB.
> It is not possible at this stage to indicate either the form which this assistance will take or the extent of it, but it may be taken that it will only be available for a limited period.[10]

By issuing the circular the War Cabinet complied with the commission's recommendation that it should make some announcement of housing policy. As a contribution to the preparation of postwar housing schemes, however, the circular was of doubtful value. Its terms were vague in the extreme. It noted that it 'may be advisable' for the state to aid public utility societies and private enterprise, but nothing definite was stated. As for the offer to local authorities, in the view of the *Municipal Journal* the circular

> carries us no further than the point at which Lord Rhondda left it … What local authorities want to know is whether the subsidy will be sufficient to justify them in embarking upon large housing schemes and to prevent losses from such schemes becoming a charge on the rates.[11]

Until the end of 1917, however, any further clarification of the postwar subsidy was vetoed by the Treasury. When Hayes Fisher suggested the issue of a further circular in October 1917, he was told by the Treasury:

> It is quite impossible for Their Lordships to commit themselves at the present time to any figure … as regards the amount which it will be possible to advance to local authorities … for that purpose….
> They would most strongly deprecate the issue of the Circular….
> They regard it as premature to make any further announcement to local authorities as regards housing beyond that contained in the Circular of 28 July last. [12]

Within a few months, however, a renewed crisis in the relationship of state and labour had created the conditions for a further announcement of housing policy. By the end of the year it was evident that the manpower needs of the armed services would compel the government to take more men from munitions works, and thus renege on the guarantees given to munitions workers earlier in the year. To counter the intense opposition that this was expected to provoke, the government launched a major tactical initiative designed to improve its own credibility and to split the moderate and extreme wings of the labour movement. The central element in this manoeuvre was the famous speech on war aims made by Lloyd George on 5 January 1918, in which he entirely endorsed the joint statement already made by the Labour Party and the TUC. The effect of the speech on public opinion, and particularly on the representatives of organised labour, was, as Thomas Jones noted, 'splendid'; but, even so, it was still felt that, if the Military Service Bill was to be carried through, the government had to 'take every possible step to remove the prevailing mistrust of the War Cabinet in the ranks of Labour'.[13]

The government was, of course, well aware of the role that housing could play in its relationship with labour. Hayes Fisher warned Lloyd George in November 1917:

Anything which retards the measures now being taken to push on preparations, or which can be interpreted as an attempt on the part of the Government to go back upon, or to 'hedge' in regard to, their pledge of 'substantial financial assistance' would have the most disastrous results and would tend largely to increase the industrial unrest of which housing is admittedly one of the causes.[14]

Accordingly, housing took its place in the government's tactical offensive, as it had in the summer of 1917. On 5 January 1918 – the day of Lloyd George's war aims speech – the Treasury lifted its veto on the issue of a further circular on housing to local authorities and consented to the 'formulation and communication of a provisional scheme' of financial assistance.[15]

The Treasury was not, however, prepared to make any 'definite pledge' on the amount of financial assistance that would be available, nor on the date at which it would commence. Moreover, the scheme that the LGB proposed, involving large capital outlay by the Treasury at the commencement of building operations, was not acceptable. Instead, the Treasury proposed a scheme of its own. Under this the local authorities would raise the capital for building by borrowing on the open market; the subsidy from the Exchequer would take the form, for the first seven years of the scheme, of three-quarters of the annual estimated deficit and, after the seven-year period, of three-quarters of the excess of the original cost over the estimated value of the scheme. In this way, the Treasury argued, local authorities would be relieved of the major part of any loss arising from building in the 'exceptional circumstances' of the immediate postwar period while the Exchequer would not be committed to the early and possibly premature issue of large capital sums. The LGB agreed to this proposal, securing Treasury consent to one significant modification: that where the loss faced by a local authority exceeded the produce of a penny rate levied on its area, the board should have discretion to extend the Exchequer contribution beyond 75 per cent.[16]

By the time this scheme was put to the War Cabinet in February 1918 the political and industrial situation had shown a further deterioration. On 1 February *The Times* carried a letter from Arthur Henderson which stated that:

At no period during the war has the industrial situation been so grave and so pregnant with disastrous possibilities as it is today.... The temper of the workmen is dangerous and the unyielding attitude of the Government is bringing the country to the verge of industrial revolution.[17]

On 5 February 1918 the War Cabinet set up a Committee on Civil

Disturbance 'to consider steps to be taken in the event of serious industrial trouble arising in connection with the attitude of the engineers to the Government's manpower proposals'. Exactly a month later the committee reported, warning of the serious danger of a general strike.[18]

Within the government supporters of a forward housing policy did not fail to point out the connection between housing and industrial unrest. George Barnes, the labour representative in the War Cabinet, recalled the recommendations of the Commissioners on Industrial Unrest of the previous summer and reminded his colleagues that 'deficiency of housing accommodation is one of the most prolific causes of industrial unrest'.[19] Hayes Fisher's memorandum to the War Cabinet of February 1918, which outlined the Treasury proposals and sought authority for the issue of the circular, was supported in writing not only by Barnes but also by the two ministers traditionally involved with the President of the LGB in the formulation of housing policy – the President of the Board of Agriculture and the Secretary of State for Scotland. Opposition in writing came from only one minister, who criticised the LGB proposal not for being too innovatory, but for being too moderate and conservative. Addison – now Minister of Reconstruction – argued that the absence of Treasury commitment on either the amount or date of commencement of the subsidy made the whole thing so 'conditional' that no local authority would proceed with the preparation of a housing scheme. Against the Treasury–LGB scheme Addison argued for the altogether more radical proposals developed at the Ministry of Reconstruction on the basis of Rowntree's memorandum of 1917.

In order to accommodate Addison's objections, the War Cabinet, with the concurrence of the Chancellor of the Exchequer, agreed to the deletion of the clause reserving the government's freedom to delay indefinitely the introduction of the subsidy. Otherwise it was decided that the circular should be issued as it stood.

> It was generally agreed that the force of some of the main criticisms made during the discussion would be best tested by the issue of the Circular to the local authorities. It would then be discovered how far they were prepared to take action on the strength of the Treasury's conditional promise, it being understood that if the result appeared inadequate it might then be necessary to issue an undertaking of a more definite kind, as suggested by the Minister of Reconstruction.[20]

The circular of 18 March 1918 set out the terms agreed between the Treasury and the LGB and asked local authorities to supply details of their proposed housing schemes (including numbers, estimates of cost, and site and house plans) 'with as little delay as possible'. Local authorities were told that to qualify for the subsidy schemes would have to commence within two months and be completed within twelve months of receiving sanction from the LGB, although this exhortation to urgency was rather weakened by the rider that 'provision will . . . be made for an extension of the term where circumstances necessitate this'. A similarly irresolute acceptance of the demands of the housing radicals was seen in the specification of housing density in the circular: 'to secure government assistance, the aim should be to provide that in ordinary circumstances not more than 12 houses (or in agricultural areas, eight houses) should be placed on an acre of land wherever this is possible without materially increasing the cost of the scheme.' The circular was issued on 18 March 1918. Only three days later the German army launched its great spring offensive and, with the sudden threat of national defeat, the internal crisis out of which the housing measures had been born disappeared almost overnight.[21]

The manpower crisis had nonetheless revealed the differences of approach between the two departments with responsibility for the formulation of policy on postwar housing. The attitude of the LGB was conditioned by its prewar experience in the administration of the Housing of the Working Classes Acts, under which responsibility in matters of housing rested primarily with local authorities rather than with central government. The board accordingly tended to see the solution to the postwar problem in terms of the government coming to the assistance of local authorities to enable them to meet their exceptional problems – in the same way as the Treasury had allowed local authorities to borrow money at reduced rates of interest before the war. A very different view was taken by the Ministry of Reconstruction, which saw housing within the context of the primary task of making a successful transition from war to peace. 'We must be ready for the emergencies of peace', said Christopher Addison shortly after his appointment as Minister of Reconstruction in 1917.[22] Demobilisation, return of troops, possible mass unemployment: the 'emergency problems' of peace would require handling as careful as those of war if disaster was to be avoided. Addison noted: 'The first thing to tackle at Reconstruction is to secure that some provision is made for the millions of demobilised soldiers, munition workers and other war workers, who will suddenly become at a loose end on the declaration of peace.'[23] If house-building was to play a significant part in absorbing demobilised personnel, a housing policy far more dynamic than anything attempted before the war would be required and – as had already happened with munitions housing – the central government would have to take the lead rather than, as in the past, leaving housing to the initiative of local authorities.

It was this outlook that lay behind the proposals put forward by Addison in March 1918 as an alternative to the Treasury–LGB scheme. As against the contributory role for the central departments envisaged by Hayes Fisher, Addison called for the government itself to take explicit responsibility for the housing of the working classes, making it a duty of local authorities to provide housing in their areas and giving itself the power to act in default of any local authority that failed in its obligations. Small authorities (which meant most rural district councils) should be replaced by county councils if they were unable to meet their housing obligations. To enable the central departments to carry out these unprecedented duties, Addison urged that the staff and organisation of the LGB should be enlarged and a number of regional housing commissioners be appointed to oversee the work of local authorities. Since, moreover, it was central government that was imposing on the local authorities the duty of providing houses at a time of exceptionally high costs, the Treasury should meet the whole of the loss in value of the houses due to the fall in costs after the postwar emergency period. Finally, Addison argued, a strict time limit should be imposed to ensure that the authorities carried out their duties immediately after the war, rather than waiting until building costs had fallen.[24]

As noted above, the War Cabinet in March 1918 retained its options on the Addison scheme, preferring to see if the Treasury–LGB proposals would prove workable but leaving the way open for the adoption of the Addison policy should it prove necessary. For, as the War Cabinet recognised, it was on the attitude of the local authorities that the decision really depended: if the government needed to get the houses built and was relying on the local authorities to do so, it would have little choice but to provide the latter with the guarantees they required. By the early autumn of 1918 it was clear that, as the *Municipal Journal* stated, the 'Government proposals ... are not satisfactory to the municipal authorities concerned'.[25] Many local authorities demanded that their financial liability should be limited to the produce of a 1d rate and in September this demand was taken up by the Association of Municipal Corporations which, as the government recognised, could 'be taken to represent the larger and more progressive urban authorities'.[26] On 1 October a meeting at Sheffield between Hayes Fisher and representatives of the local authorities failed to break the deadlock; while the latter refused to accept anything other than a strictly limited liability, Hayes Fisher could only reiterate that the 'Treasury would not agree to anything more favourable than the terms promised'.[27]

Armistice and After

Until the beginning of November 1918, the pledges made by the government on postwar housing conformed to the views of the LGB rather than the Ministry of Reconstruction. With the Armistice of 11 November 1918, however, the position was transformed. Suddenly the government found itself faced with the emergency foreseen by the Ministry of Reconstruction – the demobilisation of five million men from the services and the release of a similar number of men and women from munitions production and other war industries. In this situation the idea of a dynamic house-building campaign as a counter to unemployment assumed a new cogency. But the problem of moving from war to peace was not merely one of employment and logistics. To members of the government it appeared that the situation they faced in the wake of the Armistice, with 'general unrest and ... the presence of strikers [and] demobilised soldiers in the streets',[28] resembled in all too alarming a manner that which in other countries – Russia and Germany – had led to the overthrow of the state.

For, whether or not we now consider such fears to have been unnecessary, there is no doubt that at the time the Cabinet took the threat of revolution very seriously. Virtually as soon as the Armistice was signed, reports started to reach Whitehall of the 'very general talk of revolution' in the country.[29] At the end of January 1919, as the Cabinet faced the Clydesiders' strike for a forty-hour week, the Conservative leader and Deputy Prime Minister, Bonar Law, told the Prime Minister: 'everything depends on beating the strike in the Glasgow area, as if the strikers are successful there the disorder will spread all over the country'.[30] At the same time the Secretary of State for Scotland told the Cabinet that 'in his opinion, it was more clear than ever that it was a misnomer to call the situation in Glasgow a strike – it was a Bolshevist rising'; and Walter Long, the elder statesman of the Conservative Party, stated that 'there was no doubt that we were up against a Bolshevist movement in London, Glasgow, and elsewhere'.[31] By the beginning of February, it had emerged that the key sectors of power and transport presented the most serious danger. With the underground railway drivers on strike and the electricity workers and miners threatening to follow, the Cabinet on 4 February set up an Industrial Unrest Committee to take steps to deal with 'industrial unrest both at the present moment and in the future'.[32]

The Prime Minister, Lloyd George, warned that, if the miners' strike took place, it would be 'different in character from any hitherto ... a menace to the whole foundation of democratic government'.[33]

But while the state appeared thus threatened, the forces on which it relied for its ultimate defence seemed less than fully dependable. Early in 1919 the Cabinet anticipated a renewal of the police strike that had taken place the previous summer and, as regards the armed forces, several mutinies actually broke out in garrisons on both sides of the Channel. In immediate response to the latter, the Cabinet on 28 January decided on a pay increase for the services, 'frankly to allay unrest'.[34] Moreover, demobilisation – the real answer to unrest within the forces – presented perhaps the greatest danger of all, for the government feared that demobilised soldiers might form the military vanguard of a revolutionary movement. Throughout the first half of 1919 the government received alarming indications of discontent and radical tendencies among ex-servicemen's organisations, culminating in July 1919 in the boycott of the peace celebrations. It seemed that the mass army that had defeated the Kaiser might, now that it was demobilised, overthrow the government: as the Home Office warned, 'in the event of rioting, for the first time in history the rioters will be better trained than the troops'.[35]

How was this danger to be dealt with? Force, the last resort of government in the past, was clearly to no avail: there was no way that the government could force a demobilised mass army to do anything. The only answer was persuasion. As Lloyd George told Bonar Law in March 1919, it was ideas rather than guns that would decide the outcome of the crisis: 'the party that secures on its side either general opinion or the opinion of the working classes of the kingdom must win'.[36] On 3 March Lloyd George warned the Cabinet:

> In a short time we might have three-quarters of Europe converted to Bolshevism.... He believed that Great Britain would hold out, but only if the people were given a sense of confidence.... We had promised them reforms time and again, but little had been done. We must give them the conviction this time that we meant it, and we must give them that conviction quickly....
> Even if it cost a hundred million pounds, what was that compared to the stability of the State?
> So long as we could persuade the people that we were prepared to help them and to meet them in their aspirations, he believed that the sane and steady leaders among the workers would have an easy victory over the Bolsheviks among them.[37]

The occasion at which this declaration was made was the Cabinet's consideration of the Housing Bill. In the aftermath of the Armistice, the government promised a wide-ranging programme of social reform (including unemployment protection, hours of work, industrial democracy and land settlement), but at its heart was the promise of a great housing campaign. In the terms of Lloyd George's statement to the Cabinet, the housing campaign would give the people a 'sense of confidence' in the status quo and prove that there was no need to resort to revolution in order to improve their lot. Compared to the ends that the housing campaign would serve, cost was irrelevant: for it was believed that, as the Parliamentary Secretary to the LGB put it in April 1919, 'the money we are going to spend on housing is an insurance against Bolshevism and Revolution'.[38]

By the time the Cabinet considered the draft Bill at the beginning of March, government housing policy had, indeed, undergone a marked radicalisation. On the day following the Armistice Lloyd George announced a general election and pledged himself to secure 'habitations fit for the heroes who have won the war'.[39] At Wolverhampton on 23 November 1918 Lloyd George declared that 'slums are not fit homes for the men who have won this war'; at Basingstoke the new President of the LGB, Auckland Geddes (who had replaced Hayes Fisher a week before the Armistice) spoke in terms of a housing programme of one million dwellings; and the *Municipal Journal* noted that the 'Coalition manifesto gives housing a prominent place'.[40] Three days after the Armistice Geddes issued another circular, asking local authorities if they were prepared to build on the terms set out in the previous circular of March 1918.[41] Of the 1800 local authorities circularised some 1300 replied, of which nearly 1100 stated that they were prepared to build on these terms: but less than half of these specified the date at which their schemes would be ready for submission, and the total number of houses came to only 100 000. The conclusion drawn by the President of the LGB was presented to the War Cabinet in a memorandum dated 17 December 1918:

> Although I have no doubt that the existing proposals would lead to the provision of a substantial number of houses, I am not satisfied that they would ensure the erection of such a number or at a sufficiently early date to be regarded as a reasonable fulfilment of the Government programme.[42]

The terms offered by the government, Geddes stated, were unacceptable even to the more progressive authorities and as for the 'less progressive urban authorities and the rural districts ... more drastic methods will be required if an adequate number of houses are to be erected in these areas'. In view of this, Geddes proposed a 'considerable modification' of government policy. In the first place, powers should be given to both the LGB and county councils to act in default of a local authority; and the administrative strength of the LGB should be increased by the creation of a new Housing Department and by the appointment of regional housing commissioners. Moreover, the financial proposals should be changed to accommodate the demand of local authorities for the limitation of their liability to the produce of a penny rate: 'In view of the additional cost of providing houses for the working classes which is due to war conditions ... the whole of the burden in excess of an amount which would be produced by a penny rate should be borne by the Exchequer.' Accepting the Treasury's insistence on avoiding capital outlay from the Exchequer, Geddes proposed that during the transitional period of seven years the Exchequer should meet the excess of the annual loss on the housing scheme over the produce of a penny rate. At the end of the seven-year period the estimated annual income and estimated annual expenditure of the scheme would be compared; and if 'it appears that the future annual charge to be borne by the local authority would exceed the produce of a penny rate, the excess should be met by the State' through a capital grant. As with the government's previous proposals, the subsidy would cover only the excess cost brought about by the war; if the rents charged by local authorities fell below the economic level in relation to the normal cost of building, the LGB would have the power to reduce the Exchequer contribution accordingly.

The scheme proposed in December 1918 differed only on one or two points from that outlined by Addison the previous March. As a Ministry of Reconstruction official noted, Geddes' proposals were 'substantially those which we have urged throughout'.[43] This change of policy was not calculated to please the Treasury, which responded with scarcely concealed horror: the proposal was 'open to very serious objection ... the local authorities will have no real financial interest in the undertakings at all and will have no motive in economising expenditure'.[44] But in the face of the political crisis financial scruples had to be set aside; and by the end of January 1919 agreement had been reached between the Chancellor of the Exchequer and the new President of the LGB, Christopher Addison (who had succeeded Geddes in a Cabinet re-shuffle in the New Year). At the insistence of the Treasury, the capital grant payable at the end of the transitional period was replaced by an annual subsidy: but otherwise the terms agreed and announced in the circular of 6 February 1919 closely followed those proposed by Geddes. Initial capital for building was to be raised by local authorities on the open market, but their liability for losses on the revenue account was limited to the produce of a penny rate. During the transitional period up to 31 March 1927, this would be achieved by an annual Treasury grant based on actual expenditure and receipts; at the end of the transitional period, estimated annual expenditure and income would be reviewed and the grant fixed for the remainder of the loan period.[45]

The draft Housing Bill containing these measures was submitted to the War Cabinet on 1 March 1919 and considered, as noted above, on 3–4 March. Here it emerged that belief in the overwhelming political importance of the measure was not confined to Lloyd George and other erstwhile radicals but was also shared by the Conservative members of the coalition. Following Lloyd George's stirring introduction, the Chancellor of the Exchequer, Austen Chamberlain, stated that he 'thought they all agreed with the general attitude expressed by the Prime Minister.... He regarded housing as the first problem to be faced.... We ought to push on with it immediately, at whatever cost to the State.'[46] Such criticism of the Housing Bill as was made by the War Cabinet was not that it went too far in getting houses built at public expense but that it did not go far enough. The period allowed to local authorities for the preparation of their housing schemes was reduced from six months to three and it was decided that provision should be made so that 'where, in the opinion of the LGB, the scheme was not adequate or suitable, the LGB should be empowered to compel the local authority to prepare an adequate scheme'.[47]

Apart from these changes the draft Bill was accepted in general and referred to Cabinet committee for detailed treatment. Here it was decided that the minor clauses affecting town planning proposed by the LGB should be added to the Bill and that, accordingly, 'Town Planning' should be added to the title. More significant was the decision to excise the clause empowering local authorities to lend money to private owners for house improvements; such a clause was seen as a clear concession to the private landlord, which Addison considered a 'rather questionable' policy.[48] Otherwise the Bill was approved and, on 18 March, introduced to Parliament amid considerable publicity. 'An important part of the Government's policy of reconstruction and social reform' was the official description given in the press release. In the view of *The Times*, there was 'no doubt that the country regards this as far and away the most important Bill in the government's programme of social reconstruction'.[49]

An 'insurance against revolution'

The extent to which the housing proposals were an *ad hoc* response to an immediate political crisis was reflected in the vagueness of official statements on both the cost and probable duration of the programme. The number of houses needed had been put at a notional 500 000 in the Tudor Walters Report of November 1918 and it was this figure that was adopted by the government for its official target. The circular of 6 February 1919 stated that to qualify for the subsidy housing schemes would have to be carried out within two years of the date of the circular, but in Cabinet committee this was replaced by the more flexible formula, 'within such period as may be specified by the Local Government Board with the consent of the Treasury'. The LGB's view was that, given the inevitable delays, it would not be possible to maintain any rigid time limit, although for costing purposes the board worked on a hypothetical three-year timetable in which 100 000 houses would be built in the first year and 200 000 in each of the succeeding two years. But the official view of the board, to which it secured the agreement of the Treasury, was that the programme would continue until costs reached their postwar normal level: 'The intention is that financial assistance should be given while prices remain abnormal. . . . It is impossible to predict when prices will reach the postwar normal level. So long as prices remain at their present abnormal level financial assistance will be given'.[50]

On the cost of the scheme the government was equally uncertain. The LGB said that 'it is not practicable to do much more than guess at the ultimate annual charge' to the Exchequer. In a paper prepared by the board for the second reading of the Bill in the House of Commons, it was stated that the annual charge to the Exchequer would depend on the initial cost of the houses, the amount of the local authority contribution and the amount obtainable in rents, and that none of these could be accurately predicted. In response to a certain amount of pressure in Parliament, Addison published the board's estimates: for 500 000 houses at an average cost of £500 to £700 each, the total capital expenditure would be £250 to £350 million, on which it was considered that the annual charge to the Exchequer might ultimately be £5 to £7½ million. To neither the size nor the vagueness of these estimates, however, did Parliament take particular exception; Lord Salisbury – a supporter of the Bill – was one of the few members to express surprise 'at the way that this vast expenditure was presented to Parliament'.[51]

If the LGB was vague over cost, it was nonetheless definite as to the principles to be followed in determining the rents for the new houses. On this, the board stated, its policy was

to aim at getting rents which, at the end of the transitional period, when it is assumed that post-war normal conditions will have been reached, will approximate as nearly as possible to the economic rents obtainable for the same class of houses built at the post-war normal cost.[52]

The rents to be charged after the 31st day of March 1927 should be sufficient to cover (in addition to the expenses of maintenance and management of the houses and a suitable allowance for depreciation), the interest which would have been payable on the capital cost of building the houses if they had been built after that date.[53]

The principle of an economic rent on eventual normal cost (deriving from prewar Liberal thinking) was central to the 1919 Act. If the rents charged for the local authority houses were below what was needed to cover the normal cost of building, private enterprise would be driven out of working-class housing, forcing the state to take its place on a permanent basis. This, the government was in no doubt, had to be avoided.

The question of rent was bound up with the question of the class of tenant envisaged in the housing programme. The purpose of the programme was, ostensibly, to meet the shortage of working-class housing that had developed as a result of the war. Largely as a contribution to the complex series of negotiations held between the LGB and the London County Council, Addison announced in February 1919 that the subsidy would be available for slum clearance and rehousing as well as for additions to the housing stock. Nonetheless, the latter remained the clear priority; not until there were more houses available *in toto* would it be possible, as Addison said, for those at present living in slum conditions to move elsewhere.[54] The government's policy on rents meant that only the most affluent members of the working class would be able to afford to live in the new houses; as one MP stated, the tenant of the state house would be 'the aristocrat of the working classes, the skilled and highly paid artisan, because it is only that class of man who will have the chance, even with the subsidy . . . which the State proposes to supply', of being able to pay the rent demanded.[55] Here was the most obvious contradiction between the government's view of state house-building as an essentially temporary affair for which economic rents would be charged and the political function of the housing programme of providing houses for ex-servicemen in general. As events turned out (see Chapter 8), the combination of the high interest rates paid for capital and the fall in wages after the collapse of the postwar boom were to put the houses out of reach of any but the most affluent 'heroes'.

In the tumultuous political climate of the first half of 1919, the Cabinet, as already noted, preferred to exclude from the Housing Bill any explicit grant to private enterprise. Nonetheless, the Bill did include provisions intended to benefit employers and landowners, in the form of increased aid to public utility societies. In 1914 these had occupied a central place in the housing policy of the Liberal government and during the war their interests continued to be well represented in Whitehall, largely through the influence wielded at the Ministry of Reconstruction by the Garden Cities and Town Planning Association. After the Armistice, with the adoption of the Ministry of Reconstruction programme, increased aid to public utility societies became part of government policy and the 1919 Act included various provisions of benefit to them – not least, a Treasury grant of up to 30 per cent of their initial capital requirements. Since it was considered that 'these societies will in the great majority of cases be promoted and managed by the employers of labour', it was not surprising that the grant was attacked by labour (both inside and outside the House of Commons) but warmly supported by the Federation of British Industries.[56] It was, it seems, largely the inclusion of this grant that made the landowners regard the Housing Bill as, overall, 'an honest attempt to meet a very difficult situation'.[57]

There was, however, one section of the Bill to which landowners objected strongly. This was the section dealing with town planning, incorporating the recommendations for the simplification of procedure made by the Tudor Walters Report. Here the aim of the government was to remove the stages in the existing town planning procedure which were likely to delay the progress of housing schemes in town-planning areas. But to landowners these stages were not obstructive but protective, and they stated that they 'strongly object to these very moderate safeguards being taken away'.[58] On this, however, the tide was going against them. Once the question of town planning had been raised, its supporters in Parliament proved themselves to be an extremely well organised lobby that neither the landowners nor the government could altogether resist. Although admitting that the existing town planning procedure was 'impossible', Addison believed that 'all the energy and enthusiasm that we can command for the immediate future must be concentrated on housing needs', and he therefore resisted the idea of adding to the work of local authorities by making town planning compulsory.[59] But in the committee stage of the Bill it became clear that the town planning lobby would not be so easily persuaded. Eventually, after much argument, a compromise was reached: a new clause was added to the Bill requiring every town with a population of over 200 000, and any other town at the order of the LGB, to prepare a town planning scheme within three years of 1 January 1923. By this time, Addison conceded, the housing schemes of local authorities should have been completed.

The new town planning clause was one of the few significant alterations made to the Bill during its passage through Parliament. The property owners secured a couple of material changes: local authorities were, after all, empowered to make loans to private owners to improve their property and also, with the consent of the LGB, to sell land acquired originally for housing purposes. Apart from these and other minor alterations, mostly made by the government, the Bill reached the statute book with little objection from Members of Parliament. Matters on which the government had expected to face fierce criticism were accepted with scarcely a murmur. In the Commons the Bill passed without a division; in the Lords only Hayes Fisher, now Lord Downham, showed real hostility to the Bill. As Waldorf Astor, the Parliamentary Secretary to the LGB, said in winding up the debate, the government was 'absolutely amazed'[60] at the uniformly favourable reception given to the proposals.

The Cabinet had in fact underestimated the extent to which its own conviction that housing was the best antidote to revolution was shared by Parliament. In the debate on the second reading of the Housing Bill on 7 and 8 April 1919, one MP after another rose to testify to the belief that, as the member for Hertford, N. P. Billing, put it, the 'present housing conditions are the real, and in fact the only, reasons for social unrest',[61] and that decisive action on housing offered the best hope of an answer to the social crisis. Several MPs said it was bad housing that drove a man to thoughts of Bolshevism, and that the answer to unrest was to provide the working man with a 'real home'. Mr Billing continued: 'If a man is comfortably housed ... you will not find much unrest there'. This implied that the counter-revolutionary effect of the housing programme would stem from the direct influence of having a proper home; as another member said, 'We can never get at the root of our difficulties until we are able to give the people a home which is worth having'.[62] Other MPs advanced the more realistic argument put to the Cabinet by Lloyd George: they believed that it was by seeing the new houses being built rather than by the direct experience of living in them (which, after all, was to be confined to 500 000 families) that the people would be weaned from ideas of revolution. Sir Donald Maclean, the Leader of the Opposition, stated:

Unless this vital problem is dealt with promptly and effectively, the social conditions of this country will go from the very serious condition in which they are now to one of which we should shudder to think. . . . We are face to face with the greatest difficulties. . . . One of the great difficulties of the future will be unrest, and one of the best ways of mitigating it is to let people see that we are in earnest on this question.[63]

Whichever argument was advanced, the implications for house form and housing standards were similar. If the housing programme was to carry out this counter-revolutionary function, the new houses had to be, and had to be seen to be, in the words of J. D. Gilbert, MP for Southwark, 'on quite different lines' from those of the past and 'a great improvement on anything we have'.[64] It was a point made by no less than ten of the twenty-four members (other than government speakers) who contributed to the second reading debate. Mr Billing, whose views have already been quoted, derided the 'fatuous argument' against providing the working man with a bath and demanded that every house should have a bath and a proper hot-water system. Sir J. Bethell said that 'every house must have a bathroom'.[65] Several MPs spoke of the beneficial effects of putting the houses in quasi-rural surroundings and giving them proper gardens. The Conservative MP for Chelmsford, Mr Pretyman, stated:

> If there is one part of these proposals that appeals to me . . . it is that houses shall be provided in semi-rural conditions with good garden plots and with good transport access to the work in which the man is engaged, so that he can do his work in the factory while his family can live in fresh air under semi-rural conditions and in a properly constructed house and where, when he gets home at night, he will find not only a healthy family, but healthy occupation outside where they can go and work together in the garden. As one who knows what it means, I say that that will do more than any other part of this legislation.[66]

What was the meaning attached to the gardens, bathrooms and other improvements in housing standards that the MPs demanded? Mr Gilbert, who wanted houses on 'quite different lines', with bathrooms and labour-saving sculleries, provided the clearest answer: 'I hope that this will mark a new era for the working classes of this country'.[67] By building the new houses to a standard previously reserved for the middle classes, the government would demonstrate to the people just how different their lives were going to be in the future. In the terms of Lloyd George's Cabinet statement, the housing programme would persuade the people that their aspirations would be met under the existing order, and thereby wean them from any ideas of revolution. The new houses built by the state – each with its own garden, surrounded by trees and hedges, and equipped internally with the amenities of a middle-class home – would provide visible proof of the irrelevance of revolution.

5 A New Standard for State Housing

By the time the new housing policy reached the statute book in July 1919, its qualitative aspect (involving a transformation in housing quality) was considered to be at least as important as its quantitative aspect. This had not always been the case, however. Until the eve of the Armistice in November 1918, official statements on housing standards and design had rejected the demand for a fundamental improvement in quality, and had insisted that postwar housing should follow in the tradition of prewar municipal schemes. But, as with policy, so with standards and design, the political climate created by the Armistice soon drove the state to adopt a more radical position.

This position was generally identified with the Report of the Tudor Walters Committee, published in the week of the Armistice. Largely the work of Raymond Unwin, the report was the first comprehensive treatise on housing design; it exerted a considerable influence abroad and had a direct and profound effect on the design of state housing in Britain. Accordingly, in dealing with the development of the qualitative aspects of the new housing policy, this chapter first provides a short account of the controversy over housing standards and then examines in detail the contents of the report and looks at the response it evoked from the organs of the state in the months that followed the armistice.

Controversy over Housing Standards

It was on 24 July 1917 that the Cabinet approved the issue to local authorities of a circular announcing the government's intention to provide 'substantial financial assistance' for housing after the war. Two days later the President of the LGB, Hayes Fisher, appointed a committee to investigate the technical side of the housing programme under the chairmanship of the Liberal MP Sir John Tudor Walters. The brief of the committee was to consider questions of building construction and report on methods of securing 'economy and despatch' in the provision of working-class housing. While critics of the LGB complained that concern for 'despatch' was not a quality noticeable in its approach to the housing question, the sincerity of the LGB's interest in economy was never in doubt and it was, indeed, on grounds of economy that the board opposed any major improvement in housing standards for the postwar programme. Any improvements (such as the provision of a bathroom or parlour), the board argued, would lead to an increase in cost that would have to be borne by the Exchequer and should therefore be resisted as far as possible. In 1918 the board stated that

> Any increase in expenditure in the erection of houses by local authorities in the years immediately following the conclusion of the war will fall largely on the State.... Any such increase that can reasonably be avoided consistently with the erection of houses that shall be healthy and of sound structure must be avoided.

Accordingly improvements in standards and design should not be accepted.

> The Board are not prepared to accept the view ... that it is essential that *all* houses should have a parlour in addition to a living-room and scullery, nor do they accept the view that a separate bathroom ... is in all cases essential. Moreover they would not be prepared to insist on all houses having three bedrooms although this should be the general rule....
>
> [Since] houses providing three satisfactory bedrooms on the first floor can be designed with a 16 foot frontage ... the Board could not insist on a rigid rule that the frontage should be greater in every case....
>
> If expense were no object, or if the tenant would be prepared to meet the extra cost ... by the payment of an extra rent, the Board could readily accept the ideal arrangements desired, but as matters stand they are of opinion that less expensive arrangements must be accepted as sufficient.[1]

The extent to which the LGB in 1917–18 conceived postwar housing in terms of prewar types was indicated in the revised edition of the *Memorandum for the use of Local Authorities with respect to the Provision and Arrangement of Houses for the Working-Classes.* Dated November 1917, but not issued until January 1918, this was intended by Hayes Fisher as a guide to local authorities on the preparation of housing schemes under the circular of July 1917. The text followed that of the 1913 *Memorandum* with only the most minor changes. As in 1913, local authorities were told that their efforts should be directed 'mainly' to the housing of the 'poorer classes' rather than of the 'better-paid working class'; there was no mention of a parlour and it was again stated that 'a bath ... can advantageously be fitted in the scullery'. In fact, only two noticeable changes had been made to the text of the memorandum. The maximum desirable number of houses in a row or terrace was reduced from '10 or 12' to '8 to 10', and a specific caveat was inserted on the importance of securing a 'sunny aspect' for the living-room – both minor concessions to the views of the housing reformers. Otherwise the 1917 *Memorandum* was the same as that of 1913.[2] The new set of house plans that accompanied it showed slightly more modification: the volume of the houses had increased since 1913 by some 15 per cent and a parlour was shown in six out of twelve houses, instead of one in five. The separate bathroom, entirely absent in 1913, now appeared in four plans. Nonetheless, in most respects the plans appeared retrogressive to housing reformers, who submitted them to some harsh criticism. The architect Percy Houfton, for instance, referred to the 'unfortunate set of plans which have been issued for the guidance of local authorities ... The collection seems to have been made almost with levity, so haphazard and inconvenient is the planning in many cases.'.[3]

The conception of postwar housing indicated by the board's memorandum also informed its much-publicised cottage competition held at the same time. Following a suggestion made at a conference of 'housing experts', Hayes Fisher in August 1917 secured Treasury consent to the expenditure of £5000 on a competition for the design of postwar housing, to be organised by the Royal Institute of British Architects (RIBA). Although nominally prepared by the RIBA, the conditions for the competition were approved by the LGB and, in accordance with its instructions, emphasised the need for strict economy. Thus of the four classes for which entries were invited, one was for a cottage flat, and of the remaining three classes, only one met the demand for a minimum of three bedrooms and a parlour. Instead of a separate bathroom, the conditions specified only a fixed bath and cold water supply. In the view of *The Builder*, the conditions of the competition were 'archaic'.[4]

Under Hayes Fisher it was thus LGB policy that the type of housing to be built after the war should be essentially the same as that provided by local authorities before 1914. Before 1918 this view came under heavy criticism, from both outside and inside Whitehall. The main critic outside the government was the Workmen's National Housing Council (WNHC). Before the war the WNHC had campaigned for improvements in the standard of municipal housing and in 1915 it renewed its call for local authorities to build superior housing that would satisfy the expectations of upper levels of the working class. It was, the WNHC stated, essential 'to resist schemes that aim at building down to the poverty standard of the ill-paid and unorganised classes.' Instead, there should be 'a complete reformation in the housing accommodation of the people', with housing estates planned so as to be 'pleasant to the eye' and equipped with communal facilities, while each cottage should include a garden, a bath and a supply of hot and cold water. Of course, it noted, 'It is quite impossible to persuade local authorities to build dwellings approaching the standard the Housing Council advocates unless the State co-operates by rendering financial assistance.'[5] This remained the goal of the WNHC throughout the war: the state should provide the financial assistance to enable local authorities to build a much higher standard of housing for the skilled working man. By the time of its interview with the President of the LGB, Lord Rhondda, in June 1917, the demands of the WNHC on housing standards were precise: a minimum of three bedrooms per house, a separate bathroom with hot and cold water, and the enforcement of the minimum space standards defined by the Departmental and Advisory Committees.[6]

During the presidency of Hayes Fisher (June 1917–October 1918), the LGB remained resolutely indifferent to the demands and even the existence of the WNHC. Less easy to ignore was the Ministry of Reconstruction, which was committed to a radical line on housing standards and design as well as policy. At its first meeting in April 1917 the ministry's Housing Panel agreed on the importance of achieving a 'decent standard' in any housing provided by the state:

> The question of standard cannot be neglected. The lowest standard which decency requires is three bedrooms and two living rooms for an average family. . . . It is the duty of the State, in the emergency which will arise at the end of the War, to make adequate provision to supply the deficiency of houses of a decent standard.[7]

During the course of 1918 the ministry's belief in what Rowntree called 'the advantage which may be taken of the present situation, materially and permanently to raise the standard of houses'[8] led it into more or less open conflict with the LGB over housing standards and design. Towards the end of 1917, largely at the instigation of the Women's Labour League, Addison appointed a Women's Sub-Committee to subject to the housewife's scrutiny the houses built for the Ministry of Munitions and the prize-winning designs from the LGB's cottage competition. Their views on the former, particularly the scheme at Gretna, have already been cited in Chapter 3. It was, however, to the LGB's cottage competition and *Memorandum* that the Women's Housing Sub-Committee first turned its attention, and its interim report, signed in May 1918, constituted a scathing attack on both. On the conditions of the competition it stated:

We note with regret the minimum standards which appear to be accepted by the LGB, and we are of opinion that the general conditions of the competition are not compatible with the interests of the housewife....

We consider that the designs show no advance over those of many urban houses and we recommend a revision of minimum requirements.

The *Memorandum* was adversely criticised by the Women's Sub-Committee on a number of points. The minimum frontage of 16 feet for a three-bedroom house they described as 'insufficient' and the admission of rear projections as 'regrettable'; the minimum area specified for the main bedroom (132 square feet) was 'inadequate' and the omission of a parlour from the specification of accommodation was a 'retrograde step'. Furthermore, the Sub-Committee stated, 'In all cases we are strongly of opinion that the bath should be placed in a separate room ... The reference to the possibility of houses being built without baths is calculated to countenance retrograde action by local authorities.'[9]

Although couched in terms of the convenience of the housewife, the Women's Sub-Committee's comments amounted to a demand for a fundamental improvement in housing standards. Such a 'direct attack upon an LGB publication'[10] caused considerable embarrassment at the Ministry of Reconstruction and did nothing to improve relations between the two departments. Eventually, after awkward and protracted discussions with the LGB, the ministry decided not to make public the detailed criticisms made by the Women's Sub-Committee but only to publish in a non-polemical form their general recommendations on cottage planning and design. Together with a brief and discreet summary of the recommendations arising out of their 'observations' on the cottage competition and LGB *Memorandum*, these were published as the First Interim Report of the Women's Housing Sub-Committee in October 1918.

The Tudor Walters Report

The publication of the Women's Housing Report was followed within a few weeks by the appearance of another housing report which, by the fullness of its treatment and the authority with which it spoke, soon eclipsed all others in the public eye. This was the report of the committee chaired by Sir John Tudor Walters.[11] In the fifteen months following the appointment of the committee in July 1917 its findings were eagerly awaited by those interested in the housing question and when the report finally appeared, in the second week of November 1918, it was immediately recognised as 'the most practical and useful contribution to the general housing question published in recent years.'[12] Running to just under 100 pages, the Tudor Walters Report was the first comprehensive treatise on the political, technical and practical issues involved in the design of the small house, and in the housing debates in 1918–19, its authority became almost unquestionable. The Tudor Walters Committee was often referred to simply as the 'experts' committee' and it was indeed a distinguished body. The chairman was a respected Liberal MP with a long-standing interest in housing; the secretary, E. Leonard, was a housing inspector from the LGB. Four members of the committee were particularly noteworthy. The architectural representative, Sir Aston Webb, was undoubtedly the most famous, although he had little experience of housing. Less well-known, but rather better qualified, was the Controller of Housing and Town Planning and Chief Engineer at the Scottish LGB, J. Walker Smith. The other two leading members of the committee had first-hand experience of building in emergency conditions: Raymond Unwin and Frank Baines. But, as was shown in Chapter 3, Unwin and Baines held rather different views on housing design, and, although the report contained indications of both points of view, Baines actually resigned from the committee a month before the report was signed. As will be seen, it was the brain and hand of Unwin more than any other member that moulded the structure and arguments of the report.

The report covered four main areas. First, it put forward a number of general recommendations as to housing policy and administration, and as to the type and class of house to be built. Second, it discussed the layout of housing schemes and recommended certain procedures for site planning and development. Third, it dealt with the house itself: with the standard of accommodation to be provided, with methods of arranging the internal planning of the house, and with principles of design. Finally, the report reviewed the investigations undertaken for the committee into the costs and availability of various building materials, and into the possibilities for saving presented by standardisation and the use of new materials.

In entering the area of housing policy, the committee was certainly making a wide interpretation of its brief to 'consider questions of building construction'. The committee argued, however, that discussion of economy and despatch in the provision of housing could not take place on a purely technical level, but had to include some consideration of wider issues, such as the class of house to be built and the administrative framework for the housing programme. In any case, this provided the committee with the pretext for a discussion of general questions of housing policy, in which it endorsed the proposals, not of the LGB, but of the Ministry of Reconstruction. In order to meet the existing shortage of houses (which, it said, stood at 500 000 in 1918 and which was increasing by 100 000 a year) the report said that 'some dynamic force' would be needed: the LGB should be given powers to compel local authorities to act; a 'strong Housing Department' should be created at Whitehall and a system of regional commissioners set up to stimulate and co-ordinate the work of local authorities. Not only municipal enterprise but also private enterprise, in the form of public utility societies, should be included in the scheme. To secure the necessary materials, the committee made the recommendation (prefiguring that of the Carmichael Committee on the Building Industry after the war, of which both Tudor Walters and Walker Smith were members) that the government should take steps to stimulate production and should give priority to housing in the use of the materials available. As will be seen in Chapter 6, this was one recommendation of fundamental importance that was to be rejected by the Cabinet – with catastrophic results for the housing programme.

The radical views on housing policy expressed by the Tudor Walters Committee were maintained in its treatment of housing standards. In appointing the committee, Hayes Fisher had intended that it should examine ways of cheapening and expediting the construction of houses of the kind set out in the board's *Memorandum*. The committee, however, turned this on its head. Against Hayes Fisher's argument that economy proscribed the provision of housing of a higher standard than that generally approved by the LGB before the war, the Tudor Walters Report argued that good economy actually demanded major improvements in housing standards. Whereas in the past the function of local authority housing had been to meet the housing needs of the 'poorer classes', the problem after the war, the report stated, would be a shortage of housing of all kinds. In view of the tendency of the housing standards demanded by the working class to rise, it claimed, it would be bad economy to provide new houses of other than the highest standard. Otherwise, before the loan repayment period had expired the houses might become unlettable, with resultant losses to local authorities. Developing the argument previously advanced in 1913 by the Departmental Committee, the Tudor Walters Committee stated:

Hitherto the housing undertaken under the Housing Acts and supervised by the Local Government Boards has been mainly intended to provide for the poorer sections of the working classes, whose needs could not be met by private enterprise owing to their inability to pay such a rent as would provide adequate inducement to speculative or other private builders. The problem with which the Boards are now confronted, however, is a serious shortage of all kinds of houses for the working classes; for the building of houses during the war has ceased for the well-paid as much as the ill-paid sections. This fact must materially affect the types of house which it is most economical to build, and the standard of accommodation and equipment which should be provided.

The general standard of accommodation and equipment demanded in their dwellings by the working classes has been rising for some time; and there is every prospect that the influence of war conditions will considerably increase the force and extent of this demand for an improved standard.

The erection ... of so large a number of houses as is now contemplated must profoundly influence the general standard of housing ... which it is the desire of the Boards to see raised....

In the face of an improving standard it is only wise economy to build dwellings which, so far as may be judged, will continue to be above the accepted minimum, at least for the whole period of the loan with the aid of which they are provided, say 60 years; to add to the already large supply of houses on the margin line might prove anything but economical in the long run....

Ultimate economy in the provision of dwellings will depend upon the relation between the average rental secured over a long period and the annual amount which has to be expended to meet interest and sinking fund on the capital outlay or to defray maintenance and other charges; hence the probable future conditions must be studied as well as immediate results. (Paragraph 27)

In the report's argument for the adoption of a much higher standard for postwar housing there were thus two main strands. The committee assumed that a major objective of the LGB was to secure an improvement in the general standard of housing. As noted above, to Hayes Fisher such a goal was subsidiary to the primary task of limiting expenditure. More important to the committee's case was the contention that the standard of housing demanded by the working class had risen in the past and would continue to do so in the future. This was central to the rationale for higher standards: for only if this was so did it make sense to concentrate on the uppermost levels of working-class housing rather than provide equally for the 'shortage of all kinds of houses for the working classes' which then existed. In adopting this position the Tudor Walters Committee was thus assuming the present and future efficacy of working-class demands. In the turbulent

atmosphere of 1918 this seemed no more than common sense. Later,
however, after the collapse of the postwar boom in 1920, the political
and economic power of the working class declined considerably, with
the result that housing standards then fell sharply from those
recommended by the Tudor Walters Committee.

The committee stated that 'some of the most impoitant economies
in the provision of dwellings depend on the laying out and development of the sites, including roads, drains, etc.', and accordingly
a major section of the report was devoted to this subject. Here
the report followed Unwin's earlier publications and summarised the
principles and techniques of low-density layout developed by the
garden city movement. As Unwin had shown before the war, economy
in low-density development depended particularly on the savings in
roads and road costs that the reduction in the number of houses per
acre made possible: if estates were laid out at low densities (twelve
or eight houses to the acre) but following the layout methods of
high-density development, enormous diseconomies would result. To
avoid this, the report contained specific and detailed advice on low-
density layout: on the treatment of road junctions and the regulation
of road widths, on the elimination of rear access roads (to be replaced
by open passageways within the cottage blocks), on the location of

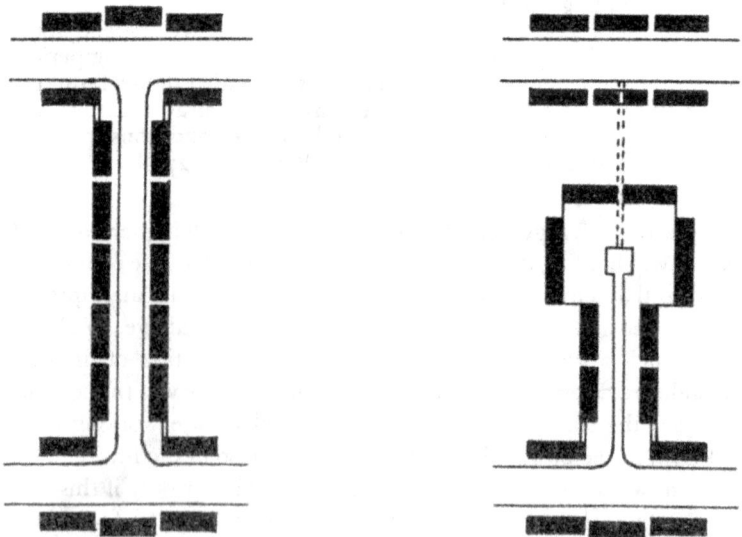

*Figure 20   Tudor Walters Report (1918): economic advantages of cul-de-sacs.
The cul-de-sac (right) provides frontage for as many houses as the through
road (left), but saves more than 50 per cent in road construction costs*

open spaces and on the uses of the cul-de-sac (see Figure 20). Many of these points were illustrated with diagrams taken from Unwin's earlier publications, most notably *Town Planning in Practice* of 1909.

On the aesthetics of planning, the Tudor Walters Report took a similar view to that advanced by the Departmental Committee in 1913: that beauty derived not from ornamental and therefore costly additions but from what were termed the inherent elements of good design, such as proportion and vista.

> To be content merely with satisfying the utilitarian ends of a scheme would be false economy; the amenities should be considered. The care and thought which are required to secure economical provision for the practical requirements, if exercised with trained imagination, may at the same time make of the necessary parts of the plan a coherent design ... Within the limits prescribed by convenience and due economy, by so planning the lines of the roads and disposing the spaces and buildings as to develop the beauty of vista, arrangement and proportion, an attractiveness may be added to the dwellings at little or no extra cost, which we consider should not only not be omitted, but should be regarded as essential to true economy. (Paragraph 56)

As an example of this combination of the practical with the aesthetically desirable, the report cited the placing of outbuildings between end houses, as at Gretna and Mancot. Apart from their practical advantages, stated the report, 'these links improve the grouping of the outbuildings and tend to remove the objectionable appearance of the repeated gaps' (see Figure 16).

The discussion of estate layout in the Tudor Walters Report was, essentially, a summary of an existing body of published knowledge. With the treatment of the house itself, this was not the case. Here the report was both more contentious, in arguing for a radical improvement in housing standards, and more innovatory, in attempting a comprehensive treatment of the design problems of the small house.

The Tudor Walters Committee was by no means the first body to call for a radical improvement in housing standards for postwar housing. As we have seen, it was preceded both by the WNHC and by the Women's Housing Sub-Committee. At the time the innovation represented by the Tudor Walters statements on housing standards lay less in what was said than in the status of the body making the pronouncements. In contrast to the WHNC and the Women's Sub-Committee, both of which appeared somewhat disreputable to the eyes of the establishment, the credentials and authority of the Tudor Walters Committee were impeccable. Appearing within the pages of such a definitive treatise, the policy of improvement in standards –

which the LGB had until this time rejected – acquired a new and quasi-objective authority.

Although the report was, as the *Municipal Journal* put it, on the 'side of the angels'[13] in the debate on housing standards, its stand was, in fact, rather less heroic than that of the Women's Sub-Committee. Apparently unqualified recommendations made in the text were all too often modified elsewhere. Thus, while the report recommended that 'every house should be provided with a bath in a separate apartment', elsewhere it suggested that 'the bath ... may be in the scullery, if no other arrangement is practicable'. Likewise, on the three-bedroom minimum demanded by working-class witnesses the Committee displayed a certain ambivalence: it stated that 'generally houses with less than three bedrooms should not be erected as part of the proposed housing programme' but elsewhere admitted that 'we recognise that there may be exceptions'. On the parlour question (rightly described as 'the most debatable point in reference to accommodation'), the report followed Unwin's earlier writings in insisting that, however much it was desired by the tenants, the parlour was not to be regarded as essential:

> The desire for a parlour ... is remarkably widespread both among the urban and rural workers. ... It is the parlour which the majority desire.
>
> Such witnesses state that the parlour is needed to enable the older members of the family to hold social intercourse with their friends without interruption from the children; that it is required in cases of sickness in the house ... that it is needed for the youth of the family in order that they may meet their friends; that it is generally required for home lessons by the children of school age, or for similar work of study, serious reading, or writing, on the part of any member of the family; that it is also needed for occasional visitors whom it may not be convenient to interview in the living-room. ... It will be seen from these instances that considerable importance is attached to the provision of a parlour. ...
>
> We consider, therefore, that whenever possible a parlour should be provided and that, in all schemes, a large proportion of houses having parlours should be included. ...
>
> We do not, however, consider that the parlour should be secured by cutting down the minimum sizes of the living-room, scullery or other essential parts of the house; and, *where it is not possible to provide a parlour except in this way, we recommend that it be omitted.* (Paragraph 86; author's emphasis)

On the issues of both the parlour and the bathroom, the Women's Sub-Committee had shown itself more resolute in its endorsement of working-class demands.

For room sizes the Tudor Walters Committee reverted to the series of minima originally published by the Departmental Committee in 1913 and endorsed by the Advisory Committee in 1915. Two sets of figures had been produced by the Departmental Committee, one for the smallholder's house and the other, less generous, for the agricultural labourer's cottage (see Table 1). Only the first of these was reproduced in the Tudor Walters Report. These, it said, were the 'minimum sizes of rooms which it is desirable to build'; and the report warned that the reduction of room sizes in order to reduce costs was not economically sound.

The question of a separate bathroom and parlour, and minimum room sizes, offered straightforward indicators of housing standards. A more complex but almost equally contentious aspect of the standards issue concerned the level and arrangement of services. In the traditional working-class house, the living-room was equipped with a coal range and served for cooking, as well as for eating and general living. As the report noted, however, 'working-class occupants generally are more and more wishful to eliminate from the living-room the dirty work and particularly the cooking of meals'. This, the report stated, had to be taken into account in planning the new houses, although (as will be seen below) by no means all the plans and arrangements it recommended conformed with this requirement. Whereas the WNHC called for the complete elimination of cooking from the living-room in all new houses, the Tudor Walters Committee argued that the separation of the cooking function from the main heat source ran into substantial problems of cost and raised a number of difficulties in relation to both the location of, and the apparatus for, the separate functions. As Unwin told the Women's Sub-Committee, these constituted 'the biggest problem in cottage planning'.[14]

The Tudor Walters Report stated that there were essentially only three satisfactory ways of distributing the heating functions between the various rooms: these three

> correspond to three methods of arranging the life and work of the house ... all the details of the planning of each room and its equipment must accord with one or other of these methods throughout, if each house is to be thoroughly convenient for one or other method of life. (Paragraph 101)

In the most economical of the three arrangements recommended by the report, the cooking-range was located in the living-room; the scullery contained both the copper (for water-heating) and a gas cooker (for use when the range was not lit) or, in the absence of gas, a small grate or stove suitable for drying clothes. Hot water would be supplied direct from the copper to the bath, which had therefore to be located either in the scullery or in a small room opening off it. In the second arrangement, the living-room contained 'a modified form of grate intermediate between a cooking-range and a sitting-room grate, so that a limited amount of cooking can be done on occasion'; there was a gas cooker or stove and a copper in the scullery, but hot water for the bath would come from a back-boiler working off the fire in either the living-room or the scullery. This involved the extra cost of a hot-water circulating system but it freed the bath from the scullery copper and meant that the bathroom could be put on the first floor. This was also the case with the third arrangement, which was the only one of the three to comply with the demand for the complete elimination of cooking from the living-room. In this the living-room contained only a 'sitting-room grate'; the scullery housed the cooking-range and gas cooker (where gas was available), while hot water for the bath came from a back-boiler in the range. A parlour could be added to each of the three methods of arrangement, making in the terminology of the report, classes Ia, IIa and IIIa. But of the total of six classes recommended it was only the most luxurious (IIIa) that provided the amenities 'desired by the majority of the artisan class'; as the report admitted, only this arrangement provided 'what is regarded by them as the necessary accommodation for the proper carrying on of family life'.

On the question of the plans that were to incorporate these different arrangements, the committee's advice was clear: true economy consisted not in following a single standard plan that was supposed to offer maximum size for minimum cost, but 'in taking advantage of all the opportunities afforded by the site, position and aspect of each house in order to secure the greatest comfort and so obtain the best value for building cost'. Standardisation, whatever its benefits in other cases, should not be applied to house plans, in the manner of the speculative builder who erected houses of the same plan regardless of site or aspect. In contrast to the demand of the Liverpool group for a 'standard cottage', the Tudor Walters Committee called for flexibility in planning, so that the most desirable house could be produced for each individual situation. Type plans, it said, should be used only as the basis for design: for every housing scheme, the report urged, it would be necessary to appoint an architect to design the layout and select and adapt the type plans for the particular requirements of the scheme.

The best economy can be secured only when these types are used and adapted by a competent architect to suit the individual circumstances of each house. The type plans will guide as to the many internal conditions which need to be considered and will suggest alternative arrangements; the adaptation of them to site and situation should be the work of the architect in charge of each scheme. (Paragraph 158)

The first question to be settled in house planning was the number of storeys, that is, whether the accommodation should be provided on one floor or two. As a cheap alternative to the ordinary cottage, cottage flats had been built extensively before 1914, both by speculative builders (particularly in the North-East) and by local authorities, but they were generally disliked by housing reformers, who considered them a very poor substitute for a 'real' cottage. The Tudor Walters Committee conceded that the single-storey flat might be admissible in exceptional circumstances (for instance, in Scotland, where it was a traditional house type) but in general considered that it involved a number of practical disadvantages and that the economies claimed for it were more apparent than real. 'On the whole', the report stated, 'the two-storey cottage is the type which should generally be adopted'. Since Baines was a strong advocate of the cottage flat and was at Roe Green providing nearly half of the accommodation in the form of flats, it is not hard to see why he resigned from the committee.

The examples of economical house plans given in the report can be broadly grouped into five types. The 'simplest type' was for a non-parlour house with a south aspect, organised around a front living-room and back scullery, with the stairs running along the party wall (see Figure 21A). The basic example given in the report, with a narrow frontage (16 ft 4 in) and with the bath in the scullery, had previously appeared in the reports of the Departmental and Advisory Committees and had been used at Gretna. The committee felt that this plan was suitable only for end houses, where the landing could be lit from the side, and even then only where the aspect permitted some sunlight to reach the two bedrooms at the back. Alterations could be made to this basic plan to make it suitable for other locations and requirements. If the frontage were widened by three feet, the staircase could be put at the back of the house and lit from the north side, the bath could be given a separate room opening off the scullery and the first-floor layout could be rearranged so that two of the three bedrooms faced south. In illustration of this the report reproduced another plan from Gretna.

Where the aspect was more or less north, the only really satisfactory solution, in the view of the committee, was to adopt 'the longer and shallower type of plan which allows the living-room to have windows at both ends' (Figure 21B). This permitted sunlight to enter the living-room from the back; two bedrooms could be placed on the south side, and the larder and stairs on the north. Again, variations and enlargements were possible. The plan itself

> has many advantages; the increased frontage on both the open sides gives better opportunity for lighting and ventilating thoroughly all parts of the house.... The reduced depth of the building requires smaller roof space, shorter rafters, less height of end gable walls, party walls and chimneys. (Paragraph 155)

These were savings that could partly compensate for the increased cost arising from the greater length of outside walls and road frontage. This was the sort of cottage 'with the principal room extending from front to back' particularly favoured on health grounds by housing reformers.

This wide-fronted plan for a north aspect house could be developed into a plan for a parlour house of the same aspect. The addition of a parlour, the report noted, 'considerably complicates the planning', making it more difficult to get the right aspect for all rooms within an economical format. Furthermore,

> If placed at the front of the house, the parlour, the entrance lobby, the staircase and the larder (provided this is the best aspect for it) do not occupy as much frontage as is required comfortably to accommodate the living-room, scullery and other accessory parts at the back; hence, in many small parlour houses, either there is a projection for the coal store and WC, or the plan assumes an 'L' shape. (Paragraph 156)

In the illustration provided in the report, derived from the bay-windowed parlour house at Gretna, the coal-store and WC were placed in an outbuilding at the side of the house which also formed a link between the pairs of houses (see Figures 21C and 16).

For a parlour house with a south aspect, the report stated that the design problems were less acute and that two type-plans were feasible. One was essentially a development of the 'broad and shallow' plan, with the staircase moved from the corner to the centre of the house which it now effectively bisected, and the parlour taking the place of the stairs in the corner (Figure 21D). In this layout, if the living-room was to be of a reasonable width 'a house of considerable frontage' was involved. This could be avoided by the alternative arrangement, which provided a house almost square in plan (Figure 21E). This might be thought of as a development of the basic narrow-fronted type (Type A): the frontage has been almost doubled to allow the

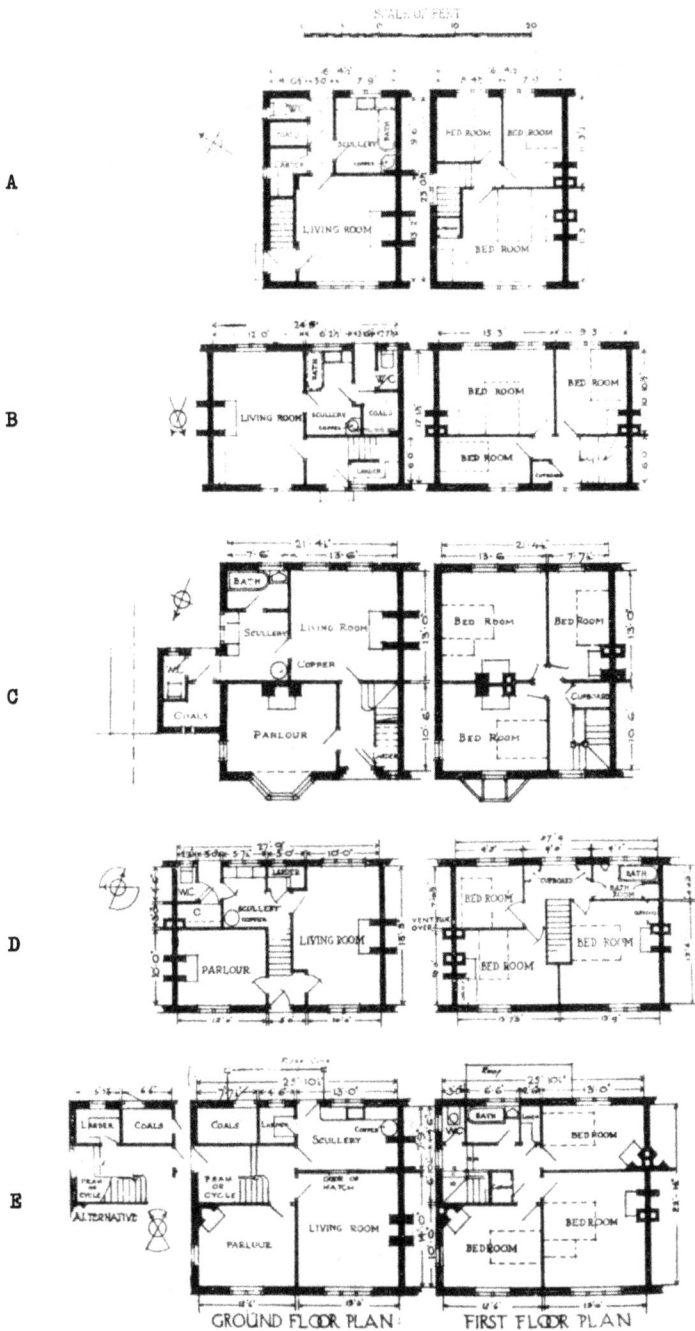

SCALE OF FEET

A

B

C

D

E

GROUND FLOOR PLAN   FIRST FLOOR PLAN

Figure 21   Tudor Walters Report (1918): recommended type-plans

parlour and side entrance lobby to be added to the basic front living-room/back scullery arrangement. In both the type plans for south aspect parlour houses the bathroom was located on the first floor: although this involved the additional expense of a hot-water circulating system, for a parlour house it gave a more equal distribution of rooms between the two floors and it was, according to the report, the arrangement desired by housewives of the artisan class.

In its discussion of the internal planning of the house, the Tudor Walters Committee aimed to impress on its readers the complexities and difficulties involved in what might at first sight appear the relatively simple task of cottage design. As Unwin had repeatedly urged, the design of the small house was not to be lightly undertaken. The report stated,

> It is evident, from the individual consideration of the rooms and other parts of the cottage, that the requirements are many and varied. The satisfying of even the more important of them, within the limited space available, involves a problem in design and planning, the proper solution of which is by no means as easy as is generally assumed. (Paragraph 143)

On design in general the committee's advice was nonetheless that it was best to aim for simplicity: 'simple, straightforward plans will usually prove most economical'. Outbuildings and projections, it said, were usually expensive in relation to the accommodation provided and should be avoided except where they were desirable for some good reason, such as in the case of Type Plan C, where they accommodated the WC and coal-store and acted as links between the buildings. Great economies could also be secured, the report noted, by grouping the chimney flues into as few stacks as possible. Simplicity should be the key to the external treatment. In place of gables and dormers, the report called for unbroken roof lines, which provided more space for first-floor rooms and saved both in initial cost and maintenance.

> An important economy can also be effected by a simplification in the design of the roof itself. It is very doubtful whether the introduction of dormers is conducive to economy . . . [rather] it will probably increase the cost of building. Generally, it is better to run the eaves in an unbroken line immediately above the first-floor window heads and avoid the numerous expenses entailed in capital cost and maintenance when the roof is broken by dormers and flats. (Paragraph 149)

Similarly, the report rejected external ornament on both economic and aesthetic grounds. In place of picturesque detail and ornament,

it called for the use of proportion and good arrangement to produce
an inherent attractiveness 'at little or no extra cost':

> Considerable economy may be practised advantageously in the
> external design. . . . Ornament is usually out of place and necessarily
> costly both in first execution and in upkeep. The best effects can
> be obtained by good proportion in the mass and in the openings,
> by careful grouping of the various parts of each cottage, by grouping
> the cottages themselves, and by well-considered variations in the
> designs to suit their different positions and the different materials
> used. (Paragraph 146)

In this emphasis on proportion rather than picturesque detail, the
influence of the Liverpool school of architects was clearly evident.

For the Liverpool group, the justification of the neo-Georgian
cottage derived from its relationship to contemporary realities of mass
production (see Chapter 3). Instead of trying to make each cottage
unique, they argued, the architect should exploit the economies of
scale offered by the large-scale production of houses (which the
speculative builder had been doing for a long time) and put them
to good architectural effect by basing the design on the repetition of
similar units, in the manner of the houses of the eighteenth century.
Although looking less to questions of aesthetics than to those of
economics and practicability, the Tudor Walters Report provided a
similarly powerful endorsement of the role of standardised components
in mass housing. The report conceded Baines' contention that
standardisation was suitable only for manufactured items: the
standardisation of timber scantlings for military huts, it noted, 'at
one time created almost a famine in the particular sections and lengths
required'. But for manufactured components the report stated that
considerable economy would be achieved by the mass-production of
standardised sizes and types. Thus it called for the establishment of
standard sizes for doors and windows, which would both simplify
building operations and 'enable standardised ferroconcrete or other
lintels to be made at suitable centres and distributed to the building
sites'. Similarly, the report urged the standardisation of iron-
mongery – grates, baths, locks, latches, guttering, etc. – which, it
said, would facilitate mass-production and would lead to better value,
even if it did not actually reduce the cost.

The section of the report dealing with standardisation was the work
of a sub-committee on materials and construction chaired by Unwin,
which was mainly concerned with the question of new materials.
Whereas questions of layout could be dealt with by summarising
Unwin's published work, and the internal arrangement of the house

by drawing on the work of Unwin's branch of the Ministry of Munitions, for new materials more active investigation was required. To this end Unwin secured in 1917 the establishment by the Department of Scientific and Industrial Research of a Building Materials Research Committee. But the work of this body was far from complete when the Tudor Walters Report was compiled, and accordingly in dealing with new materials the report was able only to review general principles and point to probable conclusions.

The committee prefaced its review of the possibilities offered by new materials with a note of caution. 'We have been repeatedly assured that the adoption of this or that method or process would secure a reduction in the cost of the cottage of five, 10 or even 20 per cent', the committee reported; yet a breakdown of the capital cost of building an average cottage showed that this was impossible. No single item accounted for a sufficiently large proportion for a 'saving in the total cost of 25 per cent, a suggestion which is not infrequently made', to be possible. Furthermore, the report noted, new methods or materials that might in the long run prove economical might equally in the immediate postwar period 'turn out to be locally or temporarily expensive owing to the absence of skill on the part of the available workmen or lack of experience on the part of local contractors'. Particularly in the early stages of the housing programme, it would be important to use methods of building to which both contractors and workmen were accustomed, which would mean making use 'of every kind of suitable material and of all classes of available labour' – as Baines had done, in a spectacular fashion, at Well Hall. The report also emphasised that local materials would prove most economical, particularly given the difficulties with distribution and transport that could be expected in the immediate postwar period.

Despite these reservations, the committee considered that in some areas, particularly where local brick was not available, the use of concrete for walls might prove economical; but it warned that any differences in cost between brick and concrete would depend on local conditions. Many of the possible ways of using concrete for walls, including the various methods for pouring it *in situ*, had not been used sufficiently for any conclusion on their economic potential to be possible; further tests on a larger scale were needed, the report stated, to establish their economic viability. It was concrete blocks and slabs that had been 'most widely used for cottage building'; they had been 'very extensively used during the war for the carrying out of various emergency works' (for instance at Chepstow and Crayford) and were the 'simplest and most reliable' form of concrete walling. Nonetheless, the scope for their use would not be unlimited and the committee believed that 'the majority of houses erected in the period immediately following the war will be constructed in brick and stone in the manner to which contractors and workmen are generally accustomed.' (Paragraph 222)

The problem with timber (which, according to figures given in the report, was the largest material element in the cost of a house) was rather different. Since a severe and sustained shortage of timber in the years after the war appeared inevitable, the question was not whether any of the alternatives were cheaper but, since some alternatives to timber would have to be used, in what ways they could best be adopted. The report looked at the various functions for which timber was employed in a cottage and discussed possible substitutes in each case. For ground floors there was little problem; the floor covering could be laid directly onto concrete to make a solid floor. For upper floors, the report recommended a modified form of the hollow brick or concrete floor used in fireproof construction; a number of these were being tested, including a hollow brick floor in a cottage designed for the Building Materials Research Committee (BMRC) and built at Teddington. As for floor coverings, the committee reported that here too a number of experiments were being made for the BMRC; Rowntree was particularly involved in the development of a sawdust-based composition that was claimed to have a surface similar to linoleum and that was tested in some experimental cottages at New Earswick.[15]

The roof was the other part of the house for which a large amount of timber was normally required. On what it said might have appeared the obvious alternative, the flat concrete roof, the committee was cautious: apart from problems of internal condensation, it was extremely difficult, the committee reported, to make a concrete roof waterproof: 'One well known concrete expert stated that cracks were always liable to form even in good concrete through which damp might penetrate'; and waterproof coverings such as asphalt were expensive. The alternative was to follow more or less traditional construction but with timber replaced by concrete or steel for the roof members. The committee reported certain misgivings to this on *a priori* grounds, saying that 'it would hardly seem . . . that the methods of construction adapted to wood are likely to prove the most satisfactory ones for utilising such a different material as ferroconcrete'. Nonetheless, it was felt that further experiments might demonstrate that this was feasible and economical, particularly if steel rather than reinforced concrete were employed; and the committee recommended that, if the timber shortage continued, steel roofs, produced in large quantities and to standardised spans, would probably provide an advantageous substitute for timber. These roofs could then be covered with slates or tiles, the type of roof-covering that the committee considered the most 'effective, lasting and satisfactory in appearance'. This was the method employed in the 'Dorlonco' system, first demonstrated at Dormanstown in 1919 and heavily promoted by the Ministry of Health thereafter (see Figure 18).

All in all, the Tudor Walters Report offered a cautious welcome to the possibilities offered by new methods of building. What distinguished the attitude taken by the committee was the fact that it combined with this sober appreciation of the general scope for new methods a determination to take positive steps to establish, by research, the precise areas in which new methods could usefully be adopted. The committee offered the conclusion that

> so far no revolutionary developments of materials or processes had been evolved that were likely to result in sensational changes in the character of housebuilding, but that there were a number of suggestions in many branches of the work which deserved investigation; that, in fact, the whole of the processes called for review, in the hope that a number of improvements and economies might be found, the accumulated effect of which might be considerable, though individually they might seem to be small. (Paragraph 177)

It was this belief that led in 1917 to the formation of the Building Materials Research Committee to undertake detailed investigations into new materials. It indicated an unusually level-headed approach to a question that was often treated in a polemical manner – an approach that separated the Tudor Walters Committee as much from architectural reactionaries at home as it did from the avant-garde abroad.

Politics and Expertise

In the context of the contemporary debate on housing, the Tudor Walters Report was a radical statement. On policy and administration, on standards of accommodation, and on layout and design, the report was recognised as an endorsement of the views of the radicals and an attack on the conservative orthodoxy of the LGB. The success and esteem enjoyed by the report rested not just on its inherent merits, but equally on the conjunction of its own political bias with the movement of the general political tide at the end of 1918. Signed on

24 October, the report was addressed to Hayes Fisher, the President of the LGB; but by the time the report was published early in November, Fisher had resigned and Lloyd George and the others were promising a massive housing campaign to bring 'light and beauty into the lives of the people'.[16] In this context, the Tudor Walters Report, which not only called for 500 000 houses of the highest standard but also showed how they could be built, became a central part of the strategy adopted by the state to deflect the threat to the social order.

The Tudor Walters Report was absorbed into government policy almost immediately. In the circular of 14 November 1918, Geddes drew the attention of local authorities to the document which, he stated, 'will be found of great service to local authorities who now have this question before them ... He trusts they will give it their early attention'.[17] Negotiations between the LGB and manufacturers over the standardisation of fittings got under way at the same time,[18] and the report's call for the 'extension of the machinery of the central department' and for appointment of regional housing commissioners was incorporated in Geddes' new proposals put to the War Cabinet in December. Other recommendations made in the report (for instance, on the need for powers of compulsion to be given to the LGB, on aid to public utility societies, on bylaws and on town planning reform) were incorporated directly into the Housing Bill. In Parliament it was actually said that it was 'on the basis' of the report that the 'Bill was largely framed'. This was probably an overestimate of the influence of the report: many of the policy recommendations made in the report derived from the Ministry of Reconstruction and their incorporation in the Housing Bill should be seen as part of the adoption by the Cabinet of the housing policy of that ministry. Nonetheless, it was a belief that the government was not anxious to destroy, giving to their proposals as it did the authority of the 'best experts dealing with this matter in England'.[19]

In Parliament also the contents of the report were seen to meet the needs of the time. As seen in Chapter 4, its recommendations on the improvement of housing standards were explicitly endorsed by a number of MPs: a garden to each house, a bathroom with hot and cold water, the incorporation of labour-saving devices – in sum, a 'great improvement on anything we have'. The report's proposals for design also seem to have met with general approval in the House: money should not be spent, it was felt, on 'making these homes artistic' or adding 'elaborate ornamentation' but on making them 'comfortable, sanitary and sound', as the Tudor Walters Report proposed.

'It must be obvious to the House', said one MP, 'that standardisation is a good thing'.[20]

In Whitehall, the appointment of Christopher Addison to the LGB in January 1919 was followed by the invasion of the newly enlarged Housing Department by what might be termed the 'Tudor Walters group' from the Ministries of Munitions and Reconstruction. Existing staff at the LGB, whose expertise lay in areas other than low-density housing, were largely passed over. The new Director General of Housing was Sir James Carmichael, whom Addison had in 1917 appointed as Chairman of the Munitions Works Board and of the Committee on the Building Industry after the war. The Deputy Director was James Walker Smith, who had been a member of the Tudor Walters Committee. Two posts of Chief Architect were created, the one in charge of layout and the other in charge of plans. The first of these was taken by Unwin, the other going to his Assistant Architect at the Ministry of Munitions, S. B. Russell. Other architects from the Ministry of Munitions took more junior positions in the Housing Department.[21]

The extent to which this represented the adoption of the Tudor Walters group by the state became clear with the publication in April 1919 of the LGB's *Manual on the Preparation of State-aided Housing Schemes*. Addison had told the Cabinet in February that the *Manual*, intended as a guide to local authorities on the preparation, design and construction of housing schemes, would contain the prize-winning designs from the LGB/RIBA cottage competition. By the time the *Manual* was published in April, however, these had been entirely eliminated, and replaced by the very different sort of plans prepared by the Housing Department in accordance with the principles of the Tudor Walters Report. The text of the *Manual* either summarised or reproduced without alteration relevant sections of the report, accompanying them where appropriate with diagrams reprinted in the report from Unwin's earlier publications. The general advice on design was summarised thus:

> It is of the greatest importance that simplicity in design should be carefully studied, and no features which are merely decorative should be introduced. Economy in maintenance should be considered in conjunction with capital cost.
>
> Suitable materials that can be obtained within a reasonable distance of the locality of the intended buildings should be employed as far as possible.
>
> Broken roofs and dormers should be avoided as far as possible.[22]

In this way the detailed suggestions made by the Tudor Walters Committee were passed on to local authorities for their schemes under the 1919 Housing Act.

Thus, by the middle of 1919 the Tudor Walters Report was accepted as a quasi-official statement of the government's housing policy. At the core of the report was the notion that economy could be secured by the expertise of the designer. By flexible planning, by the code of simplification and by the various techniques known to the experienced designer (such as grouping of chimney flues and communal drainage), considerable savings could be achieved and a substantial improvement in the standards of housing could be made without a corresponding increase in capital outlay. Whereas in the past it had appeared that the lowering of housing standards was the only route to economy, the Tudor Walters Report suggested that these savings could be achieved by expertise in design.

At a time when the state was faced with the 'confident demands of labour',[23] the message of the report had an obvious relevance and appeal. Unlike cuts in standards, expertise in design offered a method of economy that would not invoke the opposition of the labour movement. Threatened with industrial dislocation and social unrest, both Cabinet and Parliament accepted the housing programme of 1919 as the necessary price of social stability, the unavoidable premium on the 'insurance against revolution'. While the Treasury faced the unspecified but undoubtedly enormous costs of building 500 000 houses at a time of disrupted production and inflated prices, the traditional method of reducing costs – building to a low standard – was proscribed by the political function of the housing programme which, on the contrary, required the adoption of standards much higher than anything known before – standards that were, in fact, 'fit for heroes'. It was to this problem that the Tudor Walters Report appeared to hold the solution. It showed how 500 000 houses could be built to the standards needed to carry out the ideological objectives of the housing programme, while at the same time securing good economy. From the point of view of the state there was indeed, as Carmichael told Addison, a 'good deal' that depended on the investigation into design and construction carried out by the Tudor Walters Committee.[24]

6 The Cabinet and the Housing Campaign

The Housing Act of 1919 was a political creation. The balance of political forces that in 1919 determined the nature and form of the housing programme continued to exercise a decisive influence over its subsequent history and led, only two years later, to the government decision to bring the campaign to an abrupt halt. Accordingly, in turning to the building of 'homes fit for heroes', it will be convenient to deal first, in this chapter, with the Cabinet decisions that largely determined the course, and eventually brought about the termination, of the house-building programme.

In the summer of 1919 the government was pledged to build 500 000 houses in three years. Whether or not this goal would be realised depended largely on the allocation of resources; in other words, whether, in a situation in which demand for resources exceeded supply, the government had the will or the power to make available the capital, labour and materials required for the housing programme. From the start the housing programme laboured at a fundamental disadvantage as a result of the government's decision, taken against the advice of the 'housing experts', to abandon control over building materials and building activity; and its prospects suffered further as a result of government decisions concerning finance. As complaints over both the extremely slow progress and high cost of the housing campaign grew more and more vociferous, government propaganda focused increasingly on the problem of building labour and the attitude of the building union which, it was alleged, by its 'obstructive' attitude was putting the housing policy in jeopardy. But in the end it was not labour but finance that brought down the programme. For it was by reference neither to the cost nor to the slow progress of the housing programme but solely to the policy of reducing public expenditure that the government decided in July 1921 to confine the grant to houses already in tenders approved by the ministry. As a result, instead of the 500 000 originally promised, slightly under 176 000 houses were built under the Housing Act of 1919.

In general, the Cabinet declined to give resources to housing when to do so would entail the opposition of powerful interest groups. The results were shortages, delays and high prices for the housing programme and, in response, a variety of expedients adopted by the government to deal with these without reversing the fundamental decisions on resources already taken. New methods of building, the use of the Office of Works and direct labour, and the involvement of private builders in the housing campaign were the most conspicuous of these expedients. All were essentially attempts to get more houses produced without withdrawing resources from other sectors.

Although on these questions housing came second to the interests of industry and finance, until the autumn of 1920 the government's commitment to the programme remained intact. This was despite the pronounced hostility of financial interests, articulated by the Bank of England and the Treasury, which from the start were opposed to the application of state money to house-building. Throughout 1919 and the first half of 1920 Treasury cavils were rejected on the grounds that the government could not afford to break its pledges on housing. In the autumn of 1920, however, with the collapse of the postwar boom and with it of the power of labour, the balance of political forces was transformed. Cabinet ministers who had opposed the Treasury view suddenly found themselves isolated and agreed to the curtailment of the housing commitment as part of the general reduction of public expenditure. The 'insurance against revolution' was no longer needed.

The Abolition of Building Controls

From an early stage it had been apparent to those responsible for the planning of reconstruction that, unless the government took action to prevent it, a serious difficulty for any housing programme would arise due to the inadequate supply of building materials and labour. Both the building and building materials industries had been brought to a state of disarray by the war, with the labour force depleted, productivity in the industry considerably reduced and the production of building materials down to a fraction of its normal level. Yet in this incapacitated condition the building industry would be called upon in the postwar period to meet not just the normal peacetime level of demand but also the backlog of construction and repair work that had accumulated during the war, and on top of this the state housing campaign. Without state control the imbalance of supply and demand in the transition period would inevitably lead to shortages, delays and monopoly prices. Such was the conclusion of the committee of enquiry appointed by the Ministry of Reconstruction under the chairmanship of Sir James Carmichael.[1] The committee reported that it would take at least two years from the end of the war for the supply of building materials to become equal to the demand and stated that the government's aim should be to increase production as rapidly as possible in order to reduce to a minimum the duration of this transition period. In the interim, as a strictly temporary but unavoidable expedient, machinery should be established for the allocation of materials according to a system of priority. The committee recommended that the government should set up a Central Building Industry Committee, representative of all the interests within the industry, which, via a system of regional committees, would control the distribution of materials and operate a system of building licensing. This latter would work on the same principle as that operated by Carmichael as Chairman of the Munitions Works Board during the war: any building operation costing £500 or more (except for government building) would require a permit.

At the urgent instruction of the Minister of Reconstruction the Carmichael Report was hurriedly completed when the end of the war suddenly appeared imminent and it was signed on 4 November 1918. The Armistice itself, concluded a week later, revealed the government in a state of confusion on the future of wartime arrangements and controls and on the processes of economic demobilisation. In contrast, industry was in no doubt as to what it wanted: as Lord Weir stated, it was the desire 'of the whole industrial community that commerce should be put on a sound normal footing with the minimum of government control as soon as possible'.[2] This point of view was well represented in the House of Commons, where the government found itself immediately after the Armistice under strong pressure to lift all controls on trade and industry. Responding to these demands from the 'industry and trades of the country', Addison told the House of Commons on 15 November:

> The Armistice was declared on Monday. On Tuesday we released a considerable number of things, and we have released more every day since then, and ... the Standing Council on Priority, which is composed almost exclusively of merchants, traders and businessmen ... is sitting daily with the sole purpose of getting rid of any embarrassing regulations in restraint of the development of trade....
> I am just as anxious as the Hon. Member ... that we should get rid of these embarrassing restrictions as fast as we can.[3]

The views of industry were as well represented in Lloyd George's 'businessmen's government'[4] as they were in Parliament. This became evident during December 1918 at the sessions of the Cabinet Demobilisation Committee that were to settle the future of building controls. Addison reminded the Committee that the system of licences was regarded by the Carmichael Committee 'not as a detail ... but as fundamental and, in their view, a *sine qua non*'[5] of the efficient organisation of the building industry. Against this, the Director General of Civil Demobilisation, Sir Stephenson Kent, argued that the Carmichael plan would seriously impede the growth of employment in the building industry, to which the government looked to counter unemployment during the period of demobilisation. Little support for the Carmichael proposals was offered by Auckland Geddes at the LGB, who suggested instead that the Ministry of Munitions should be used as a buying agency for bricks and other materials. Senior ministers were entirely in favour of decontrol; Austen Chamberlain and the President of the Board of Trade, Sir Albert Stanley, agreed with Churchill when he 'advocated sweeping away the impediments which confronted anyone who wanted to build'.[6] The Ministry of Labour also opposed the Carmichael scheme. Faced with this alignment Carmichael's arguments and protests were in vain, and on 20 December 1918 the Cabinet Demobilisation Committee decided that 'all existing restrictions on building should be removed'.[7]

The consequences for the housing campaign were more or less as Carmichael had predicted. With the supply of both labour and materials falling far short of the demand generated by the postwar boom, prices rose enormously, resources flowed to those best able to pay inflated prices, and housing was choked of supplies. With an abundance of industrial and general repair work available, builders were unwilling to tender for local authority schemes; to induce them to do so the Ministry of Health was compelled to adopt for the housing programme forms of contract[8] under which increases in prime costs were met not by contractors but by local authorities or the ministry. Prices of materials, tender prices and wage rates rose sharply, while local authorities all over the country complained that shortages of materials and labour were preventing them from building.

The result was that by the autumn of 1919 the government was faced with allegations that the housing scheme had broken down. A year had passed since the Armistice but only a handful of houses had been built and the number in approved tenders was less than 10 000. In view of this the Cabinet decided on 14 November 1919 that 'immediate action was necessary to stimulate and increase the output of houses'.[9] Among a number of possible remedies (discussed below) the Cabinet reconsidered the question of building controls. The shortage of building labour was such, said the Minister of Labour,[10] that if the housing programme was to be 'completed within reasonable time and at reasonable cost', the control of building wages and of building activity through a permit system was unavoidable. Addison argued that full control would be unacceptable both to the House of Commons and to the trade unions; instead he proposed that, as Minister of Health, he should be given powers (for two years) to prohibit non-essential building. Opposition to the reintroduction of building controls came principally from the Treasury in the form of a memorandum signed by the Chancellor, Austen Chamberlain. It was, he said, 'difficult to believe that we shall ever get out of our troubles by such a method.... The more controls we have and the longer they continue, the more difficult it becomes for trade to resume its normal course.'[11] The same objection, Chamberlain said, applied to Addison's proposal: 'He felt it would be a great misfortune to start new control at a time when we should be freeing ourselves of all controls and returning to normal conditions.'[12] The outcome was that Addison's plan was recast and substantially weakened. Instead of power to prohibit 'luxury building' being given to the Minister of Health, where it could have been used to provide a centralised, national system of control, this power was given to local authorities, who were much less independent of local pressures and interests. A clause to this effect was included in the Housing (Additional Powers) Bill, which was introduced to Parliament on 4 December and received Royal Assent on 23 December 1919.

Addison commented that his proposal for the control of building 'had not been accepted in any effective form'.[13] By the summer of 1920 it was clear that the 'luxury building' clause had not succeeded in directing available resources to house-building, and several of the larger and more energetic local authorities were pressing the government to introduce effective measures. In the face of this the Cabinet in July 1920 approved a proposal to empower the Minister of Health to prohibit building where a local authority was failing to exercise its power to do so. But the clause, included in the Ministry of Health (Miscellaneous Provisions) Bill, got caught up in the parliamentary imbroglio that developed over the Bill and never reached the statute book; the Miscellaneous Provisions Bill was defeated in the House of Lords and when the housing clauses were reintroduced as a separate Bill in March 1921[14] the prohibition of building clause had disappeared. For by this date the government had decided to place a limit on the housing programme and labour and materials had anyway become easier to obtain with the onset of the recession in the winter of 1920/1. The effective control of building, which to the planners in 1917–18 had been a *sine qua non* of a successful postwar housing campaign, was never introduced.

Capital and the City

In November 1919, faced with what was alleged to be the virtual breakdown of the housing programme, the Cabinet in effect reaffirmed its decision that building labour and materials were not to be transferred to house-building at the expense of other types of building activity. At the same time the Cabinet made a comparable ruling for the other resource that house-building required but for which demand exceeded supply – capital. Here again it was the Treasury that took the lead; and as with building controls, so with capital, the effect of the Cabinet's decision was to perpetuate the shortages, delays and high costs encountered by the housing programme. But the question of capital had an additional significance, for it was financial policy that was to lead in 1921 to the termination of the housing programme. For this reason a brief description of the issues involved is needed.

The First World War created demands for the expenditure of state capital far greater than anything experienced or contemplated before 1914. War expenditure was far in excess of the yield of taxation, however much augmented, and the difference had therefore to be financed by credit and borrowing. The basic principle that governed the issue of bank notes before the war – that notes must be convertible into gold on demand – was abandoned and what were called 'currency notes', which had no gold backing, poured off the presses. To those gaining their first experience of public finance during the war years it seemed that credit was endless and that money was no object when matters of national importance were at stake. It was in this atmosphere that the new housing policy was approved by the Cabinet in March 1919. With five million heroes returning from the war, the questions of employment and housing appeared as much a national emergency as the military danger for which funds had been so readily provided for the previous four years. Eric Geddes voiced the dominant view: 'You must be prepared to spend money on after-the-war problems as you did on during-the-war problems. That [money] must be found and added to our debt if necessary. It is the period of reconstruction and money has to be spent.'[15]

But such an open-handed attitude to public expenditure ran directly against the interests of the country's financial institutions. The role of the City as the central financial market of the world depended, its pundits believed, on the convertibility of sterling into gold. This view was set out in the reports of the Committee on Currency and Foreign Exchanges after the war. The chairman of the committee was Lord Cunliffe, the Governor of the Bank of England, and its membership consisted of representatives of the main banking interests. The committee's interim report, published in August 1918, stated that in order to effect a return to gold, a 'sound monetary position' would have to be established. The measures necessary to achieve this included the cessation of government borrowing 'at the earliest possible moment after the war'; the repayment of the floating debt via a sinking fund to be established out of the surplus of revenue over expenditure; and the absolute avoidance of fresh capital expenditure by the government. Postwar demands for expenditure on reconstruction, stated the report, would have to be resisted; on the contrary, public expenditure would have to be sharply reduced in order to provide a surplus for the repayment of debt.[16]

For a year after the Armistice, the Cabinet, preoccupied with the problems of military and civil demobilisation, effectively ignored the Cunliffe Report. In December 1919, however, the Chancellor announced the government's formal acceptance of the recommendations made by the report, and thereafter government policy moved rapidly to implement its recommendations of a balanced budget, strict control of public borrowing, reduction of the floating debt and high interest rates.[17] But even before December 1919 the housing programme had been substantially affected by the policy advocated by the Cunliffe Report, for its main points, especially the need to avoid large capital outlay by the Exchequer, were accepted by the Treasury, and it was in line with these that the financial arrangements for the housing programme had been made. Local authorities themselves had to raise the necessary capital; the annual loss but, so far as possible, never the capital cost of the housing schemes was to be met by the Exchequer. In the case of the smaller authorities, which might be simply unable to raise the capital they needed, the Treasury conceded that recourse might be made, as a last resort, to the Local Loans Funds administered by the Public Works Loans Commissioners. But the larger local authorities (defined by the Treasury as those with a rateable value of £200 000 or more) had to raise the money themsevles; to them, the Local Loans Funds, on which all local authorities had been eligible to draw before the war, were closed. The Ministry of Health was told by the Treasury in July 1919, 'Unless [the larger] local authorities raise the necessary capital themselves, it will be impossible to carry out the housing scheme ... This should be made quite clear to the authorities in question.'[18]

A few months' experience revealed the difficulties facing local authorities competing for funds in the capital market. As Addison told the Cabinet, 'many of them are floundering about in the market, the banks declining to help them, and many of them have practically suspended action.'[19] The problem was particularly acute for some local authorities in London and the South-East, where traditions of municipal saving were not established as they were in the Northern towns:

> Certain local authorities of a predominantly working-class character like West Ham and Edmonton, although with rateable values above £200 000, were finding it impossible to raise the money required for their housing schemes; and it was urgently necessary that some plan for assisting them should be devised.[20]

Indeed, these were precisely the areas with some of the worst housing shortages. The answer, Addison stated, was for capital from the Exchequer to be provided in the form of loans in cases of proven need. But the Treasury did not agree: the Exchequer 'was already over-burdened with its commitments in regard to housing'.[21] On 20 November 1919 the Cabinet met to discuss the proposals for salvaging the housing programme prepared by the Cabinet Housing Committee. Addison repeated his view that the government had either to help in financing certain local authorities or else accept that no houses would be built in those areas. The Chancellor of the Exchequer, Austen Chamberlain, voiced the Treasury's opposition to any such plan; as it was, he claimed, an estimated £60 million would be needed in the year up to September 1920 for the local authorities with rateable values below £200 000, but the liquid assets of the Local Loans Fund stood at only £15 million and the remainder would have to be borrowed by the Treasury. The Chancellor told the Cabinet that 'the best opinion in the City had been consulted, and was found to coincide with the view of the Treasury, namely, that at the present moment the Government could not borrow any more money'.[22] The Cabinet accepted this and ruled that no central funds should be made available for the capital requirements of the larger authorities.

While throwing the local authorities back onto the open market, something had to be done to make them more successful in raising the capital needed for house-building. A Treasury committee was set up to look into this and reported on 27 November.[23] The committee approached the question of housing finance from the point of view of the Treasury and the Bank of England: any further borrowing by the Exchequer would, it stated, have very serious effects on the national finances and should be avoided; capital for the housing programme would therefore have to be raised by local authorities. The committee proposed the introduction of a new sort of local authority security, Local Housing Bonds, through which, it thought, substantial sums might be raised. Despite the objections of principle, the committee conceded that more cash would probably be raised through short-term than through long-term borrowing and proposed therefore that the terms of the bonds should be five and ten as well as twenty years. The general aim should be to make not the Exchequer but those who would benefit from the houses – workers and employers – supply the money to build them.

> Every effort should be made to obtain money by subscriptions from the particular classes which will most benefit by the whole housing scheme.... Local residents should be impressed by ... the necessity of their subscribing to the Bonds, if the requisite houses are to be erected.... The restriction upon output which is caused by the lack of accommodation for employees ... should be explained, and such firms should be urged to interest themselves in the local housing schemes.[24]

The committee's proposal for Local Housing Bonds was accepted and incorporated into the Housing (Additional Powers) Bill, which was hurried through Parliament in December 1919.

In the eyes of the Treasury the main function of the housing bonds was not to solve the problems in raising capital encountered by the housing programme but rather to protect the Exchequer from heavy capital outlay. The government made no secret of this fact; when in February 1920 representatives of local authorities pressed for the capital for housing to be provided by the Exchequer, the Chancellor explained at some length that the commitment to the funding of the short-term debt made this impossible.[25] It was therefore no surprise that capital remained a problem for local authorities even after the Additional Powers Act had been passed. First of all the issue of housing bonds was delayed, in order, as Addison complained to the Cabinet, 'to keep the field clear for the new Exchequer Bonds'.[26] It was not until February 1920 that local authorities were invited to apply to the ministry for sanction to issue bonds and not until April that local campaigns to raise subscriptions got under way. Meanwhile local authorities found that their sources of investment had been drained by the increase in the interest rate on Treasury Bills announced on 14 April. The result of this increase, Addison told the Cabinet, was that 'many authorities in the Metropolitan area are practically at a standstill for lack of funds'.[27] When it eventually started, the housing bonds campaign showed very mixed results. Some local authorities raised large sums with little effort, but in other cases great efforts produced practically nothing. Thus the campaign at Wood Green, held up by the ministry as a model to other authorities, raised £230 000 at a cost to the council of only £1400, but in Hereford only 5 per cent of the bond issue was taken up, and at Aldershot 'after a very active campaign, only £3150 was obtained, at a cost of over £400'.[28] Overall the results of the campaign fell far short of the target. Instead of £10 million per month for twelve months, only £4 million was raised in the first two months and it took two years, not two months as intended, to raise £20 million. The government responded with further expedients. In May 1920 a small committee of 'City experts' was set up to advise local authorities on the timing of issues and placing of loans and in August 1920 it was announced that as from 1 October up to half of the proceeds of the local sale of National Savings Certificates were to be made available for housing.[29] While these measures helped some authorities, others continued to find shortage of capital an active constraint. At the beginning of 1921 it was still reported that several local authorities, most notably Birmingham, were holding back on their housing schemes for lack of capital.

To sum up: although officially accepted by the government only at the end of 1919, the policies on public finance recommended by the Cunliffe Report had, through the medium of the Treasury, exerted a large influence on the housing programme since its inception. Following the report's insistence on the reduction of the national debt and the avoidance of capital outlay by the Exchequer, it was left to local authorities to raise the capital for the housing programme on the open market. Here, while there was apparently plenty of money for other purposes, housing remained chronically under-subscribed. While an estimated £500 million was made available by the banks alone for industrial and commercial purposes in the financial year 1919/20, local authorities in England and Wales raised only £67 million for housing in the twenty-eight months between the Armistice and March 1921.[30] Shortages and delays for housing were the results. By the middle of 1921 the Cunliffe policy had exerted an even more dramatic influence on the housing programme, for as part of the economies imposed in line with the Cunliffe recommendations the housing programme was brought to a halt. Before looking at this, however, something must be said about the government's response to the problems encountered by the housing campaign, and about its attempts to deal with those problems without reversing its own decisions on the allocation of resources that had helped to bring them into being.

Other Answers

The attempt to build 500 000 houses in the three postwar years was one that, but for political imperatives, would scarcely have been imagined feasible. Before the war the building industry had produced on average about 80 000 houses a year. Yet with the supply of labour and materials depleted by the war, the government was expecting it to produce 200 000 houses a year. As the Astor Committee at the Ministry of Health noted ruefully in assessing the prospects for 1920, there was at the beginning of that year 'a large shortage of bricks for the execution of the housing programme even before a single brick had been supplied'[31] for all other building purposes. Furthermore, as has been seen, while calling for 500 000 houses the government refused to give priority to housing in the allocation of resources. With the economy enjoying an intense boom, available resources (capital, labour and materials) were channelled by the mechanism of the free market to those best able to pay for them, with housing coming last. Contractors preferred more lucrative private and commercial work; labour mysteriously disappeared from housing schemes and appeared at building sites elsewhere. Only a small portion of the overall capacity of the building industry was devoted to housing: in July 1920, only 11 per cent of those employed in the building industry were engaged on municipal housing schemes.[32] The result was extremely slow progress. Sixteen months after the Armistice, in March 1920, only 1250 houses had been completed by local authorities; a year later the figure was 25 000; the figure of 100 000 (the original target for the first year of the scheme) was not reached until March 1922. At the same time, in the absence of controls and with demand far in excess of supply, prices rose dramatically, from an estimated £600 per house in 1918 to an actual cost of £1200 or more in 1920.[33]

As has been shown, the Cabinet refused to allocate to the housing programme the resources it needed. Nonetheless, so long as the government was committed to providing 'homes fit for heroes' some attempt had to be made to increase the rate of progress and, if possible, reduce the cost of house-building. Squeezed between, on the one hand, the need to produce the houses and, on the other, the opposition of powerful interests to the transfer of scarce resources to housing, the Cabinet attempted to resolve the contradiction and conjure up the houses without withdrawing resources from other sectors. In attempting this feat government thinking focused on three possible answers: finding a substitute for the local authorities as building agents; organising the building process without the building contractor; and expanding the resources available for housing by the use of additional labour and new methods of building. The use of these various expedients was considered by the Cabinet at two main points: in October–November 1919, when the serious difficulties facing the housing programme became apparent; and in the early summer of 1920 when it emerged that these difficulties had not been eliminated by the measures of the previous autumn.

In November 1919 it was agreed that the housing campaign was in a perilous condition and that strong measures were needed to revive it. While the Cabinet (as shown above) refused to reintroduce general control of building or to supply capital for housing from the Exchequer, a number of *ad hoc* proposals put forward by Addison were regarded in a more favourable light. The most immediately significant of these involved the attempt to bring building agents other than local authorities, particularly private enterprise, into the housing scheme. Faced with the obvious difficulties experienced by local authorities, Addison proposed in October 1919 that a grant should be introduced for private builders. Although such a grant had been rejected, as Addison stated in his memorandum, by 'every committee which has reviewed the housing problem', he believed that in the present circumstances it would produce the houses.[34] The Cabinet readily agreed, and allocated £15 million for the purpose: the grant was to be £150 per house and available only for houses completed within a year. A clause to this effect was included in the Housing (Additional Powers) Act passed in December 1919.[35]

At the same time as the grant to private builders, Addison announced two expedients to help local authorities overcome the difficulties experienced in obtaining tenders. These aimed to obtain a more extensive involvement by private enterprise – both building contractors and speculative builders – in local authority housing schemes. In a number of cases it had been reported that partially developed sites owned by speculative builders were available on which houses might be rapidly erected. Under section 3(12) of the Housing Act a local authority was empowered to purchase houses for the working classes. In November 1919 Addison reached agreement with representatives of the speculative builders for the erection and sale to local authorities of 'houses of a type similar to those already built' by speculative builders in the past.[36] Some qualms were felt by the ministry at this deviation from the commitment to higher standards, particularly the rule of twelve houses to the acre. But with only 10 000 houses in approved tenders it was apparent that it was taking a long time to get local authorities to the stage at which building operations could begin. In this situation, the agreement for the use of partially developed sites was seen as a means of getting at least some houses built quickly.

Considerably more faith was put in the agreement with the building contractors, also announced in November 1919, which, it was hoped, would result in houses being built in large numbers. The arrangement was that local builders' federations would undertake to build a certain number of houses for local authorities at an agreed price, and would then distribute the contracts among their members and see that they were fulfilled.[37] The scheme was energetically pursued by the ministry, which arranged conferences at local level between municipalities and local builders' federations with the aim of reaching agreement on a three-year building programme. But the problem was that in practice, given the availability of commercial and private work, contractors were no more interested in local authority contracts obtained in this way than in those obtained by the normal method. In February 1920 only ten schemes had been agreed and no building had actually started. The ministry considered that the prices quoted by the contractors were excessive, in the case of the London builders being £300 per house above the figure produced by the ministry surveyor.[38] A considerable number of houses were eventually built under the agreement with contractors but mostly after the boom had ended and tenders had become much easier for local authorities to obtain.

While the Cabinet approved Addison's agreements with the builders and the proposal for the £150 grant, a suggestion made by Addison for supplementing the efforts of local authorities by another channel was rejected. This involved the government building department, the Office of Works, through which, Addison said, the Ministry of Health should be empowered to build houses when a local authority proved unable or unwilling to do so, the cost of the housing scheme being reclaimable from the local authority. The idea of using the Office of Works on housing schemes was not new. In December 1918 Sir Alfred Mond had proposed that his department should be responsible for the entire housing programme, a case for which he continued to argue intermittently during 1919 and 1920. But any scheme of this sort was unacceptable to the Treasury since it meant that the initial capital would have to come from the Exchequer, and at the Treasury's instigation the Cabinet in November 1919 rejected Addison's proposal.[39] The following June, however, Addison raised the idea again and this time it was accepted, with the significant modification that the Office of Works was to act on behalf, not of the ministry, but of the local authority. This avoided the Treasury objection, since it left the local authority to raise the capital in the normal way. In the late summer and autumn the Office of Works, at the instruction of the ministry, approached a number of authorities with the offer to undertake housing schemes on their behalf and by the end of October 1920 the Office of Works was negotiating schemes for over 17 000 houses and had started work on schemes for 2700.[40]

All the expedients discussed so far attempted to increase the agencies involved in the housing programme. They did not attempt to relieve the scarcity of resources. While the Cabinet rejected proposals for the state to use its position to allocate the necessary capital, labour and materials for housing, the question of resources was not altogether ignored. Two proposals were floated by Addison in November 1919 which aimed to expand the resources available for housing construction, particularly in terms of labour; both were endorsed by the Cabinet and implemented thereafter. The first involved the much wider use of new methods of building which, it seemed, by eliminating bricks and bricklayers from the construction of houses offered a means of circumventing the shortages of both materials and labour. In November 1919 the Ministry of Health launched a major campaign to persuade local authorities to adopt one of the new systems 'as a supplement to houses of ordinary construction already in hand': a demonstration centre was organised at Acton, where local officials could inspect houses built with the new concrete systems, and at the ministry a special commissioner was appointed, to be 'responsible for pushing the new methods of construction'.[41] From the vast number of patented systems that had appeared since the end of the war, the ministry selected a small number which, it said, could be safely recommended. In particular, the ministry favoured the 'Dorlonco' steel-frame system, which, although expensive, could be produced on a large scale and economised on skilled labour to a high degree. The result of all this was that by the summer of 1920 most of the major municipalities (Birmingham, Bristol, Cardiff, Doncaster, Hammersmith, Leeds, Liverpool, Manchester, etc) had signed contracts for houses to be built by one or other of the new methods.

At the same time as increasing the use of new methods of building, the Cabinet also decided to intensify its efforts to release the manpower constraint through another means: by persuading the building unions to accept an increase in the labour force, the dilution of skilled trades, and the introduction of piece-rates. Addison had already begun negotiations with building labour over these proposals and, following Cabinet endorsement, in December Lloyd George addressed the Joint

Industrial Council on the Building Trade. In February 1920 Addison
followed this up with an approach to the TUC. But the building unions
saw in dilution only a recipe for future unemployment and would
not agree to the government's proposals.[42]

As the difficulties of the housing campaign intensified, the Cabinet
became more and more convinced that, as the Cabinet Housing
Committee put it in June 1920, labour was 'the crux of the problem'.[43]
In an uncontrolled market the shortage of labour was undoubtedly
one of the main constraints on housing progress. Furthermore it was,
so far as the government was concerned, the constraint that could
be 'solved' by the least unpalatable measures. For the government
to provide capital for housing would involve the opposition of the
financial world; to provide materials via control of building would
arouse the opposition of industry and commerce. In contrast the only
obstacle to solving the labour problem appeared to be the building
unions. From July 1920 the government was involved in intensive
negotiations with the building unions in an attempt to persuade them
to suspend trade union practices in return for certain guarantees –
'the policy which was adopted during the war with such good results',
as the Cabinet Housing Committee noted.[44] In return for a guaranteed week and increased unemployment insurance the unions were
asked to agree to the introduction of piece-rates, the upgrading of
unskilled men and the admission of ex-servicemen as adult appren-
tices. In the autumn of 1920 government propaganda increasingly
attacked the building unions, to whose 'obstructive' and 'unreason-
able' attitude the problems encountered by the housing campaign
were attributed. The unions, however, refused to accept the dilution
proposals.[45]

From the latter part of 1920 until July 1921, it was building labour
that was blamed by the government for the high cost and slow progress
of the housing campaign. In the latter part of 1919 it had been local
authorities that the government had been inclined to blame. In
between there was a brief period, at departmental rather than Cabinet
level, when the building contractor assumed the role of villain, and
for a short time the Ministry of Health became interested in alternatives to the ordinary system of contracting. In February 1920 it was
reported at the ministry that

> Builders had now formed themselves into rings; competition had
> been killed; estimates were being based on costs agreed by builders
> among themselves instead of on competition.... Direct labour,
> whether by a municipality or through a guild, might assist the
> Government in getting a check on prices.[46]

Pressure for the use of direct labour had arisen in 1919 from local authorities who had found that they could not obtain satisfactory tenders from contractors. The ministry at first was unenthusiastic and did nothing to encourage direct labour, although it accepted that where a local authority could make out a good case direct labour schemes on a small scale should be permitted. As costs rose, however, and suspicions increased over the prices quoted by contractors, the ministry became more tolerant of direct labour as a means of checking costs and prices. The pioneer scheme at Newbury (commenced in December 1919) was followed during 1920 by others at Liverpool, Walsall, Glasgow and Taunton, and by October 1920 it was reported that the use of direct labour had been sanctioned by the ministry in the case of sixty-five local authorities.[47]

Another way of eliminating the contractor was offered in 1920 and 1921 by the short-lived guild movement. Unlike a trade union, a guild could be registered as a company able to contract for the erection of houses or the supply of labour. But, although Unwin was reported to be a convert to the ideas of 'guild socialism' and Addison claimed to sympathise with the movement, in effect if not in intention the ministry's attitude to the building guilds was ambivalent. In January 1920 the Manchester Building Guild submitted a tender for 100 houses to Manchester Corporation and in May the Guild of Builders, London, Ltd was registered, but it was not until August 1920 that a model contract for guild schemes was approved by the ministry and the first contract was not signed until October. A limit of twenty was imposed by the ministry on the number of guild contracts for housing schemes but even so the contractors felt threatened and made their opposition felt. In December 1920 Stephen Easten, the President of the National Federation of Building Trade Employers, resigned from the ministry over what he considered the favouritism shown to the guilds and for a time Addison put an embargo on guild contracts altogether. Although this was lifted, relations between the ministry and the guilds remained strained and in the wake of Addison's departure from the ministry they were eventually severed.[48]

A curious offshoot of these ideas for the reorganisation of the building industry involved the entrepreneurial First Commissioner of Works, the chemical millionaire Sir Alfred Mond. In June 1920 Mond proposed to the Cabinet the restructuring 'of the building industry for housing on National Guild lines, the contractor to be eliminated'.[49] The Office of Works would collaborate with the guild and supervise the work; in return for a guaranteed minimum week and guild recognition, the guild would implement agreements on dilution, adult apprenticeship and piece-rates. This perhaps accounted for what otherwise appeared the bizarre alliance between Mond, the millionaire creator of ICI, and guild socialism. A scheme of this sort, Mond told the Cabinet, was already being carried out by the Office of Works for the Borough of Camberwell, where the scheme had been, in Mond's words, 'conceived and organised' by the Director of Works, Sir Frank Baines. At Camberwell 290 houses were being built for the council jointly by the Office of Works and the Labour and Trades Council; labour was provided by the Trades Council and had been 'completely satisfactory from the start', with no disputes or stoppages, and dilution of skilled trades had been accepted and carried out. The Camberwell scheme (see Figure 1) was regarded as a great success and, although Mond's sweeping proposal was (not surprisingly) not accepted by the Cabinet, a number of the schemes undertaken for local authorities by the Office of Works later in 1920–1 were on a direct labour basis.[50]

In all, the various expedients discussed in this section were responsible for a considerable number of houses. Of the 160 000 houses for which contracts had been signed in April 1921, 20 000 involved the use of new methods, 13 000 were in contracts with builders' federations and a further 4500 in contracts for the sale to local authorities of houses erected by speculative builders, 1500 were in guild contracts, 8800 in direct labour contracts, and 5200 were being built by the Office of Works.[51] This makes a total of 53 000, or one-third of the number of houses in local authority contracts at the time. If we assume (for lack of alternative data) that these were all built and add the 39 000[52] built with the grant to private builders, the various expedients account for more than 40 per cent of the total number of houses built under the 1919 Housing Acts. In this sense the expedients adopted by the government cannot be accounted a failure. But while they were responsible for a large number of houses, the expedients did not offer solutions to the fundamental problems faced by the housing campaign. Whether building was carried out by direct labour, the Office of Works, speculative builders or contractors, the overall shortage of resources was unaffected and costs remained high and overall progress slow. The use of new building methods, which at one stage appeared to offer an answer to shortages of both materials and labour, soon ran up against almost equally severe shortages of capital. It was only as general demand began to fall that resources became available for housing. As the boom turned to recession in the autumn and winter of 1920/1, prices fell, contracts, labour and materials became easier to obtain and the rate of completions showed a marked increase. Average tender prices fell from £930 per house to £800 in the nine months after October 1920. The number of men employed on housing schemes doubled (to 81 000) between July and December 1920. The average monthly rate of completions of local authority houses in the year after March 1921 at 5900 was three times what it had been in the year before.[53] In other words, as the general level of economic activity fell, the resources of which the housing programme had been largely starved became available. The irony was that the end of the boom, while making house-building possible, also removed the political imperative operating on the government to proceed with the housing programme. As the numbers out of work increased, the power of labour as perceived by the government visibly weakened and the 'insurance against revolution' appeared no longer necessary.

Housing and the Collapse of Labour

To those committed to the policies of the Cunliffe Report, housing was nothing but an impediment to the re-establishment of sound finance and the restoration of the gold standard. The attitude of the financial world towards the housing programme was, accordingly, one of more or less complete hostility. This can, perhaps, be best appreciated from the following extracts from two memoranda written in June and July 1921 by A. W. Hurst, the permanent official responsible for housing at the Treasury:

> As regards the private builders subsidy, the Treasury attitude in the last year or two has been to press the Ministry more and more to rely on this method of dealing with the problem, and to restrict to a corresponding extent the activities of local authorities, who are unsuited by their very composition to be either builders or managers of housing on an economical basis.
>
> As long as local authorities have a considerable share in it, the increase in production and rate of working and the decrease in wages will proceed but slowly. Furthermore the standard of materials and design will be kept on an expensive level. A large proportion of the population lived in jerry-built houses before the war, and we cannot afford better-built homes now, still less the luxury of semi-detached garden suburb villas. We can only get back to cheap houses of the pre-war type under private enterprise and any move of the State should I submit be directed to fostering such enterprise.[54]

It was this attitude that characterised Treasury pronouncements on housing from 1919. By the autumn of 1919 the Chancellor, Austen Chamberlain, had lost the open-handed attitude to housing that he had articulated in Cabinet in March: in October 1919 a Cabinet memorandum bearing his signature raised the question whether the housing programme should not be abandoned altogether in view of the increase in costs.[55] At this stage the point was ignored, but the following summer, with the Cabinet again compelled to consider the problems and prospects facing the housing campaign, the Chancellor raised the question again. In a memorandum of 20 May he asked whether 'notwithstanding the extent to which the Government is committed to proceeding with the scheme, it may not be desirable to suspend further action'.[56] Senior officials at the Ministry of Health echoed these doubts. The First Secretary, A. W. Robinson, advised Addison to seek renewed support from the Cabinet in the light of the greatly increased cost of the programme:

> The final justification for the housing programme originally was, I suppose, that it was an insurance against something a great deal worse. It may be that the insurance is still necessary, that the Cabinet are ready to accept the heavy increase in premium.[57]

The Cabinet's decision at this point (June 1920) was that, 'in view of pledges given', the proposal to cut back the housing programme was 'not feasible at present'.[58]

In the winter of 1920/1, however, the position was transformed. Due in part to the measures introduced by the Chancellor earlier in the year, the postwar economic boom was, by the autumn of 1920, turning to slump, with prices falling and unemployment suddenly on the increase. In October a massive demonstration of unemployed workers took place in London, to which the government responded quickly with new measures for unemployment insurance and relief works. In November the Unemployment Insurance Act came into operation and in December the Unemployment (Relief Works) Act was passed. By this date, with full employment fast disappearing, the conclusion was, as the Cabinet noted, that 'the trade unions were no longer in so strong a position as they had been'.[59] It was also apparent that the slump had weaned the ex-servicemen from any ideas of radical politics and that they were going to establish, not the 'Red Guard' that had once been feared, but the British Legion.[60]

While the growth of unemployment was undermining the strength of labour in general, the Cabinet recognised that the 'crucial contest with labour' was that with the miners.[61] By the summer of 1921 this was a battle that the government had joined and won. The autumn of 1920 saw a preliminary skirmish, in which the miners sought the support of the railwaymen and transport workers. But the 'Triple Alliance' – the ultimate threat wielded by organised labour – failed to operate and the miners went out on strike on their own. This strike was settled indecisively on 3 November but the conclusion drawn by the government was that the miners had suffered a tacit defeat. Three months later, in February 1921, the Cabinet precipitated a final show-down by announcing that the date for the return of the mines from public control back to the owners would be brought forward to 31 March. For the miners, this meant not just the failure of their campaign for nationalisation but also a wage-cut of 40 to 50 per cent. On 31 March, accordingly, the miners struck again; on 8 April the government declared a state of emergency and mobilised the armed forces. For the government the real danger was not the miners' strike itself but the general strike that would follow if the Triple Alliance operated: on 8 April the strike order was issued to the railwaymen and transport workers to take effect from 12 April, but the strike was first postponed and then, on the notorious 'Black Friday' (15 April), called off. Although the miners stayed out until the end of June, the threat of a general strike had passed, and for the government the crisis was over. Thus on 18 April the Cabinet met in an atmosphere of self-congratulation, passed a vote of thanks to the Prime Minister and Minister of Labour, and dispatched letters of thanks to the volunteers who had helped in what was already termed the 'recent industrial crisis'.[62]

The Cabinet was fully aware of the implications of this change in the balance of power for its reconstruction programme and for the housing campaign at its heart. Since the Armistice the pattern had been that while the Treasury called for the reduction of public expenditure, the Cabinet was led by political imperatives towards generous expenditure on reconstruction, as an insurance against something 'a great deal worse'. Now, however, the danger was receding and the insurance was becoming superfluous. On 29 November 1920 the Cabinet Finance Committee agreed to Treasury proposals for general cuts in public expenditure, including the imposition of a 'definite limit ... [of], say, 100 000 houses' on the local authority housing programme.[63] Addison agreed in principle to this curtailment, for, as he put it in January 1921, 'it was to be noted that the housing problem assumes a different complexion in present conditions of trade and industry'.[64] Accordingly at the end of February Addison instructed his officials that no further tenders for houses were to be approved except where 'a very substantial reduction on past prices is secured'.[65]

At the same time he negotiated with the Treasury over the extent of the curtailment; by 11 March he and Chamberlain had agreed that, for the present, local authorities would be confined to the 180 000 houses believed to be in approved tenders, but that when prices had fallen they would be permitted another 70 000 under the financial terms of the 1919 Act. Public announcement of this major change of policy was postponed, however, until after the Triple Alliance crisis had been settled, and it was not until 12 May that the curtailment of the housing programme was officially revealed.[66]

Although the new terms meant a cut of 50 per cent in the target of the housing campaign, they were not enough to satisfy certain sections of the political establishment. In the changed economic and political conditions, the social reforms so readily promised in the wake of the Armistice took on the appearance of unnecessary and unjustifiable extravagance, for which it was now expected that heads would roll. The Beaverbrook and Northcliffe press launched an 'anti-waste' campaign, attacking 'squandermania' in general and Addison and the housing programme in particular. At the end of March 1921 Lloyd George attempted to deflect this attack by moving Addison from the Ministry of Health (appointing Sir Alfred Mond in his place); but in June, following another byelection defeat of a government candidate at the hands of an anti-waste campaigner, Lloyd George decided that more dramatic measures were needed. On 10 June he wrote to Austen Chamberlain that the byelection result at Westminster St George's was a 'great warning': 'the middle classes mean to insist upon a drastic cut-down ... nothing will satisfy them next year except an actual reduction in taxes'.[67] Two years earlier, political considerations had led the Cabinet to lavish expenditure on housing, but now – with squandermania, not the danger of revolution, as the dominant consideration – they pointed in the opposite direction. At the end of June unemployment had risen to over two million and the Cabinet noted that 'now that the coal dispute was settled ... [there was] not much danger of active unrest in Great Britain'.[68] The danger against which the insurance had been taken out had disappeared.

The Treasury responded swiftly to the opportunity presented by this change in the political climate and in May 1921 set out the case for further drastic reductions in public spending. The position, it stated, for the following financial year (1922/3) was that the estimates for ordinary supply services (£602 million) were some 20 per cent above the available revenue (£485 million). Further borrowing, it said, would depress sterling; increased taxation would hamper the recovery of trade and industry. There was therefore, in the Treasury view, no alternative but to cut expenditure for 1922/3 by 20 per cent, to bring it into line with revenue. A draft circular setting this out was approved by the Cabinet on 11 May 1921 and issued to all spending departments.[69]

It was in this context that Sir Alfred Mond, the new Minister of Health, produced on 22 June a Cabinet memorandum offering unsolicited reductions in housing expenditure. Mond stated that, under the terms agreed by Addison and Chamberlain, the estimated cost to the Exchequer of the housing programme would rise from £10 million in 1921/2 to £14 million in 1922/3. Unless, therefore, there was a 'modification of the agreement', there would be, not the 20 per cent cut desired by the Treasury, but a 'heavy increase' in housing expenditure in the next financial year.[70] It was not possible, Mond stated, actually to reduce expenditure on housing; all that could be done was to limit the amount by which it would increase. Mond proposed to do this by confining local authorities to houses already in approved tenders (176 000) and by taking administrative action to limit the number of houses built by state-aided private enterprise. At the same time, however, Mond considered that something would have to be offered towards the cost of the slum clearance schemes which local authorities, under pressure from the ministry, had prepared on the understanding that they would qualify for the Addison grant. For this purpose he proposed an Exchequer grant of up to £1 million per annum, of which a maximum of £200 000 would be drawn in the year 1922/3. Overall the estimated expenditure for 1922/3 would be £11.5 million, which represented a saving of £2.5 million compared to the provisional estimate. At the Treasury Hurst commented, 'The offer now made by the Minister of Health concedes as regards local authorities' ordinary housing schemes practically what we asked for in January last'.[71]

But in Cabinet Finance Committee Lloyd George and Chamberlain now showed an enthusiasm for cost-cutting that exceeded even that of Mond and the Treasury. Meeting on 30 June, the committee resolved that 'in view of the difficult financial situation ... there was no alternative open to the Government but to decide housing questions not on merits, but on financial considerations only'.[72] The grant to private builders should be stopped immediately. The grant to local authorities should be made not to all houses in approved tenders but only to those for which contracts were 'already entered into from which it is impossible to obtain release'. Only a nominal sum should be allocated for the slums, £200 000 for two years being the terms agreed.

These measures even Mond considered excessively draconian and over the next fortnight he secured a number of modifications designed to make the change of policy appear less embarrassingly abrupt.[73] To conceal the precipitance with which the subsidy was withdrawn, it was decided that the annual grant for slum improvement would have to be made for the sixty-year duration of the loan period. The change of policy was particularly awkward in the case of the grant to private builders: for on 1 July 1921 Royal Assent was given to a Housing Bill which extended for another year the deadline for the completion of houses eligible for the grant. On this Mond got the Cabinet to agree that although in general no payment would be made on houses begun after 1 July 1921, where commitments had been entered into on the basis of previous government assurances the grant would be payable provided that building was commenced by the end of August 1921. On local authority schemes two modifications were made to the conclusions of the Finance Committee. Instead of cancelling contracts, the limitation to approved tenders was reinstated; and Mond was authorised to state that the cuts did not necessarily represent the government's last word on the housing problem. In view of what he called 'the widespread disappointment that would be felt among the working classes at the suspension of house-building', Mond in a memorandum of 7 July sought authority to state that the limitation on the programme was not necessarily final.

> I am quite certain that it will be impossible for the Government to leave the housing position just where it is, and I am convinced that some further schemes will have to be evolved which I fear must contain an element of State assistance, in order to reduce the housing shortage to reasonable dimensions. While I am not at present prepared to place a definite scheme before the Cabinet I should like authority to indicate on behalf of the Government – what I have already indicated as my personal view – that the Government ... intend further to explore the whole situation.[74]

This item, recast in a slightly less definite form, was included in the ministerial statement agreed by the Cabinet and made by Mond in the House of Commons on 14 July 1921. In view of the 'very grave financial difficulties' confronting the nation, the statement ran, the government had decided that 'for the time being at any rate' housing expenditure would be limited to 176 000 houses in the case of local authorities and public utility societies; in the case of the private builders' subsidy, to houses begun before 1 July or, at the discretion of the minister, within six weeks of 14 July; and for the improvement of slum areas, to an annual contribution of £200 000. The statement ended:

It is the intention of the Government to keep the housing problem closely under review. They fully recognise the importance of that problem from the point of view of the health and social conditions of the people but it is impossible to incur greater commitments than our finances will allow.[75]

Allowing for the time-lag involved in building operations – which meant that a considerable number of houses included in the 1919 programme would not be completed for another two years – this marked the end of the 'homes fit for heroes' campaign.

7 The Ministry and the Housing Campaign

The previous chapter recounted the history of the housing programme only as it was perceived in Downing Street. It is now time to turn to the building campaign itself and look at what was actually built. This chapter deals with the administrative superstructure devised for the housing campaign, and looks in detail at the instructions on housing design issued to local authorities by Whitehall. The next chapter examines the house-building activities of two sample local authorities and sees how the wide-ranging political, ideological and economic issues involved in the 'homes fit for heroes' campaign worked out at local level, in the provision and design of the houses themselves.

The New Organisation

With the housing campaign of 1919 prime responsibility for state intervention in housing moved from local authorities to central government. State housing was no longer (as it had been before the war) primarily a local issue in which local conditions led to local decisions. It was now the central element in the government's programme of social reconstruction and the major weapon in its propaganda battle to stave off revolution. This transfer of responsibility had important administrative implications. The government considered it both undesirable and impracticable to attempt to build the 500 000 houses itself. Accordingly, local authorities were still to build and own the houses but they were to do so under the closest supervision from Whitehall. The result was a unique and elaborate administrative superstructure. As Geddes told the Cabinet in December 1918, a new administrative system was required both to ensure that the government's promises of 'homes fit for heroes' were realised and to protect the Treasury against local authorities whose own financial liability was limited to the produce of a penny rate. Drawing on the plans prepared at the Ministry of Reconstruction, Geddes proposed a three-tiered structure, with an expanded Housing Department in Whitehall and – the unique feature of the new organisation – a system of regional housing commissions to act as intermediaries between Whitehall and local authorities.

In order to enable the Local Government Board to perform the
dual function of expediting the erection of houses and of protecting
the Treasury from uneconomical construction or management, a
considerable extension of the machinery of the Central Department
and a large measure of decentralisation will be needed.

For the purpose of expediting the provision of houses, I propose
to appoint a Chief Commissioner of Housing [later called the
Director General of Housing], who will be in charge of a separate
Department which will devote its whole energies to the rapid
erection of houses during the resettlement period.

This Department will deal with both administrative and technical
questions, will secure uniformity in the procedure of the required
Housing Commissioners, and will constitute a central bureau of
information and advice in regard to provision of houses, laying out
of sites, types of cottage design and their construction, building
materials, and standardisation of fittings....

I propose further to appoint eight, or perhaps nine, Housing
Commissioners.... Each Commissioner will have his own local office
and his own staff of expert advisers and clerks. The Commissioner
will consider and discuss with the local authorities the needs of their
districts in regard to housing, and will advise and assist each local
authority in his district on questions of the provision of houses and
planning of sites.... He will conduct all preliminary discussions and
will submit sufficient information and sketch plans to enable the
Central Department to give an immediate decision as to whether
the scheme of the local authority should be allowed to proceed.[1]

The new organisation was in operation by the middle of 1919. It
put the provision and design of local authority housing schemes into
a new and very different position. Whereas before 1914 Whitehall
had exercised only a limited influence over the provision and design
of municipal housing, under the system adopted for the implementation of the 1919 Act a local authority had to obtain the approval
of the Ministry of Health (either at central or regional level) for every
aspect of its housing scheme. There were, in fact, seven distinct stages
at which approval had to be obtained: for the number of houses needed
and the type of houses to be built; for the choice of the site and its
acquisition; for the layout plan; for a loan for the construction of streets
and sewers; for house plans; for a loan for the erection of the houses
on the basis of the tenders received; and for the rents to be charged,
as part of the estimated receipts and expenditure on the scheme. As
a ministry official stated, without exaggeration, local authorities were
subjected to a 'large degree of control' from the ministry 'at every
stage of the business'.[2]

At the top of the new organisation stood the Housing Department of the Ministry of Health. This consisted of the Housing Department inherited from the Ministry's predecessor, the LGB, augmented by staff from other divisions of the ministry and by a number of temporary senior posts. Most of the permanent positions went to officials from the LGB; Unwin himself was one of these, for he had been appointed Chief Town Planning Inspector at the board in 1914, and he now became Principal Architect in charge of housing layout. The major temporary appointments, however, as has been seen, were filled, not from the LGB, but from the Ministry of Munitions and the Tudor Walters Committee: Carmichael (Director-General), Walker Smith (Deputy Director), and Russell (Principal Architect in charge of house plans).

The function of the department was to direct and control the housing programme. There were two aspects to this, deriving on the one hand from its statutory duties under the Housing Act, and on the other from the political pressures on the government to realise its promises and get the houses built quickly. Between them these involved the department in the issue of a mass of directives and regulations covering every detail of the planning, building, and management of houses and of the organisation of a major house-building campaign. For example, in August and September 1919 the department issued standard forms of tender and contract and a standard specification to be used in all housing schemes. The impact of the latter with, for instance, its specification for fencing of '4 × 3 inch tapered reinforced concrete posts' with 'three rows of no. 8 gauge galvanised steel wire',[3] was to be seen in housing schemes all over the country. The department had also to deal with the chaotic position in relation to the supply of materials created by the government's rejection of building controls, and a special staff under a Production Officer was appointed to assist local authorities to obtain the materials and transport required. Early in 1920, when the problem of materials supply appeared insoluble, Major Wightman Douglas was given responsibility for 'selling' new materials and methods of building to local authorities. In addition, to stimulate and inspire local authorities, a special publicity branch was set up under B. S. Townroe; it organised booklets, press releases and exhibitions, and published a fortnightly journal, *Housing*. This supplemented the ministry's more formal communications and kept local authorities up to date with ministry thinking.

The Housing Department in Whitehall set out the general conditions for the housing programme; dealings with individual local authorities were largely delegated to the housing commissioners. There were eleven of these for England and Wales, mostly located in the major regional centres (Liverpool, Manchester, etc) and each supported by a sizeable staff, including Architect, Surveyor, Production Officer, etc.[4] The role of the housing commissioners was to see that local authorities proceeded with their housing schemes at the pace and in the manner desired by Whitehall, and to counteract what was seen in Whitehall as the natural tendency of local authorities towards lethargy and error. In addition, the task of approving or rejecting local authority designs, which at first was undertaken in Whitehall, was soon delegated to the regional commissions. From July 1919 house plans, and layouts for up to 100 houses, were submitted for approval to the commissioners rather than to Whitehall and from December 1919 only layouts involving more than 500 houses were sent to the central Housing Department.[5] Local authorities were urged to keep in close contact with the housing commissioner and seek his advice on all questions, including sites, layouts, types of houses, specifications, and contracts.

But while they were subject to this formidable system of direction and control, the local authorities were still responsible for building. The ministry specified the requirements that had to be met and ensured that they were observed; but it was the local authorities that actually acquired the sites, selected the designs, entered into contracts with builders and owned and let the houses. Critics of the Act such as Sir Alfred Mond at the Office of Works complained that before the war local authorities had shown themselves unfit to build and manage houses and that they were no better suited to the task after the war than they had been before.[6] Whether or not this was true, two changes had in fact been made that affected the way in which local authorities managed and designed their housing schemes. The first change involved the decision-making process: most local authorities complied with the ministry's instruction that they should appoint separate housing committees to assume the full powers of the council in relation to housing. The ministry hoped that this would remove some of the causes of delay in municipal house-building. The second change directly affected design. Before 1914 municipal housing schemes (like any other type of municipal building work) had normally been designed by the Borough Engineer or the Borough Surveyor; the involvement of architects (as on the LCC housing schemes) had been exceptional. For the 1919 programme, however, the ministry followed the recommendation of the Tudor Walters Report and strongly encouraged local authorities to engage architects for their housing schemes. Local authorities were told in April 1919 that

> All schemes submitted should be prepared by competent architects, whose duties should include the preparation of the layout plan and the design and planning of the houses.
>
> It is recognised, however, that where a local authority have a properly qualified engineer or surveyor, that they may consider it desirable that the schemes shall be prepared by him, with the assistance of a competent architect.[7]

Not surprisingly, this intrusion by architects was resented by municipal engineers and surveyors. In Norwich, for instance, the City Engineer, A. E. Collins, was a man of some reputation who had previously designed some municipal cottages using the 'Winget' concrete block system. The appointment of Stanley Adshead as Consulting Architect for the city's 1919 Act schemes was resisted by Collins, albeit unsuccessfully, and led to considerable controversy in the local press. In some places, however, mainly in small or medium-sized towns, borough surveyors and engineers were able to maintain their position and were responsible for the design of housing schemes; this was the case, for instance, at York (examined in Chapter 8) and at Luton, Slough, Southgate, and Evesham. But, in the majority of cases, the housing schemes built under the 1919 Act were designed by architects. Salaried architects were appointed only by the largest municipalities (London, Manchester, Sheffield, etc.), where the volume of work on housing was sufficient to justify a full-time appointment. Elsewhere, outside architects were used, paid according to a scale of fees drawn up by the ministry and the Royal Institute of British Architects and issued in September 1919.[8] In these cases, local authorities tended to select either local architects, or well-known housing specialists, or, in some cases, a combination of the two working in collaboration. For instance, local architects alone were responsible for schemes at Bristol, Burnley and Guildford, while the schemes at Brighton and Norwich were designed by local architects in collaboration with a layout 'expert' (in both cases, Professor Adshead). Architects who had made their names in housing or town planning before or during the war now found their services greatly in demand for municipal housing schemes. For instance, Adshead and Houfton designed the Dover housing scheme, and Adshead and Alexander Harvey collaborated at Newburn-on-Tyne; Houfton was also responsible for the Aberavon scheme and Harvey for Widnes. Another stalwart of the garden city movement, T. Alwyn Lloyd, designed Sedgley's scheme; Dunn and Curtis Green designed the Stanmore estate at Winchester; and R. S. Bowers, a former member of the Gretna team, and his partner E. G. Culpin of the Garden Cities Association, undertook schemes for Reading and a number of other local authorities.

After 1921 the scale of fees for architects employed on municipal housing was reduced and local authorities were no longer able to attract architects of the first rank: the high architectural quality of 'homes fit for heroes' was not maintained. The pursuit of economy also brought about the demise of the administrative superstructure after 1921 when the decision to limit the subsidy to houses in tenders already approved by the ministry made the expanded organisation more or less redundant. Unfortunately, little information is available on the housing activities of the ministry from 1921 to 1923; virtually none of the unpublished records appear to have survived, and publications (such as *Housing*) that give information for the period 1919–21 were terminated as part of the economy measures. Nonetheless, it is clear that the ministry's staff was severely pruned. In August 1921 Mond announced a reduction of 300 in the staff of the Housing Department, both in the central office and in the regions. While permanent officials (including Unwin) were immovable, those on temporary appointments had no security. Carmichael and Walker Smith had already left the ministry; in October 1921 they were followed by Russell, and it seems likely that the other temporary architectural appointments were terminated at this point. In the regional offices the reduction of staff was even more dramatic: by March 1922 all the offices of the housing commissions had been closed.[9]

The Layout and Appearance of Housing Schemes

The notion of improvement was central to the housing policy of 1919. If, in Lloyd George's phrase, the housing programme was to win the confidence of the people by showing them that the government was going 'to meet them in their aspirations', then the houses had to be of a very different sort, and very much better, than those of the past. This commitment to the improvement of housing quality was clearly stated in the *Manual* published in April 1919: 'It is the intention of the government that the housing schemes to be carried out with State assistance should mark an advance on the building and development which has ordinarily been regarded as sufficient in the past.'[10]

One of the basic elements in this advance lay in the adoption of the garden city model of low-density development: the *Manual* stated

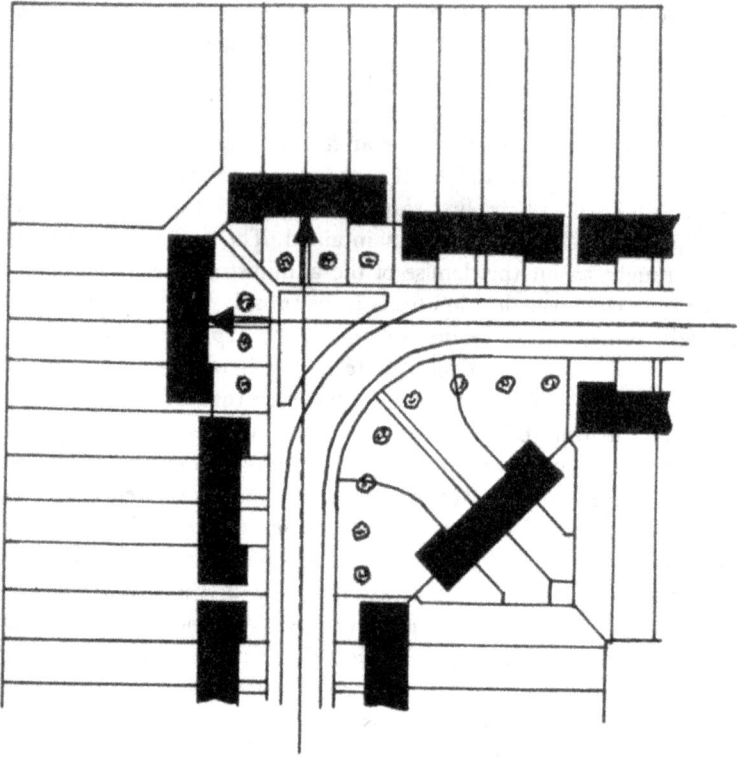

Figure 22 Manual (*1919*): *treatment of right-angle bends, producing terminal features to the street-picture in both directions. The drawing was based on one previously published by Unwin in* Town Planning in Practice

that densities should not exceed twelve houses to the acre in urban districts and eight to the acre in rural districts. The *Manual* drew on Unwin's earlier publications, not just for a resumé of the techniques involved (see Figure 22), but also for the economic rationale of this method: 'in normal circumstances', it said, 'the increased area of the plot obtained by adopting the standard of 12 houses to the acre is well worth the slight extra rent per plot needed to pay the ground rent'.[11] This was merely the abstract of Unwin's argument in *Nothing Gained by Overcrowding!* (see Chapter 1); it did not attempt to take into account the relative change in costs brought about by the war which had, in fact, reduced the extra cost involved in the low-density method. Between 1914 and 1919, while the cost of building roads and sewers had doubled, the cost of land had scarcely changed, and so any system (such as low-density development) that economised on roads and sewers by using more land was made relatively more economical. An article by Unwin in the ministry's journal, *Housing*, in December 1919 estimated that the additional cost per plot entailed by building at twelve rather than twenty-one houses to the acre had fallen from 19 per cent in 1914 to less than 4 per cent in 1919. Subsequent movements in prices continued this trend and in 1921 the Committee on the High Cost of Building Working Class Dwellings concluded that the reduction of density was not responsible for any significant increase in cost. The cost of the additional land required had been outweighed, it stated, by the savings in development costs made by the use of light roads and cul-de-sacs: low density did not mean high cost.

The *Manual* of 1919 referred to another general argument on residential development that Unwin had publicised before the war. In his Warburton lecture at Manchester University in 1912, Unwin had called for a policy of promoting not fully-fledged garden cities on the lines of Letchworth but what he called 'satellite towns', large but only semi-autonomous developments located on the perimeter of existing cities. This idea was taken up by the ministry in 1919: the housing schemes of larger municipalities, it recommended, should take the form of detached suburbs or small towns.[12] Thus encouraged by Whitehall, a number of the larger city councils made plans for providing their housing schemes in the form of satellite towns. In 1920 Manchester Corporation commissioned Professor Abercrombie to investigate the feasibility of the purchase and development of the 4500-acre estate at Wythenshawe. In the metropolis, early in 1920 the London County Council envisaged not only the huge settlement at Becontree (with a planned 24 000 houses), but a further satellite scheme on the 570-acre estate of Grove Park in South-East London. Other towns planned similar developments on a more modest scale. Bristol, for instance, planned a series of five independent garden suburbs of 1000 houses each and Grimsby Town Council early in 1919 agreed to the Housing Commissioner's suggestion that, instead of four small sites, they should acquire a single site for a 'large garden suburb' of 1200 houses. Many of these ambitious proposals were aborted by the withdrawal of the Addison subsidy in 1921 and while some (such as Wythenshawe and Becontree) were undertaken or completed later in the 1920s, others remained unrealised.

Under the procedure instituted for the housing programme of 1919, layout plans had to be prepared by the local authority and approved by the ministry before house plans could be considered for approval, let alone put out to tender and placed in contracts. As Unwin stated, the result was that in order to expedite the stages of the construction process, the job of preparing the layout plan was often rushed:

> In many cases plans have had to be prepared under pressure and in great haste. Sufficient experience of this type of development has not always been available, and the urgency of housing needs has not always allowed enough time for the full study of the problems involved.[13]

Accordingly, the ministry encouraged local authorities in such cases to undertake revisions of their layout plans in the light of greater experience. In some cases the mistakes were purely technical: inadequate attention had been given to the preliminary site survey, or through-roads had been used in places where cul-de-sacs would have been more economical. But in general, Unwin stated, the most serious defect in the layout of the schemes was not technical but aesthetic. Instead of relating the buildings to one another and to the site, local authorities were too often content, in Unwin's words, 'with the mere repetition of groups of houses, and with the setting back or forward of one or two groups here and there to produce variety, without really taking the matter up thoughtfully'.[14] What the local authority layouts really lacked, in the eyes of the ministry, was 'grouping'. It was grouping that, according to the ministry, could make a good visual effect even from plain and simple houses; it was the creative side of the town planner's skill; it meant giving greater importance to the overall effect or street picture than to the individual building; and it was, as an article on the subject in *Housing* declared, virtually impossible to achieve with semi-detached houses. The ministry's preaching, however, was to a large extent in vain. For the thing that most local authorities desired above all was the 'semi'; it was the 'semi' that fulfilled most popular aspirations and it was not something that local authorities were prepared to give up readily in order to satisfy the notions of the architects at the ministry.

Another question on which the 'educated' architectural opinion of the ministry ran into conflict with the more popular taste of the municipalities was the elevational treatment of the houses. The *Manual* followed the Tudor Walters Report and adopted simplified design; the ministry said of the plans and elevations in the *Manual* that

> simplicity of construction with economy of material were the governing factors in their design; [also] the elimination of all unnecessary and costly appurtenances, such as outbuildings, outside

porches, projecting wings and gables, dormers, broken outlines in roofs, and tall and elaborate chimney stacks.[15]

Also omitted was the inventive detailing that had relieved the severity of simplified design at Gretna: the ministry believed that if it had 'succumbed to the temptation of indulging in these luxuries', it would not have been able to prevent local authorities from indulging what would, in all probability, have been their own much less restrained

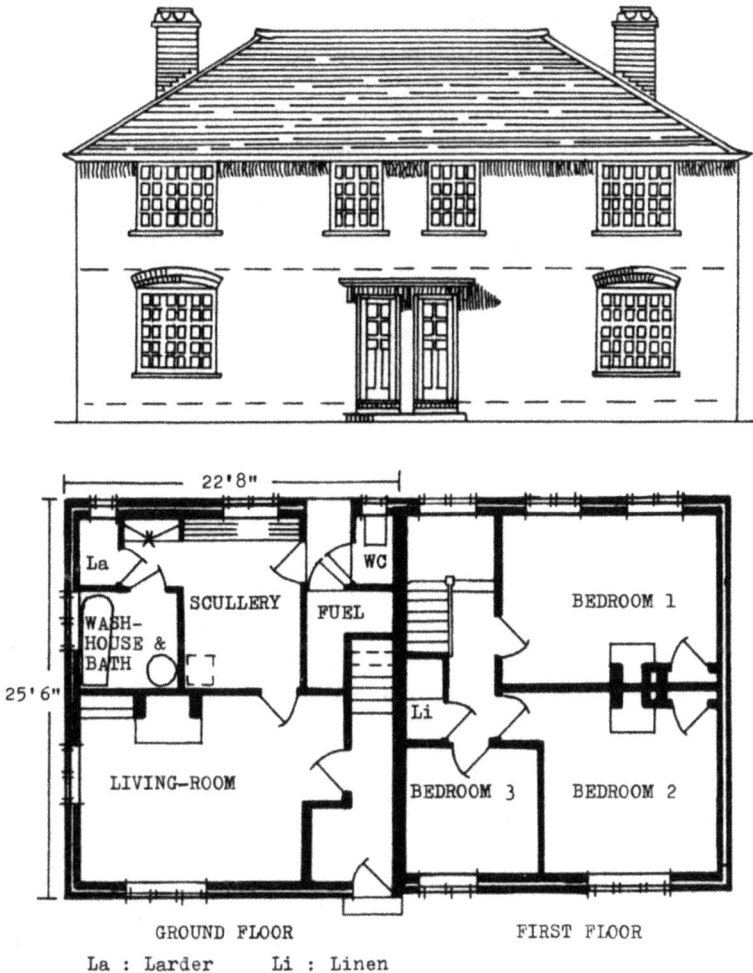

Figure 23 '*Boxes with lids': typical design from the* Manual *of 1919*

taste for ornament and detail.[16] Accordingly, interesting detail was largely eliminated, and the designs in the *Manual* retained only the general Georgian characteristics of neat hipped roofs and symmetrical disposition of doors and windows. They were immediately dubbed 'boxes with lids' (see Figure 23).

Nonetheless, while eschewing excessive detail in its own designs, the ministry was not averse to the adoption of a stronger neo-Georgian treatment by local authorities. In fact, this was specifically recommended in an article in *Housing* in November 1919. While for the less conspicuous parts of an estate, it was stated, it would be necessary to rely for effect on the 'grouping of the simpler blocks', for the main frontages and the parts open to public view a 'Georgian treatment of the elevation' was recommended. Symmetrically spaced sash windows and an 'eaves cornice of reinforced concrete' were the elements suggested.[17] The ministry also recommended that a formal or axial layout could be adopted for these prominent parts of the estate. This contrast between the smart neo-Georgian front displayed by the conspicuous parts of the estate and the rather reduced treatment given to the remainder was adopted at a number of the larger schemes built under the 1919 Act, including, for instance, the highly praised Moulescombe estate at Brighton, for which Adshead designed the layout (see Figure 24).

The endorsement of neo-Georgian by the ministry was motivated, at least in part, by its desire to lead authorities away from their own decorative inclinations. For the most part, local authorities did not share the elevated architectural opinions of Whitehall and preferred instead to decorate their elevations with gables and bay windows in the manner of the speculative builder (see Figure 2). These probably corresponded much more closely with the taste and aspirations of the tenants than did the rigours of simplified design but to the architects in Whitehall they were anathema. 'The gable should be used only when the plan or the section demands it', stated the ministry, not, as the speculative builder used it, to add breaks to the roof-line purely for effect. Likewise the bay window, another feature beloved by local authorities, was permitted by the ministry only when it was needed to bring the room concerned up to the minimum size. 'Sham half-timber, superabundant gables and bay windows endlessly repeated ... are consistent neither with good architecture nor with low prices', declared the ministry.[18] To architects such as Unwin, raised on the teachings of Pugin, there could be no doubt that external features should not be superimposed for effect but should derive from the internal arrangement of the building; gables should appear only

Figure 24   Moulescombe estate, Brighton (1920): part of the neo-Georgian façade presented to the main Brighton–Lewes road

when they were 'inherent in the plan adopted', not as a result of what the ministry called 'straining after effect'. But local authorities and tenants did not belong to this architectural tradition. They could see no reason for omitting decorative features which, in their view, effected improvements in appearance very much greater than the increase in cost. York Corporation, for instance, was only one of many authorities under the 1919 Act that resisted to the utmost the idea of building houses without any projections or gables; and when in 1923 the Corporation decided to build under the 1890 Act, without financial assistance from Whitehall, it immediately restored the decorative feature eliminated by the ministry from the houses in its 1919 scheme (see Figure 35).

While the ministry struggled against the incursions of what it regarded as the sham picturesque, it did not uphold the doctrine of simplification without modification. Indeed it found that, in the conditions of building faced by the housing programme, significant departures from the design principles enunciated by the Tudor Walters Report were necessary. Instead of the simple 'box with a lid', the ministry's designs in the second half of 1919 and for most of 1920 showed breaks from the cube both horizontally, with projecting wings, and vertically, with dormer windows. In May 1920 the Ministry published a collection of *Type Plans and Elevations*, in which the majority of designs were not simplified but had dormer windows, gables and broken eaves-lines (see Figures 25 and 27). This change of policy substantially affected the appearance of the 90 000 or so houses commenced between the middle of 1919 and the end of 1920: instead of the invariable 'boxes with lids' implied by the *Manual*, many of the houses showed a complexity of form of this sort. How had this departure from the doctrine of simplification come about?

The answer seems to have been that serious problems arose when simplification was applied to roofs of tile rather than slate. At Gretna and Mancot local slates had been used for the munitions schemes, but for the postwar housing programme all building materials were in short supply and the condition of the transport system made it essential that, wherever possible, local materials should be used. Accordingly the ministry ruled that in tile districts (primarily the southern counties) tiles were to be used. Being more porous than slate, tiles had to be laid at a steeper pitch (45° was the minimum specified by Whitehall for tiles, as against 27° for slates) and so, if the doctrine of simplification were followed and the eaves-line run unbroken above the first-floor windows, the result would be a roof of considerable height. This involved not only a large and unused roof space, but also an unnecessary and expensive addition to the height of the end walls, party walls and chimneys.

There were, essentially, only two ways of eliminating this unnecessary cost: either the roof span had to be reduced or the roof had to be broken. In the case of a non-parlour house, a short roof span could be achieved by using a wide and shallow plan. In the volume of *Type Plans and Elevations*, what the Tudor Walters Report had called the basic type for a non-parlour house, the deep and narrow Type A, was eliminated altogether, and only broad-fronted plans with short roof-spans were included. For the larger parlour houses, a short span could be obtained either by following a wide and shallow plan (Tudor Walters Type D) or otherwise by adopting an L-shape for the ground plan. With a plan of this sort, a house of considerable area could be covered by a roof with a relatively small span and

Scale of Feet.

FRONT ELEVATION   REAR ELEVATION

GROUND FLOOR PLAN   FIRST FLOOR PLAN

Figure 25   Type Plans and Elevations (*1920*): *typical L-shaped plan with broken eaves-lines (south aspect)*

therefore with a relatively low ridge (see Figure 25). The L-shaped plan had been mentioned but not illustrated in the Tudor Walters Report; it was nonetheless adopted for the majority of plans for parlour houses in *Type Plans and Elevations* and for a large number of parlour houses for which local authorities obtained ministry approval in 1919–20.

The L-shaped plan was one way of keeping down the height of the roof ridge. The alternative was to retain a wide span but reduce the height of the ridge by putting the first-floor rooms into the roof, lowering the eaves-line and breaking it, where necessary, with dormers. This was the traditional way of solving the problem in tile districts, widely exploited for visual effect by the prewar garden city movement, and in 1920 it was endorsed for reasons of economy by the ministry. An article in *Housing* in May 1920 set out the approved method, based on an 'asymmetrical roof' (see Figure 26). On the more sunny aspect, where most of the windows would be placed, the eaves-line was run at 7 feet above the first floor, just above the first-floor windows; on the other side of the house the eaves-line was

Figure 26   The 'asymmetrical roof': drawing published by the Ministry of Health in 1920

brought down to a height of 5 feet above the first floor and any necessary windows inserted in the form of dormers. In this way both the span of the roof and the height of the roof ridge above the ceiling of the first-floor rooms was minimised while at the same time the number of dormers required was reduced as far as possible. Wall-cutting for dormers, the ministry conceded, was notoriously costly; nonetheless it stated that this method, with dormers on one side only and with 45° hip and valley tiles used in place of lead, was likely to prove cheaper than an unbroken roof of tiles (see Figure 27).[19]

These non-simplified types of design were adopted by the ministry in 1919–20 only because the priority was to get houses built, rather than to minimise cost. It was recognised that building with tiles involved additional cost, whether the roof was broken and dormers inserted or whether it was left unbroken and chimneys and party walls increased in height. But, given the state of the transport system and the scarcity of materials, tiles had to be used and their additional costs accepted if anything like a reasonable rate of completions was to be obtained. Once it was decided that the priority was no longer to build as rapidly and extensively as possible, but instead to minimise the cost of building, the position on design was transformed. If cheapness, not output, was the goal, as the Committee on the High Cost of Building Working Class Dwellings stated in 1921, the width of frontage occupied by each house would have to be reduced; only narrow-fronted houses on a deep plan were acceptable. To minimise the cost of construction, breaks from the cube, whether in the form of wings projecting horizontally or dormers projecting vertically, would have to be eliminated, and unbroken tile roofs at 45° pitch would also have to be avoided. If the priority was to build as cheaply as possible, then plain rectangular blocks with low-pitched slate roofs were needed.

This change of policy took place in the winter of 1920/1. In February 1921 housing commissioners were instructed that fresh tenders were to be approved only where 'a very substantial reduction on past prices is secured'.[20] The decision to impose tight cost limits on future approvals had however been taken at a meeting of Addison with senior officials on 9 December 1920 and the change of policy was reflected in the plans published by *Housing* from the end of December (see Figure 28). In place of the wide and shallow types previously favoured, narrow and deep plans were now shown. Projections and recessions in the main walls were eliminated, as were breaks in the eaves-line; instead an unbroken slate roof rested on an unbroken rectangular plan. Brick arches were replaced by concrete lintels over the ground

Front Elevation.

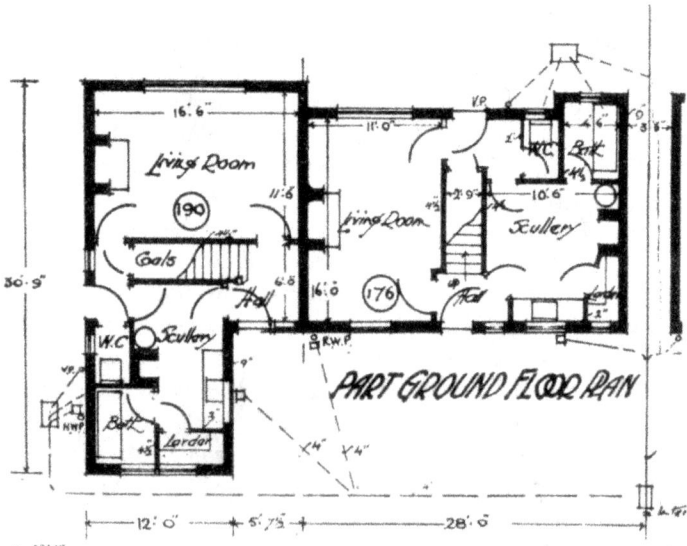

Figure 27 Type Plans and Elevations (1920):

Back Elevation.

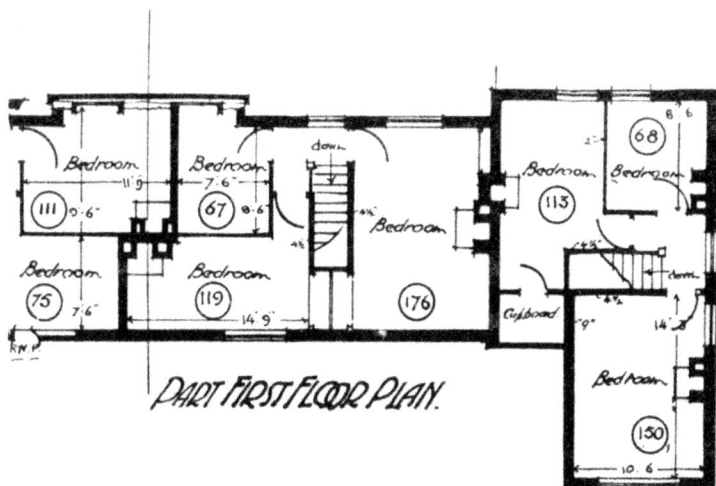

PART FIRST FLOOR PLAN.

Scale of Feet.

symmetrical roof on double-fronted plan (north aspect)

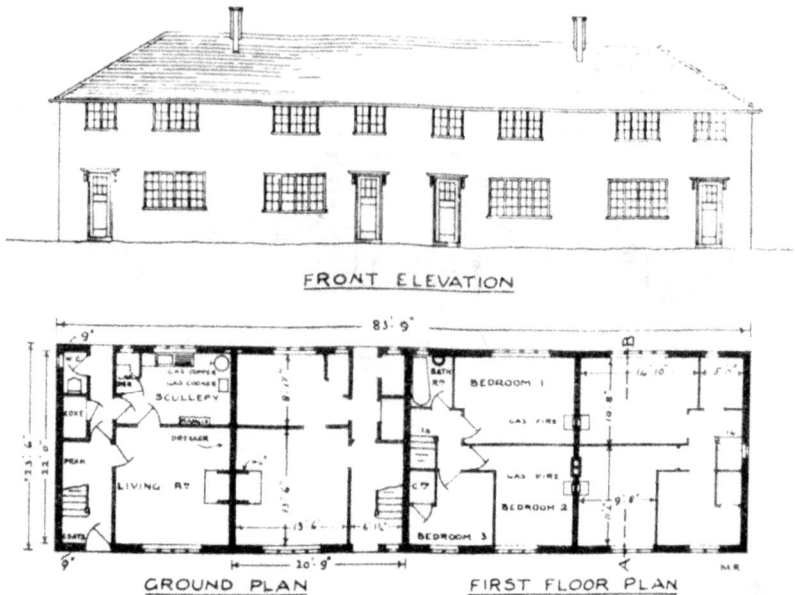

FRONT ELEVATION

GROUND PLAN   FIRST FLOOR PLAN

Figure 28   Economical cottage 1921: design published by the Ministry of Health in January 1921

floor windows. A standard internal depth of 21 ft 8 in was specified; in changed market conditions, it was believed that standardisation of timber lengths might at last prove economical.

Simplification was taken further by Mond. At the date of his appointment as minister (1 April 1921) there were some 60 000 houses in approved tenders that had not been commenced. Mond immediately instructed his officials to undertake a revision of standards with the object of economising. The revisions were to apply to the houses in approved tenders that had not been started, as well as to the remainder of the local authority programme which, at this stage, it was still anticipated would be undertaken in the future. On questions of construction, the ministry pressed local authorities from the middle of 1921 to make four general changes: to reduce the width of frontages; to reduce the number of type-plans used on each estate; to increase the number of houses in each block; and to simplify roofs and walls. This renewed advocacy of simplified design might be seen as a return to the philosophy of the Tudor Walters Report, even if, by its association with a very different housing policy, simplification no longer possessed the heroic connotations of 1918–19. But on the basic question of housing density Mond directly contradicted the recommendations of the Tudor Walters Committee. Immediately on his appointment as minister, Mond told his officials that 'the possibility of increasing the number of houses to the acre needed to be considered'.[21] In pressing local authorities to revise their layouts, Mond urged not just the more extensive use of light roads (as the Committee on High Cost recommended) but also an increase in density to twenty houses to the acre.[22] As will be seen below, from 1921 the interest of the ministry in the Tudor Walters Report was largely confined to the suggestions for economy that it contained; it did not extend to the ideals of improvement at the heart of the report.

House Plans and Housing Standards

Despite apparently extensive preparations, when the war suddenly came to an end in November 1918 the housing programme was in no condition to be put into immediate operation. The problems of demobilisation and the postwar transition had suddenly arrived, but the housing campaign that was to provide both jobs and houses was not ready. Accordingly, on his appointment to the LGB in January 1919 Addison ruled that, in view of the urgency of commencing building, local authorities that were ready to build should not be held back on the grounds that their plans fell below the standards required. On 27 January he told Carmichael, the Director General of Housing,

> We cannot wait until the last word in architecture is met before we begin to sanction schemes. With the present state of unrest and unemployment it is of great importance that work should be begun as soon as possible, and I would rather an authority got to work in erecting houses which were not up to the ideal in every respect ... rather than that we should hold them up for the settlement of all details.[23]

Such a liberal attitude on the part of Whitehall was, however, entirely uncharacteristic and thereafter local authorities building under the 1919 Act were required to conform with both the letter and the spirit of Whitehall's views on housing standards and design. Internally as much as externally the house was to follow the recommendations of the Tudor Walters Report. The *Manual* stated that flats or bungalows were to be built only in exceptional cases: the general dwelling-type was to be the two-storey, self-contained cottage. Two classes were permitted: the first, the 'most general type of house', comprised a living-room, scullery, larder, fuel-store, WC, bath in separate chamber, and three bedrooms; the second contained, in addition, a parlour. While three bedrooms was to be the norm, the *Manual* stated that houses with two and four bedrooms would also be permitted. The minimum size of rooms was to be that recommended by the Tudor Walters Report (see Table 4).

The *Manual* also included a number of type plans which, it was stated, had been 'prepared with due regard to the areas desirable for the different rooms' and illustrated generally what was required. The plans were, however, 'for guidance only': the intention was not that the type plans should be built without alteration, but that they should be taken as the basis for design and adapted to suit particular requirements. This was in line with the recommendation of the Tudor Walters Report and, likewise, the plans themselves followed the arrangements approved by the report. Of the twelve plans contained in the *Manual*, there were four for special requirements (bungalows, cottage flats, agricultural cottages) and four each for the two main sorts of cottage. For the latter the *Manual* provided new plans, designed by the Housing Department, and these followed the five types recommended by the Tudor Walters Report. For non-parlour houses, there were two plans of Tudor Walters Type A (south aspect, narrow frontage) and two of Type B (north aspect, wide frontage). For parlour houses, there were two plans of Type C (north aspect) and one each of Type D (south aspect, double-fronted) and Type E (south aspect, square type).

The Tudor Walters Report had recommended three methods of arranging the heating and cooking functions but only the most basic of the three was indicated by the plans published with the *Manual*. The cooking range was located in the living-room and was the main heat source for both cooking and space heating; a gas cooker or stove was provided in the scullery, as a supplementary heat source for cooking or drying clothes when the range was not lit. In the plans for non-parlour houses a combined wash-house and bathroom was provided opening off the scullery; this was equipped with a fixed coal-fired copper, from which hot water was supplied direct to the bath (see Figure 23). In only two of the plans, both for parlour houses, was there an upstairs bathroom, requiring a hot-water circulating system. In other respects, however, the plans in the *Manual* compared favourably with those in the Tudor Walters Report. This was particularly true of space standards. The ministry measured the size of houses by the gross area of the ground floor alone: measured in this way, the range of sizes for non-parlour houses in the *Manual* was 500 to 578 square feet, as against 441 to 536 square feet in the Tudor Walters Report. Furthermore, in June 1919 the ministry decided to permit local authorities to build in excess of these figures to a maximum ground floor area of 600 square feet for a three-bedroom non-parlour house and 700 square feet for a three-bedroom parlour house.[24] In all, it was agreed that the standard of houses specified in the *Manual* and permitted by the ministry represented a considerable improvement over that of prewar working-class housing.

As word reached Whitehall of the tender prices received by local authorities, however, this generous attitude to house-sizes soon changed. In July 1919 the official estimate for the average total cost per house (including land, roads and sewers as well as the building itself) was £500 to £750; but even in June 1919 the average price in tenders for house construction (excluding the cost of land and development) was £740, and this excluded increases in prime costs that brought the figure, by the time building was completed, to an actual figure of £1000.[25] In view of these prices the ministry decided at the end of July 1919 that the scale of maximum permitted sizes was too generous and instead ruled that 'the sizes of houses set out in the plans in the *Manual* must be regarded as the normal maximum size for houses for the type in question. The floor areas for the houses as a whole must not be exceeded'.[26] Over the next year, as the ministry struggled to realise the government's ambitious house-building targets and costs escalated, space standards offered one area in which it seemed that general, albeit minor, savings were possible, and by the end of 1919 it appears that the ministry was using the table of room sizes, not as minima as envisaged by the Tudor Walters Report, but as maxima. The Committee on the High Cost of Building Working-Class Dwellings stated in 1921:

> At first, in view of the fact that the standard [of room sizes] had been laid down as a minimum, some latitude was allowed to local authorities provided that the increase in size proposed was not unreasonable and did not involve much additional expense. Owing, however, to the steady increase in the cost of building during the first year of operations, the minimum gradually became the standard, and after the first few months the Ministry of Health were not able to approve tenders for houses exceeding the standard.[27]

Political pressure for a trimming of standards came with the Cabinet discussions on housing in November 1919. As one of many possible remedies for the high cost of the housing programme, Addison on 11 November proposed the adoption of 'new and cheaper types of houses'.[28] Following this it was decided that a 'selection of economical plans', based on the experience of the regional housing commissions, should be prepared, and this eventually appeared as the volume of

Type Plans and Elevations in May 1920.[29] The thirty-four plans provided, as the Committee on High Cost stated, a somewhat lower standard of accommodation. The range of house-sizes was down by about one-tenth compared to the *Manual* and on one point the plans in the 1920 volume showed a clear departure from Tudor Walters minima. The Tudor Walters Report and the *Manual* had given a minimum size of 180 square feet for the living-room; but in a three-bedroom parlour house, the area needed on the ground floor was greater than that required on the first floor, particularly if (for reasons of economy) the bathroom was located on the ground floor. Accordingly, in these cases the ministry reduced the size of the living-room to 160 to 165 square feet. This did not go unnoticed: in May 1920 the Housing Commissioner for the Northern Region resigned in protest against, among other things, the 'reduction of the standard of housing from that indicated in the *Manual*'.[30] Nonetheless, seen in the long term, this represented an extremely minor abrogation of established standards. The case of the living-room in the parlour house was the exception that proved the rule: far from the drastic changes that Addison's 'new and cheaper houses' had implied, in all respects except this one the standards of the Tudor Walters Report were observed in the volume of *Type Plans and Elevations*.

In one respect the plans shown in *Type Plans and Elevations* represented an improvement over those in the *Manual*: several of the plans for non-parlour houses followed the double-fronted arrangement with central staircase (see Figure 27). This was a type that, although considered highly desirable by housing reformers, had not been included in the Tudor Walters Report or the *Manual*. But it was now adopted by the ministry in response to the problems of roof construction discussed above. Apart from this one change, however, the plans in the 1920 volume followed the five types established by the Tudor Walters Report. In some cases, only detail alterations had been made to the arrangement recommended by the Tudor Walters Report; in others, more substantial re-working had taken place. Substantial modification was most obviously required if an L-shaped plan was used to reduce the roof-span, which was the case with some two-thirds of the plans for parlour houses in the 1920 publication. Apart from this, only one general change was made to the internal organisation recommended by the Tudor Walters Report. The plans published both in the report and in the *Manual* had, like Unwin's prewar designs, eliminated internal passageways on the ground floor and used the living-room for circulation. This however was not popular with prospective tenants; apart from any other disadvantages, it meant that the slop-pail from the bedrooms had to be carried through the living-room in order to be emptied. This criticism was accepted by the ministry as early as July 1919 and thereafter it attempted to avoid the objection by providing direct access to all rooms from a central circulation space. Figure 25 shows a typical plan from the 1920 volume in which one of the Tudor Walters types (Type D) has been reworked both to produce an L-shape for the plan and to avoid the use of the living-room for circulation.

It had been stated in the *Manual* that the ministry's house plans were intended only as the basis for the designs of local authorities. But with such slow progress it was soon decided that in cases of great urgency a local authority might be pressed to use the ministry's plans without alteration. On 4 July 1919 housing commissioners were told: 'It is so necessary that some houses should be built at once that the Commissioners should urge in suitable cases the adoption as they stand of appropriate plans in the *Manual* for these urgent schemes'.[31] The idea that the ministry's designs could be used without modification was the reason for including such a large number of plans in the *Type Plans and Elevations* volume. In the preface it was stated:

> It is unnecessary to point out that a considerable amount of time has been saved by adopting the type plans and quantities, and it is hoped that in the present period of extreme urgency a much more extended use will be made of them.... The full working drawings can be obtained by Local Authorities and Public Utility Societies from the Ministry of Health, Whitehall, or from the Housing Commissioners. The quantities appertaining to each type can be purchased from HM Stationery Office.[32]

These hopes, however, appear to have been largely disappointed. Local authorities were prepared to adopt the type plans issued by the ministry as the basis for their own designs. Indeed, I have not found any local authority plans that did not correspond to one of the ministry's types in general arrangement. But actually to use the plans and quantities produced by the ministry was another matter. A ledger from the ministry has survived which records the number of parlour houses built by local authorities to plans supplied by the ministry: it shows that in the period between February 1920 and April 1921, contracts involving ministry plans were entered into by seventy or so local authorities, ranging in size from Tunbridge RDC to Manchester Corporation, but that the total number of houses involved was less than 3300.[33] If we assume that this is an accurate record (which there seems no reason to doubt) and allow a figure of even double this for non-parlour houses, the number of houses built to the ministry's plans would still account for less than 10 per cent of the total number for which contracts were signed in this period. This points to the conclusion (corroborated by the case studies presented in the next chapter) that, however much they all resembled the plans of the ministry, the number of houses actually built to those plans by local authorities was relatively small.

Until the end of 1920, the housing standards of the Tudor Walters Report were maintained. With the decision, in the winter of 1920/1, to limit future contracts to cases where tender prices were substantially reduced, however, house plans and housing standards underwent a marked change: wide-fronted types were proscribed and narrow and deep types exclusively adopted. In contrast to the broad-fronted plans of the *Type Plans and Elevations*, from December 1920 *Housing* carried a series of plans designed by the ministry, intended for both aspects, with a frontage of 20 ft 9 in. These plans reverted to the basic arrangement of Tudor Walters Type A (see Figure 28). Furthermore, this same arrangement, with the same frontage, was employed for a new class of house published in *Housing* in February 1921. This was described as intermediate between the parlour and non-parlour types. It was essentially a non-parlour house with the cooking range transferred from the living-room to the scullery and the scullery proportionately increased in size to the detriment of the living-room. It was stated that

> In the average housing scheme ... it should be possible to obtain considerable economy by substituting some of these ... houses for the parlour houses, since the living-room practically constitutes a parlour without the serious increase in cost which this room usually entails.[34]

Following Mond's appointment to the Ministry of Health this suggestion was taken further. Housing commissioners were told that in the case of houses to be built with the 1919 grant but yet to be commenced, any parlour houses were to be replaced by the new 'intermediate' type.

In making its recommendations on the internal arrangement of the house, the Tudor Walters Committee had sought to avoid the combination of cooking, eating, washing-up, washing and drying of clothes, and general 'living' in any one room. Its plans had been specifically intended to prevent this by splitting these functions between living-room and scullery and, in the case of the non-parlour house, by discouraging the use of the living-room as a parlour. The new intermediate type, by providing a living-room that could function as a parlour and thereby allowing the scullery to become a general living-room clearly contradicted the advice of the report. But in the pursuit of immediate savings the recommendations of the Tudor Walters Report were set aside. From the middle of 1921 substantial cuts in housing standards were imposed by the ministry. Where houses were in signed contracts but had not been commenced, room sizes were to be reduced; in the numerically far smaller category of additional houses for which approval was still to be given, local authorities were told by the ministry that 'the type for additional houses could not be on the same basis as those already erected'.[35] Small dwellings, with no parlour and with only two bedrooms, were advocated by Mond and plans on these lines were drawn up by the ministry's architects; and cottage flats, of the sort used at Well Hall, were revived and recommended by the ministry. Eventually, in January 1923, the ministry abandoned one of the most basic improvements effected in 1918–19 and stated that it was prepared to approve local authorities building houses without bathrooms.[36] For, after 1921, the houses were no longer intended as proof for the heroes of the beneficence of the state; indeed, in so far as they contained any directly political message, it was something rather different. As the *Municipal Journal* noted approvingly in July 1922, these smaller houses showed that the government and local authorities were no longer 'led astray by visionaries', but were simply getting on with the job of supplying 'the cheapest form of housing which will actually provide accommodation for the poor'. These small two-bedroom houses (see Figure 31), it was claimed, were 'more likely to solve the housing question than the model houses with parlours and palace-like amenities in picturesque surroundings' that local authorities had been told to build only two or three years earlier.[37]

8 House-building in London and York

The previous chapters have given an account of the process by which the housing programme came to be adopted and implemented by the government in the post-war years. It now remains to take the last link in the chain and see how the ideas, objectives and contradictions of the 'homes fit for heroes' campaign were given embodiment in built form in the housing schemes of local authorities.

Two local authorities have been chosen: the London County Council and York City Council. As the largest housing authority in the country, the LCC is an obvious choice. London was the largest conurbation in the UK and its housing problem was regarded as the most serious of any city in the kingdom; the LCC housing programme was the most ambitious and most widely reported of any in the country; and, even though cut short by the government decision to axe the housing campaign, it still accounted for one in twenty of the houses built by local authorities under the 1919 Act. While London was, to some extent, representative of the large cities, the experience of the LCC was necessarily atypical of the majority of local authorities and for this reason the study of the LCC is complemented by a shorter account of municipal house-building in York. In 1921 York was the fifty-ninth largest town in England and Wales, with a population of 84 000, and it was considered by R. L. Reiss that housing conditions in York were 'typical of those which existed ... in most industrial towns' with a population between 30 000 and 250 000.[1] Moreover, social conditions in York are exceptionally well documented as a result of the investigations undertaken by Seebohm Rowntree, and the proximity of Rowntree's New Earswick permitted a ready comparison between municipal housing and one of the early garden city schemes.

The most obvious difference between York and London was, of course, size. The estate built under the 1919 Act in York, although on the edge of the built-up area, was only a mile from the centre of the city; whereas to find a site to meet the housing needs of the eastern part of London, the LCC surveyor had to travel 10 miles from the Royal Exchange. The idea of using low-density housing on the edge of the city as the answer to the shortage in the centre made

sense in York in a way that it could not in London. This relative
advantage of the small over the larger town was reinforced by the
financial system incorporated in the 1919 Act. Before the grant from
the Exchequer could be obtained, there had to be an annual loss on
the housing scheme greater than the produce of a penny rate. In York,
the produce of a penny rate (£1688) was only one-hundredth of what
it was for the LCC: whereas York had to build only a small number
of houses before the Exchequer came to its aid, the LCC had to build
thousands of houses before this position was reached. This perhaps
accounted for the fact that, although both councils were controlled
by the local equivalent of Conservatives (in York called Independents;
in London, Moderates or Municipal Reformers), the LCC was very
much the less enthusiastic of the two about the duties and opportunities conferred by the 1919 Act.

One further difference between the housing schemes of the two
councils should be noted: whereas the LCC schemes were designed
by architects (as recommended by the Tudor Walters Report), York
was one of the relatively small number of local authorities that
entrusted the design of its housing scheme to its City Engineer. The
LCC Architect's Department had a distinguished record in housing
design and was responsible for all the architectural work on the 1919
Act scheme, initially under W. E. Riley and from October 1919 under
his successor, G. Topham Forrest. In York the City Engineer, F. W.
Spurr, had undertaken a small amount of housing work for the council
prior to 1919 and was responsible for both the layout and house design
of the 1919 Act scheme. In this respect, neither example is, strictly
speaking, typical, for most local authorities engaged outside architects
for their 1919 Act housing schemes. Nonetheless, in terms of the
architectural quality of estates built under the Act, the LCC Roehampton estate and the York Tang Hall estate stand, roughly
speaking, at the two ends of the spectrum, and in this way they are
illustrative of the general standard achieved in the products of the
'homes fit for heroes' campaign.

London County Council

Since 1907, when the Conservatives or Moderates had won control
of the council, the LCC had shown a decided reluctance to undertake
building in relief of the housing shortage. Nonetheless, it had not been
able to eliminate this sort of activity entirely and, for such building
as could not be avoided, the LCC had developed a number of precepts
before 1914 that were to directly influence its programme after the

war. In the first place, the council had decided that any housing of
this sort should be directed not towards the more affluent members
of the working class (who should be left to private enterprise), but
to the poor. This meant small houses, as built at Old Oak after 1911
(see Chapter 2). Second, the LCC showed a persistent interest in the
use of suburban housing as a cheap alternative to the provision of
rehousing on cleared sites in central areas. Between 1911 and 1913
the council persuaded the LGB to accept houses built on suburban
estates as a substitute for new housing for the population displaced
from cleared sites, and it was only on this basis that in 1919–20 the
council agreed to the purchase of Roehampton and the other new
estates. The third idea concerned the size and social mixture of cottage
estates. Economic considerations applying to both initial construction
and subsequent management made it desirable to provide the housing
in what the Housing Committee called 'the largest practicable units'.
On the other hand, the concentration in one area of a large working-
class population deprived of contact with other classes was regarded
with apprehension: as the Housing Committee put it in October
1918, 'on general social and political grounds' it was considered 'not
desirable to develop the whole of a large area entirely by the provision
of houses for the working class'. The answer was what was termed
'mixed development'. This involved the purchase of a large estate,
part of which could be leased to private builders for the erection of
middle-class houses while still leaving a portion for working-class
housing large enough for economies of scale to be obtained. It was
this concept that was embodied in the garden suburb scheme adopted
for the White Hart Lane estate in 1912 and in the three estates
(Roehampton, Becontree and Bellingham) acquired and developed
under the 1919 Act.

It was with these preconceptions that the LCC responded to the
offer, made by the government in March 1918, of a Treasury grant
towards the cost of postwar housing schemes. The LCC programme
was set out in a Report of the Housing Committee adopted by the
council on 23 July 1918. Claiming that there was insufficient
information available with which to justify a policy aimed at meeting
the housing shortage, the Committee proposed to continue its prewar
emphasis on the qualitative rather than the quantitative aspect of
the housing problem. Slums would be dealt with by clearance,
rebuilding and improvement. At the same time, in order to 'create
a healthy draught from insanitary to wholesome property', additional
houses would be built both on the existing suburban estates (Old Oak,
Norbury and White Hart Lane) and on new estates to be acquired

close to the areas of worst housing. In all a sum of £3.5 million would be spent on capital account over a period of seven years.

In seeing postwar policy as a development of, rather than a radical break from, that of the past, the LCC programme of 1918 corresponded with the view taken by the Local Government Board under Hayes Fisher and contained in the circular of March 1918. It did not, however, correspond either with the new policy announced by the government in February 1919, or with the reality on which that new policy was based, that it, the emergency created by the Armistice and by the large-scale influx of ex-servicemen and other war workers into an already overstretched housing market. Figures for empty houses on LCC estates revealed the seriousness of the position: in 1911 8 per cent of LCC houses had been vacant; in 1914 the figure was 1.25 per cent but by 1919 it was less than 0.1 per cent. To make good the shortage, before any margin was supplied to permit slum clearance, the Housing Committee estimated that accommodation would have to be provided for 50 000 persons. Moreover, as the Housing Committee pointed out, the change in housing policy announced by the government in February 1919 made a revision of the LCC programme more or less unavoidable. Under the new policy local authorities had the duty instead of merely the power to carry out housing schemes adequate for the needs of their districts, and under the new financial terms the annual loss on housing schemes had to exceed the produce of a penny rate before any assistance from the Exchequer was received. The Housing Committee stated that

> The effect of the revision of terms in the case of London is to rule out the Council from any State assistance until a programme of housing work far in excess of the large scheme hitherto contemplated shall have been carried out.

The new scheme was prepared by the Housing Committee and adopted by the council on 3 June 1919. A five-year programme was proposed in which 29 000 dwellings for 145 000 persons would be built on suburban estates, including 10 000 dwellings in the first two years. At the same time the worst insanitary areas, ·with a total population of 40 000, would be cleared and 10 000 further dwellings provided as rehousing for 50 000 persons on cleared sites. The estimated capital expenditure was £24 million for the 29 000 cottages and £5.4 million for slum clearance and rehousing; and the estimated annual deficit on the entire scheme was between £1.1 and £1.2 million, equivalent to a special county rate of 7d to 7½d in the pound.

As to the location of the proposed 29 000 additional dwellings, a report to the Housing Committee in May 1919 showed that 40 per cent of the 789 000 people living in unsatisfactory housing in the county were to be found in the eastern district to the north of the river. Accordingly the majority of the additional houses were to be directed to the relief of this area. No large sites, however, were available within this sector of the county and the Housing Committee therefore proposed to acquire, by compulsory purchase, a large site outside the county with good rail connections 'to give access to this open land from the congested area' where, it was assumed, people would continue to work. On this site, located between Becontree and Dagenham, 24 000 houses would be built. The remaining 5000 houses would be distributed between the existing estates and two new estates to be acquired in the south-west and south-east, at Roehampton (1200 houses) and Bellingham (1750 houses).

It was with this programme that the LCC started building. Of the remaining portions of existing estates acquired under Part III of the 1890 Housing Act, those at Old Oak and Norbury had been developed with roads and sewers in 1914, and it was with these that the postwar programme got under way, with the issue of invitations for tenders for houses on the two estates in June 1919. At White Hart Lane delays arose from complications over the garden suburb scheme and constructional work on roads did not start until June 1920. For the LCC, as for other local authorities, land was one of the few resources needed for the 1919 programme that did not present major difficulties. New estates were acquired at Roehampton (147 acres), Bellingham (252 acres) and Becontree (3000 acres). Purchase of the Roehampton estate had been proposed under the council's 1918 programme, and as a result its development proceeded in advance of the other two: ministry approval for the acquisition of the estate was secured in July 1919 and construction work began early in 1920, at about the same time as the purchase of the Bellingham and Becontree estates. In addition, at the suggestion of the ministry, an estate of 575 acres at Grove Park in south-east London was acquired by compulsory purchase in May 1920, but, owing to the premature closure of the 1919 subsidy scheme, was not developed until later in the 1920s and 1930s.

The LCC's programme was at an early stage of implementation when the curtailment of the Addison scheme was announced. In May 1921 only 244 houses had been completed at Old Oak, 134 at Norbury and 17 at Roehampton, and none at all at Bellingham, Becontree or White Hart Lane. Following the cutback of July 1921, both the Old Oak and Norbury estates were completed under the contracts approved under the 1919 Act; but at White Hart Lane houses in approved tenders covered only 56 of the 98 acres available, and the development of the remainder had to await later legislation. Of the three new estates, only Bellingham was completed under the original contract, the McAlpine contract for 2090 houses being completed by January 1923. At Roehampton, the ministry insisted that the contracts be broken after only 624 houses had been completed; the remainder (588 houses) were built with the 1919 subsidy but not completed until 1927. At Becontree, the ministry in October 1921 authorised the erection of a further 1000 houses under the 1919 scheme, in addition to the 2876 houses in the first section; but the remainder of the houses (more than 20 000 in all) were not permitted under the 1919 scheme. In all, just under 9000 houses were built by the LCC on cottage estates under the 1919 Act.

From the start, the LCC house-building programme was beset by problems arising from the Cabinet decisions on resources discussed above in Chapter 6. To obtain tenders for the Norbury and Old Oak houses in June 1919, it was found necessary both to supply bills of quantities (something that the council had never done in the past) and to include in the contract an 'up-and-down' clause protecting contractors from subsequent rises in wage rates and prices of materials. Without the 'up-and-down' clause, as the ministry tacitly admitted with its standard contract of September 1919, tenders were unobtainable. Even so, only four tenders were received from the thirteen firms invited to tender for each of the LCC contracts, and the lowest of the Norbury tenders was subsequently withdrawn, necessitating the invitation of fresh tenders. In October 1919 the new LCC Architect, G. Topham Forrest, faced a crisis over the housing contracts: on 15 October the contractors for the first 130 houses at Old Oak withdrew their offer to extend the contract to include the further 520 houses to be built on the estate; on 20 October the contractors for the second Old Oak contract withdrew from the contract, stating that they were prepared to build only if the council would guarantee them a 10 per cent profit on the net cost; and two days later the contractors for the completion of the Norbury estate withdrew their tender altogether. Out of the council's entire programme for 29 000 houses, it seemed that only the 130 houses at Old Oak might be built. In an attempt to deal with this, the Housing Committee decided not to revert to direct labour (as Progressive and Labour members urged), but instead to meet the contractors' demand for a guaranteed profit on housing schemes. On 29 October the Housing Committee authorised the use of 'cost-plus-profit' contracts, in which tenderers were asked both to state the 'fee' (covering profit and expenses) that they would require on a stated expenditure and to provide the schedule of prices for which they would undertake typical houses. This type of contract was immediately adopted for the second Old Oak contract and subsequently for the other major contracts in the LCC housing programme, including those for the development (both roads and houses) of Becontree and Bellingham in the summer of 1920. The only other type of contract used in the council's 1919–23 housing programme was that in which an agreed price was arranged with the local builders' federation. At the instigation of the Ministry of Health, this was adopted by the council for the contract for the houses at Roehampton in May 1920, at the spectacular average price of £1150 per house.

The contractors said that their reason for withdrawing from the Old Oak contracts in October 1919 was the unavailability of materials and throughout 1919 the Housing Committee was under strong pressure to circumvent this constraint by adopting timber or concrete for walling in place of brick. Timber, however, was rejected on the grounds that its disadvantages in terms of maintenance, long-term cost and durability outweighed any initial advantage in availability; and on concrete, the Architect reported that the shortage of transport was at least as pressing as the shortage of bricks, and that, accordingly, concrete construction should be adopted only where aggregate was available on the site. This strategy was followed in the LCC programme up to 1923: at Roehampton and Bellingham concrete was used only to a small extent (for instance, for partitions and party walls) but at Becontree 2200 of the 2876 houses on the first section were built of concrete, using the 'Winget' method.

The shortage of building labour was the major constraint on the housing programme from the autumn of 1919 until the spring of 1921. The exceptional position of the LCC exempted it from the difficulties in raising capital encountered by other authorities; subscriptions to its housing bonds and issues of stock permitted the council between 1919 and 1921 both to meet its own needs and to lend some £4.4 million to the Metropolitan Borough Councils. But on the question of labour the LCC suffered as badly as other authorities from the excess of demand over supply and the greater attractiveness, in terms of wages and conditions, of non-municipal work. In October 1920 fewer than 1500 men were employed on what was nominally a programme to build over 7000 houses per year. Only when the boom broke in the autumn of 1920 did the size of the labour force employed on the LCC schemes begin to show a marked increase: by March 1921 the figure had increased to 5600 and by July stood at just under

10 000. As a result the rate of completions increased dramatically: in September 1921 only 709 houses had been completed but a year later the number was 5673.

On questions of design it was Roehampton that, as the first of the new generation of LCC estates, set the standard for LCC building in general. Before the war the LCC cottage estates had been built at a density of twenty-five to twenty-seven houses to the acre and for Roehampton the ministry agreed to a higher than normal density in view of the central location of the estate: the houses were built at 15.8 per acre gross, giving 1194 dwellings on the 75.6 acres of the estate retained for working-class housing. The layout plan (approved by the ministry in December 1919) showed the usual low-density techniques, including the placing of houses around three sides of a green, the use of backland for allotments, and set-backs in the building line (see Figure 29). One of the usual forms, however, was missing: the cul-de-sac. When the London Building Acts Committee (the body responsible for London building bylaws) learned of the Architect's intention to include several of these in the Roehampton plan, it complained that 'some of the present-day slums were, no doubt, originally pleasant cul-de-sacs of a similar design'; and, although the Housing Act of 1919 conferred exemption from bylaw requirements on housing schemes approved by the ministry, the Housing Committee preferred to avoid the possibility of censure. Accordingly cul-de-sacs were eliminated and replaced by through roads, despite the waste of frontage (at Roehampton, sufficient for fifty-four houses) that this entailed.

For Old Oak and Norbury, where roads were already constructed, the ministry agreed with the LCC that in order to avoid delay house plans similar to those used before the war should be adopted. The houses built at Old Oak were described as following 'prewar designs, with some additional amenities'. The main addition consisted of a bathroom instead of just a bath in the scullery. But the room sizes were substantially below the Tudor Walters minima; a third of the houses had only two bedrooms; and the frontages were, as with the prewar designs, extremely narrow, in some cases as little as 12 feet. Accordingly, the LCC was told by the architects at Whitehall that 'they would require compliance with the standards [of the *Manual*] in future proposals'. New type plans had therefore to be prepared for Roehampton and the other new estates. These were submitted to the Housing Committee by Topham Forrest in October 1919. Officially described as being 'of much improved design, intended to meet the post-war demand for a superior class of accommodation',

Figure 29   London County Council, Roehampton estate: layout (1919)

Table 2   *Contrast between typical houses erected at Old Oak and Roehampton, 1920 (figures in feet and inches, and square feet)*

	Old Oak	Roehampton
Frontage	14'3	21'2½
Depth	25	23'7
Net floor area	656	839
Living-room area	142	192
Scullery area	55	80
Bedroom 1 area	126	145
Bedroom 2 area	99	110
Bedroom 3 area	55	80
Offices	WC in bathroom	Separate WC
Amenities	Hot-water supply	Bathroom with lavatory basin; linen cupboard; large cupboards and larder; hot-water supply; covered way to back.

Source: LCC Minutes, 14 December 1920.

they differed markedly from those adopted for Old Oak and Norbury a few months earlier (see Table 2). The rooms were larger and generally conformed to Tudor Walters minima. Frontages were noticeably wider; most of the plans, instead of being narrow and deep as at Old Oak, were square, and the minimum frontage (which the majority of the plans considerably exceeded) was 18 ft 6½ in. A high level of equipment and services was provided: a bathroom (in almost every case on the first, rather than the ground, floor) equipped with bath and hand-basin; a separate WC; fitted cupboards in the living-room and bedrooms; and an internal tool-shed. These were luxuries unprecedented in LCC houses, and they were not to outlast the Addison programme. The most impressive item was the hot-water system. There were essentially only two answers to the question of water-heating: the cheap but unsatisfactory method by which water was heated in a copper and drawn off direct to sink and bath and the satisfactory but expensive circulating system, requiring a boiler, hot-water cylinder and cold water tank. Only the circulating system permitted an upstairs bathroom and a heated linen cupboard, but on cost grounds the Tudor Walters Report had regarded it with caution and it was not included in the ministry's plans of 1919–20.[2] In the Roehampton Type Plans of 1919, however, a hot-water circulating system was provided in all but the smallest (one and two-bedroom) dwellings.

The type-plans adopted for Roehampton derived from the Tudor Walters Report. But in keeping with the higher density of the LCC estates, there was a lower proportion of houses with very wide frontages; the houses were generally square in plan rather than broad and shallow and rarely provided for the living-room to be lit from both ends. The double-fronted types from the Tudor Walters Report were little used: parlour houses were mostly derived from Tudor Walters Type C, and non-parlour houses either followed the basic Tudor Walters Type A or, where the aspect was northerly, adopted an unusual type, in which the living-room and scullery occupied opposite corners in a square plan (see Figure 30). This was a type

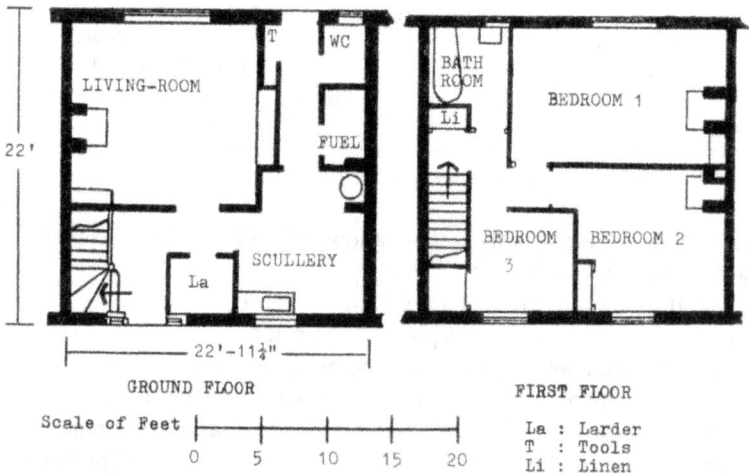

Figure 30   London County Council: typical plan from the set adopted for the Roehampton estate in 1919 to meet the requirements of the Manual

that the Tudor Walters Report had mentioned but not generally recommended (preferring the wide-fronted Type B) and it was not one that was generally endorsed by the ministry.

There were a number of other respects in which the LCC plans diverged from the orthodoxy of the Ministry of Health. In keeping with its prewar traditions, but in opposition to the general policy of the ministry, the LCC provided a high proportion of small dwellings intended for the poorer classes. Again it was Roehampton that first raised the general question for the new LCC estates. In November 1919 the council's Director of Housing proposed that since Roehampton would appeal to 'those of the working class whose standards and ideals are the highest', 80 per cent of the houses should be parlour houses of three and four bedrooms. This, however, implied a dramatic break from the traditions of the council which the Housing Committee preferred to avoid and for the first instalment at Roehampton a middle course was adopted. There were to be no four-bedroom houses at all, but 40 per cent were to have three bedrooms and a parlour; 40 per cent were to have three bedrooms but no parlour; and 20 per cent were to be small dwellings with only one or two bedrooms, mostly built as cottage flats. But the high proportion of three bedroom parlour houses was a concession to the location of the Roehampton estate. At Bellingham and White Hart Lane, the proportion of this class of house was only 20 per cent – the same as that followed on the prewar section of Old Oak, which had been specifically intended to meet the needs of the poorer classes. Overall, in the houses built by the LCC under the 1919 Act, there was a much lower proportion of accommodation for the higher-paid sectors of the working class than that envisaged in the *Manual* (see Table 3).

Table 3   Proportion of houses of different classes in LCC estates (per cent)

	1-room	2-room (L & 1 bed)	3-room (L & 2 bed)	4-room (L & 3 bed or L, P & 2 bed)	5-room (L, P & 3 bed)
1. Old Oak, prewar section (as built)	5	8	33	33	20
2. Roehampton, first instalment (adopted 1919)	—	10	10	40	40
3. Roehampton, second instalment (adopted 1919)	—	5	15	30	50
4. White Hart Lane, postwar section (adopted 1919)	—	5	35	40	20
5. Bellingham, as built (1920–23)	—	6	16	58	19

Note: L = living-room; P = parlour.
Sources: *Municipal Journal*, vol. xxvi (5 October 1917) p. 975; LCC Housing of the Working Classes Committee, Building and Development Sub-Committee 5 November 1919, 3 December 1919 and 17 December 1919; LCC Minutes 12 June 1923.

On the question of priority in the allocation of tenancies, the ministry provided no specific guidance beyond suggesting some form of preference for ex-servicemen and it was left to individual local authorities to formulate their own schemes. Most authorities, including the LCC and York City Council, adopted complicated systems in which preference was given to ex-servicemen, those who had lost their homes through war service, the war-widowed and those living in conditions of overcrowding. In the LCC system, adopted in October 1919, preference was given to those who had lost their homes through undertaking war work or war service, but there was preference also for certain classes of the council's employees. Membership of these categories, however, was only the first step to an LCC tenancy; a prospective tenant had also to demonstrate a 'good record for cleanliness and punctual payment of rent' and have an income at least five times greater than the total of rent, rates and fares. In practice, in view of the high rents charged for the postwar houses, this income requirement was as effective a barrier to tenancy as the formal priority system.

Under the open-ended grant provided by the 1919 Act, the question of rents was one in which the Exchequer had a direct financial interest, and over which, accordingly, the ministry attempted to exercise strict control. But, in setting the level of rents, the ministry was caught between opposing forces. On the one hand, the government was committed to restoring economic rents, once the abnormal costs brought about by the war had disappeared. In practice, the target adopted by the ministry was a rent that in 1927 covered two-thirds of the actual cost of building, this being the extent to which it was thought that costs would eventually fall. On the other hand, given the enormous increase in the cost of building, if rents calculated on this basis were charged immediately, the political function of the housing programme – of providing and being seen to provide ex-servicemen with homes – would clearly be negated. The answer was to distinguish between initial and eventual rents. An economic rent on two-thirds of the building cost remained the goal to be achieved by 1927. Initial rents, however, were to be determined by reference not to building costs but to existing rents and the amount that tenants could pay. In its regulations the ministry specified four factors for the determination of initial rents: local rents for working-class houses; the substantial increase in those rents permitted by the Rent Restriction Act of 1920; any superiority in condition or amenity of the new houses; and 'the class of tenant in the district for whom the houses are provided'.[3]

It was in accordance with these instructions that the initial rents of the new LCC houses were settled by the Housing Committee. But the outcome was rents substantially greater than those of prewar houses. In 1920 the rents charged for the postwar houses at Old Oak were 50 per cent higher than those for prewar houses on the same estate, and the rents adopted for Roehampton were, in view of the superiority of the houses, even higher: for a non-parlour house with three bedrooms, the weekly rent adopted in 1920 (exclusive of rates) was 7s 4d and 11s respectively for prewar and postwar houses at Old Oak, and 15s 6d at Roehampton. Even so, the proportion of the annual cost (including maintenance, interest on capital, sinking fund, etc.) covered by the rent was only 30 to 35 per cent. As the Finance Committee pointed out in December 1920, if the ministry's aim of notional economic rents was to be realised by 1927, at some stage the rents of the new houses would have to be doubled.

It was the deficiency of the rent in relation to the cost of building that in December 1920 provided the opportunity for a 'review' of housing standards on the council's estates. By this date the postwar economic boom had turned to slump and it was emergency measures for the relief of unemployment, not the threat from labour, that filled the headlines of the national and local press. The initiative came from the LCC Finance Committee which on 8 December suggested that the ministry should be asked whether the improved standard adopted in 1919 should still be maintained. The ministry's answer, dated 14 January 1921, was that there should not be 'any substantial reduction in the general standard' but it suggested that the LCC should investigate the possibility of economies through changes to individual plans and grouping, the layout of sites, and construction. Many changes of this sort were adopted in the new set of type plans approved by the Housing Committee in April 1921. In addition, longer rows of houses were introduced with less variety in types; more extensive use was made of narrow roads, particularly for providing access to houses grouped

Table 4 *Minimum room sizes adopted by the LCC in 1921, compared with those of the Ministry of Health followed in 1919 (square feet)*

	LCC, 1921	*Manual*, 1919
Living-room	144	180
Parlour	100	120
Scullery	60	80
Bedroom 1	144	150*
Bedroom 2	100	100*
Bedroom 3	60	65*

* These were the minima for bedrooms in non-parlour houses. The *Manual* stated that when a parlour was provided and the number of bedrooms not increased, the sizes of the bedrooms 'should be increased in size proportionately'.
Source: LCC Housing Committee, Building and Development Sub-Committee, 2 February 1921.

around a central green; and constructional economies, such as the
omission of hand-basins from bathrooms and plastering from
sculleries, were adopted. Most important of all, the Housing
Committee decided to abandon the minimum room sizes specified by
the ministry in 1919 and revert to the smaller sizes that had been
followed at Old Oak (see Table 4)

While smaller room sizes were adopted in the 1921 set, the plans
remained in arrangement similar to those adopted for Roehampton in
1919. Most of the plans in the 1921 collection were square in shape and
the figure for the lowest frontage was comparable to that in the 1919
plans. Reversion to the narrow and deep plans of the sort used before
the war was effected with the further review of standards undertaken
by the Housing Committee in the autumn of 1921 and the issue of a
new set of type plans in February 1922. Constructional savings
included the use of stocks instead of red facing bricks, the reduction of
roof pitch and the simplification of the roof, as well as minor economies
such as the omission of picture rails. Many of the improvements
inherited from the Tudor Walters Report and the *Manual* were
discarded. For instance, in the two-bedroom non-parlour houses the
bathroom and WC were combined and the only access for both the

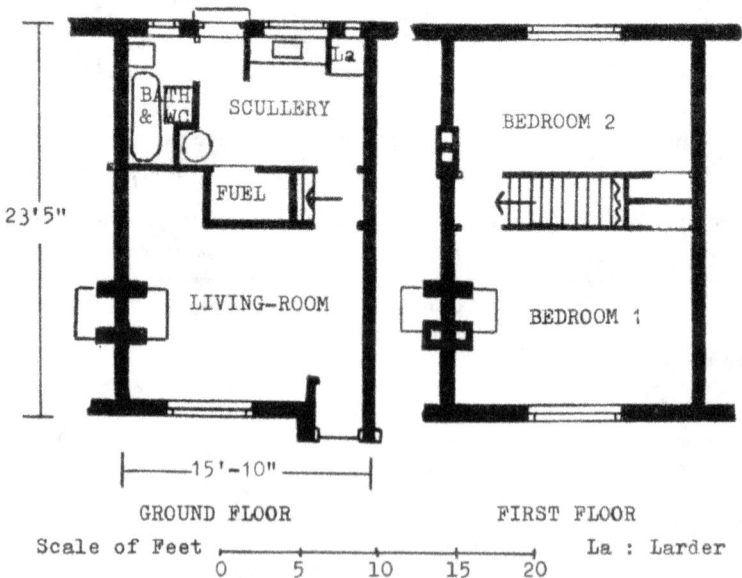

*Figure 31   London County Council: typical narrow-fronted plan from the set
adopted in 1922, based on prewar designs*

delivery of coal and the collection of refuse was through the living-room. The plans themselves were based on those used before the war, with very narrow frontages (see Figure 31) – in some cases as low as 14 ft 7½ in.

The architectural precepts embodied in the LCC estates should rightfully form a subject of their own. Suffice it here to state that with the LCC estates, as one might expect from a department long known as a favourite haunt of the pupils of Philip Webb and W. R. Lethaby, one is confronted with a level of architectural design absent from the York scheme examined below. In terms of the conflicting claims of picturesque and simplified design, the designs made for Roehampton in 1919 (and also those for Bellingham and White Hart Lane made the

Figure 32   London County Council, Roehampton estate: photograph taken in 1922

following year) showed a greater resemblance to the enclosed effects of the prewar Old Oak estate than to the simple repeated units of Gretna or Dormanstown. With blocks complex in both section and plan, Roehampton followed Hampstead Garden Suburb in its allegiance to the romantic concept of buildings 'growing out of the earth' (see Figure 32). In the early stages of building, up to 1922, the LCC architects were able to use both the good quality materials (facing bricks and clay tiles) and the inventive detailing (relieving arches, stringcourses and diaper brickwork) essential to this kind of architecture. But in the later houses, particularly those well concealed from the perimeter and the main thoroughfares, both the good materials and the expensive detailing disappeared. At Roehampton these later houses (dating from the period up to 1927), with their low-pitched slate roofs and unrelieved rendered surfaces, were much closer to the dowdy image of the stereotyped interwar council house than to the high quality architecture of the early parts of the estate.

York City Council

The outbreak of war in August 1914 prevented the implementation of plans adopted by York City Council earlier in that year for a substantial scheme of 220 houses on a suburban site. However, during 1917 and 1918 these plans were revived and it was on the site selected in 1914, known as the Tang Hall estate, that the council's scheme under the 1919 Act was built.

Before 1914 the only housing built by the council was a small group of cottages provided under the rehousing obligation of a street improvement scheme in 1912. In 1914, however, the council had accepted the proposal of the Medical Officer of Health for the building of a suburban estate as part of the city's public health and slum clearance programme. Two distinct types of housing were to be provided on the site: 'cheap cottages' would be built 'to cope with the immediate needs of dispossessed persons'; and to meet the housing shortage in the city and provide a margin for slum clearance, larger houses would be built for the more affluent sectors of the working class.

While forestalling the plans of the council for dealing with the housing shortage, the war also led to a decline in, and eventual suspension of, building, thereby making the shortage even more severe. In the decade before 1914, an average of eighty working-class houses were built each year in York; but in the three years 1915–18, only fifty-two were built altogether. In its reply to the Ministry of Health's form of survey in 1919, the city council estimated that 300 houses were needed to meet the shortage – a figure which Liberal and Labour councillors said was far too low – and a further 950 to rehouse those displaced by slum clearance. The council estimated that 300 houses would be built by private enterprise, leaving 950 to be built by the corporation.

The same estate was to be used both to rehouse the poor and to provide houses for the better-off in relief of the housing shortage. This fact allowed what was essentially a conflict over housing policy to take the appearance of a technical debate over house types. In February 1919 the council intended to provide equally for the slum dwellers and the better off; its proposal for the first instalment at Tang Hall comprised 118 houses without parlours for the poor and 120 houses with parlours for the more affluent. The government, however, believed that meeting the housing shortage should take priority over clearing the slums and in response to suggestions from Whitehall the number of parlour houses in the first instalment was increased to 138. This emphasis on housing for the more affluent was further increased as a result of pressure exerted by the labour movement in York. When the proposal for the first instalment of houses was announced in March 1919, the response of local labour was prompt and effective: the York branch of the National Union of Railwaymen and the Poppleton Road Allotment Holders

> expressed the opinion that of the first four hundred houses, 10 per cent should be four-bedroomed and the rest three-bedroomed houses (the latter being built first), and that 90 per cent of these latter should also be parlour houses – all the four bedroom houses also having parlours.

The outcome was a set of amended plans prepared by the City Engineer and 'arranged as far as possible to meet the demand with regard to the provision of more parlours'. In this the proportion of parlour houses was increased to 64 per cent. These plans were accepted by the Health Committee on 2 May 1919 and were followed for the first instalment of 185 houses in the Tang Hall scheme.

None of the houses in the council's original proposal of 1914 had included a parlour. Houses intended for the more affluent had been distinguished from those for the dispossessed slum dwellers by the inclusion of three as against two bedrooms, and by the provision of a separate bathroom. Compared with this, the scheme followed in 1919 showed changes in two directions. The proportion of houses for the better-paid artisan had increased; slum clearance now took second place to the housing shortage. Second, the standards of housing had improved; all houses had a bathroom and at least three bedrooms, while those for the superior class included a parlour. In agreeing to these changes, the city council had bowed to the combination of pressure from Whitehall and local labour.

This debate over house types took place at a time when, due to the postwar boom, labour was, in the words of the *Municipal Journal*, 'in the saddle'. This situation did not last in York any more than in the country as a whole; 1920 was a year that, as the York and District Trades and Labour Council ruefully commented, 'began with great promise but ended in tragedy', with the city 'haunted by the dread spectre of unemployment'.[4] Labour was thus in a much weaker position when in March 1921 the council decided, in view of the uncertainty over the future of the 1919 Act subsidy, to proceed immediately with the second instalment of 150 houses at Tang Hall. With the spread of unemployment and the fall in wages, the 'better-off' sector of the working class was definitely worse off than it had been two years earlier. Accordingly little resistance was offered to the council's decision to provide only non-parlour houses in the second instalment. With the pressure from labour removed, the council was therefore able to return to the original 1919 conception for the Tang Hall scheme of meeting equally the needs of those affected by the qualitative and quantitative aspects of the housing problem. But before tenders had been accepted the housing programme was abandoned by the government and in August 1921 the council was informed that it could not proceed with the second instalment.

In implementing its housing programme York City Council suffered from the same problems of materials and labour scarcity as other local authorities; these have been described in the case of the LCC and need not be repeated. But on the other vital resource – capital – the position of the LCC was quite unrepresentative, and so the experience of York, as a more typical municipality, is worth recounting. As an authority with a rateable value in excess of £200 000, the city council did not qualify for assistance from the Public Works Loans Board and had therefore to raise the capital for building by itself. Measured by rateable value per capita, York was a relatively affluent borough and did not experience the severe difficulties encountered by some local authorities in this respect. Even so, the problem was serious, for the sums that had to be raised were enormous in comparison with any previous borrowing undertaken by the council. Up to February 1921 £73 000 had been spent on capital account on the first instalment of 185 cottages at Tang Hall but only £55 000 had been raised in housing bonds, including subscriptions from local employers (Rowntree's and the North Eastern Railway) made in return for the nomination of tenants. Even without the additional 150 houses that the council proposed to build, capital expenditure on housing for 1921/2 was estimated at £281 000, of which it was estimated that only £115 000 could be raised from housing bonds and savings certificates. At a special meeting of the council on 14 March 1921 the Finance Committee reported that 'at present prices it is estimated that to build the houses we require we shall have to raise a larger sum than the whole of our Corporation debt before this burden was put upon us.' Relief was clearly felt in certain quarters a few months later when the government's abandonment of the housing programme removed the immediate prospect of having to raise funds on this scale.

For the first instalment of the Tang Hall scheme, there were only two type plans; both were for blocks of four cottages with open-passage access to the rear, and both were designed by the City Engineer in 1918. The non-parlour type, which came in both three and four-bedroom versions, was the basic Tudor Walters Type A, with a generous scale of room sizes (including an extremely large living-room of 240 square feet) and an upstairs bathroom. Whereas houses of this type were located on the north–south roads of the rather grid-like layout and the plans were suitable for houses on either side of the road, the parlour houses were placed on the east–west roads and therefore had to be modified according to whether the houses faced north or south. In the plan for parlour cottages, the middle two units were double-fronted, while the end two were 'turned', in effect creating a 30 foot frontage along one side (see Figure 33). The middle houses were of Tudor Walters Type D, with the stairs centrally placed and living-

FRONT ELEVATION

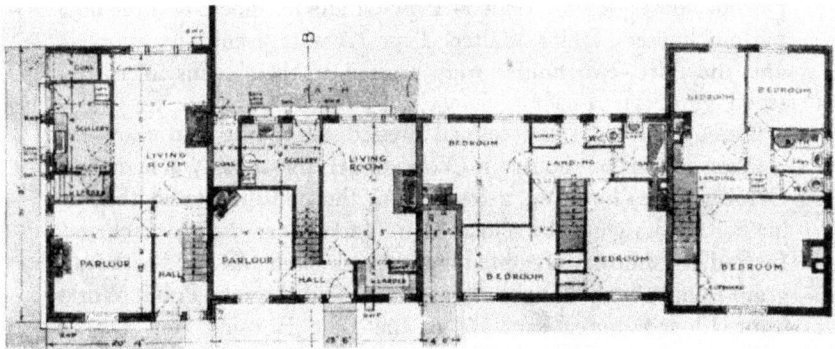

GROUND FLOOR   FIRST FLOOR

Figure 33   Tang Hall estate, York: elevation and plans of parlour houses
1919

room on one side and parlour and scullery on the other. For the end houses, the plan submitted to the LGB in January 1919 showed a rather unsatisfactory arrangement, with the parlour and scullery adjacent to the end wall. In March 1920 this was replaced, at the instigation of the Housing Commissioner, by an L-shaped unit of Tudor Walters Type C: this reduced the number of chimneys per block from five to three and permitted direct access to all main rooms from the entrance lobby and staircase.

It was these type-plans that were included in the initial contracts for 185 houses at Tang Hall signed in 1920. These had been intended only as the first instalment of an eventual total of 400 houses to be built at the Tang Hall estate under the 1919 Act; but the council's intentions were cut short by the government announcement of 14 July 1921. In November 1921, however, the Ministry of Health agreed to the erection of a further thirty-two houses under the 1919 subsidy arrangement to 'fill up vacant sites between houses already erected'. This necessitated small units of two or three houses rather than the larger units generally favoured by the ministry. The Housing Committee proposed that both parlour and non-parlour houses should be built, 'with the same accommodation as existing houses': but the Housing Commissioner insisted that the 'type for the additional houses could not be on the same lines as those already erected'. In practice this meant the reduction of room sizes and the omission of the hot-water circulating system, with the bathroom returning to its former place next to the scullery. After considerable altercation with the Housing Commissioner, plans for pairs of parlour houses (Tudor Walters Type C) and for blocks of three non-parlour houses (Tudor Walters Type A) were eventually adopted, and the thirty-two houses were erected to these plans in 1922–3 (see Figure 34).

Throughout 1922 the council pressed the ministry to allow the erection of further houses in York under the subsidy scheme. In October 1922, however, a letter from the ministry stated that no further houses could be allocated to York under the 1919 scheme. Instead, the ministry suggested that the council should build without a grant from Whitehall, but with capital provided by the Public Works Loans Board under Part III of the 1890 Housing Act. On 20 November 1922, by a large majority, the council decided to complete the Tang Hall scheme on this basis and the following month tenders were invited for the erection of thirty parlour houses, to plans prepared by the City Engineer. For these houses the council was able to please itself on matters of design in a way that had not been possible when

Figure 34   Tang Hall estate, York: the early portion. On the right are the non-parlour houses built in 1920; on the left, the in-fill houses permitted by the Ministry under the 1919 Act scheme, built in 1922–3

Table 5   Sizes of principal rooms in parlour houses built by York City Council, 1919–23 (square feet)

	Living-room	Parlour	Scullery	Gross area of ground floor
LGB minima, 1919 (*Manual*)	180	120	80	---
Tang Hall, first instalment (1919–21):				
end houses	189	142	72	634
middle houses	181	117	74	551
Tang Hall, additional houses permitted under 1919 Act	156	80	62	514
Tang Hall, houses built in 1923 under 1890 Act	165	111	86	558

Source: York City Archives, Corporation Housing Scheme at Tang Hall, plans A104 (1919), A158 (1922) and A173 (1922).

building under the 1919 Act. The plan was altogether more lavish than that adopted to meet the ministry's requirements earlier in 1922. Room sizes were larger (see Table 5). The bathroom returned to the first floor and the hot-water circulating system was reinstated. The roof was hipped instead of merely pitched and, instead of being unbroken, contained a central projection (see Figure 35). For all this, however, the plan of the houses followed a standard ministry type (Tudor Walters Type E).

In December 1919, in the wake of the tenders received for the first houses at Tang Hall, the Health Committee had decided to inspect the plans prepared for houses at New Earswick to ascertain 'if the Corporation's plans could be amended and the estimates reduced'. Here was the possibility for the municipal scheme of direct fertilisation from one of the pioneer estates of the garden city movement. Following the announcement of financial assistance for public utility societies in the 1919 Act, plans had been put in hand at New Earswick for building on a large scale, but these were undermined by the escalation of building costs in 1919–20, and in the event only 110 houses were built with the assistance provided by the 1919 Act. Even so, the designs for these houses, by Barry Parker, attracted considerable interest in the specialist press.[5] But Parker's ideas seem to have made little impact on the York Corporation scheme, and there was nothing in the latter that showed a response to Parker's particular points of emphasis. For instance, the through living-room for non-parlour houses, on which Parker insisted absolutely, was noticeably absent from the 1919 portion of the Tang Hall estate, whereas the detached tool-shed, on which Parker placed an equally absolute embargo, was all too conspicuous (see Figure 34).

The relative neglect by the council of the example provided just outside the city by New Earswick might be seen as the grounds for the rather adverse comments on the council's estates made in *Poverty and Progress* by Seebohm Rowntree. He wrote:

> It is perhaps invidious to criticise the elevations of the houses, for tastes vary. I think, however, it is fair to say that anyone familiar with building estates where the houses have been designed by first-rate architects who specialised in designing cottages, would place the York houses in the second class.[6]

To my mind, however, this is a fair assessment. While the improvements in standards and amenities inside the houses were undeniable, the layout of the estate was dull, making little use of the low density of ten houses to the acre, and the elevations of the houses were very much

FRONT ELEVATION

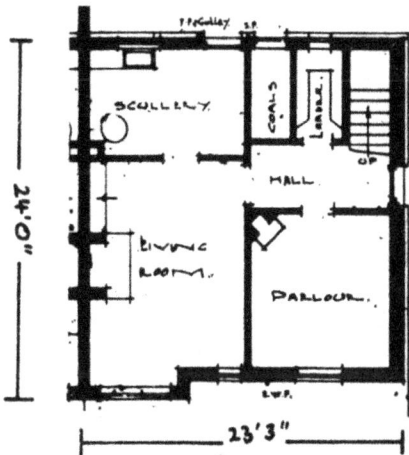

GROUND FLOOR

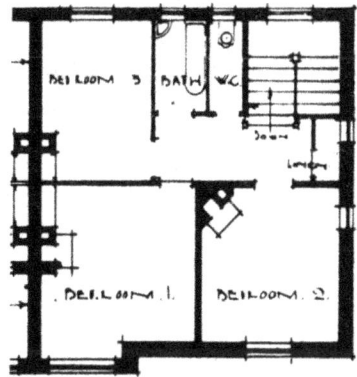

FIRST FLOOR

Figure 35   Tang Hall estate, York: elevation and plans of parlour houses built in 1923 under the Housing Act of 1890

less inventive than the council's earlier housing ventures. Other local authorities got much better architectural results for their 1919 Act schemes, at no extra cost to themselves, by the employment of outside architects. The shortcomings of the layout can be attributed to inexperience in low-density layout but the elevations require more explanation. In part their ineffectiveness derived from the intervention of the Housing Commissioner, who insisted on the substitution of slates for the tiles originally intended by the City Engineer: the first 1919 Act houses look considerably stronger in the contract drawings, with 45° tile roofs, than they do as built with low-pitched roofs of slate. But the basic problem was the difference between the views of the corporation and the ministry on the question of architectural treatment. The inclination of the City Engineer and the council, as the 1912 scheme showed, was entirely towards a quaintness based on dormer windows and gables. In the early part of 1922, when discussing with the Housing Commissioner the plans for the additional thirty-two houses permitted by the ministry, the Housing Committee went to considerable pains in its attempts to ensure that 'the gables as shown on the plan should be retained'. The Housing Commissioner insisted on their elimination from the Exchequer-aided houses but a similar feature was included in the houses built the following year without the Exchequer grant (Figure 35). The corporation had no conception of the supposed aesthetic benefits that were claimed for the architectural doctrines of simplicity and honesty; but the 'features' such as gables which were central to the corporation's notion of what was desirable were unacceptable to the architects at the ministry, particularly when used in the purely ornamental manner that the corporation envisaged. Under the 1919 system, design was in the hands of the local authority but subject to the control of Whitehall. The outcome was a thoroughly unsatisfactory compromise. The corporation was compelled by the ministry to omit the features they would have liked to 'beautify' the elevations, while at the same time the doctrines of austerity and simplicity were too foreign to the thinking of the corporation to be adopted in any effective way. Having neither the quaintness of its own earlier ventures nor the positive tautness of simplified design as, for instance, in the Parker houses at New Earswick, the corporation's houses in the 1919 scheme (see Figure 34) were plain, without producing the effect of simplicity and repose for which the architects at the ministry were hoping.

Homes fit for Heroes in London and York

Under the Housing Act of 1919, the LCC and the York City Council built a total of slightly more than 9000 dwellings, with a significantly higher standard of accommodation than any prewar housing built by either body. The houses built under the Act were the outcome of a collaboration between central and local government, into which the two sides entered for slightly different reasons. The factor common to the motivation of both central and local government was the shortage of housing which had been greatly exacerbated by the war and which, it appeared, would not be met without state intervention. The prime motive of the government in launching the housing programme was to secure an 'insurance against revolution'. To show how much better life was going to be in the future, the government wanted local authorities to build houses of a much higher standard than ever before, aimed not at slum-dwellers but at ex-servicemen and the organised working class. The case-studies have shown that local authorities were less concerned with questions of ideology and revolution than with those of public health. In both York and London the shortage of housing was making it impossible for the councils to carry out their public health programme, which both councils regarded as their main concern. Accordingly, they looked more to the provision of housing for slum-dwellers than was considered desirable by Whitehall. In York this inclination was checked by the combined pressure of the ministry and local labour; but the LCC was given considerable latitude by the ministry – on this as on other matters – and was able to include a high proportion of small houses in its 1919 Act scheme.

It was crucial for the ideological function of the housing programme that the houses be indisputably better than working-class houses of the past. Housing on garden city lines was not only unmistakably different from the usual forms of working-class housing but it had also been regarded as beyond the means of working-class incomes, and for that reason it was just what the government needed in order to validate its claim to the loyalty of the returning heroes. Under the 1919 Act the financial liability of local authorities was limited, and so they had no financial interest in resisting the government's pressure for an improvement in housing standards. Accordingly, the houses built under the Act by both the local authorities were of a considerably higher standard than anything proposed or built by either authority before the war: the changes have been detailed in this chapter and related both to internal accommodation (number and size of rooms, level of equipment and services, etc.) and to dwelling type and layout, for which the model of the garden city movement was followed. In the case of both authorities, until the curtailment of the housing programme in 1921, it was houses of the sort recommended by the Tudor Walters Report that were built.

The number of houses built under the Act by the two councils fell short, by more than two-thirds, of the targets adopted in 1919. This short-fall was the result, first, of the slow progress of building due to the scarcity of resources, and then of the government's abandonment of the programme. In 1921 the government decided that the insurance against revolution was no longer needed and required local authorities both to curtail their building programmes and to cut their housing standards. The two local authorities examined in this chapter differed in their response to this demand. York City Council resisted both but was able to obtain only a very small addition to its 1919 scheme. In contrast, the LCC, which in 1919 had adopted a large-scale programme and improved housing standards only under pressure from the government, now showed itself willing to adopt the changed views of the ministry on both quantity and quality. Nonetheless, the size of the council's programme, combined with the slow rate of building, meant that a considerable number of its 1919 Act houses were started after 1921. For these, the standards of accommodation were much lower than those approved between July 1919 and December 1920 and the house plans resembled those that had been used before the war.

For the most part, however, and particularly in the portions of the schemes approved before 1921, the houses built by the two councils under the 1919 Act were remarkably similar inside and out. Principles of layout, room sizes and standards of accommodation and amenity, and even some house types, were common to both. There were, as one would expect, architectural differences, deriving from the very different kinds of offices responsible for design in either case. Overall, however, it is a question of resemblance rather than contrast. In keeping with the specific intention behind the 1919 programme, the impression created by Tang Hall as much as Roehampton was, as said at the time, that 'whatever else these houses may be, they are at least different ... from pre-war "working-class" houses.'[7]

Conclusion

In August 1921, wrote Elie Halévy, 'capitalism emerged the victor from a crisis that had lasted for two years'.[1] 'Homes fit for heroes' was one of the main weapons adopted by the state in order to secure that victory.

This was the first occasion on which the provision and design of public housing had been used to such telling political purpose. Long before the First World War the state had been compelled to take action to relieve certain aspects of the housing question – most notably where the health of the classes that controlled the state was threatened by the existence in the cities of large areas of festering slums. In the decade prior to 1914, increasing problems of housing provision (related particularly to the rise in the rate of interest and the problem of rural areas) led the state to take further measures and made housing into a recognised element of national debate. Nonetheless, housing policy at Westminster remained essentially a passive response to particular problems outside. The really significant development in these years was the emergence of the garden city movement – which was significant less for its architectural innovations *per se*, than for the contention of its industrialist patrons that these innovations, involving the transformation of housing and environmental conditions, held the key to a contented population. But while admiration of the garden city achievement extended to most shades of the political spectrum, the response of the state to the garden city example was constrained by the limited nature of state intervention in housing provision. Thus the 1909 Housing and Town Planning Act attempted to promote garden city development *without* increasing the state's expenditure on housing provision and even in the Land Campaign the limited role still envisaged for state housing remained an effective constraint on the promotion of garden city housing.

The position at the end of the First World War was very different. In the wake of the Armistice the government believed that unless drastic measures were taken Britain would follow Russia and Germany into Bolshevik revolution. How was a mass army to be induced to return peaceably to a civilian life of which the realities – poverty, unemployment, insecurity, bad living conditions – were so unattractive, when they held the weapons that could be used to overthrow those realities? This was the overwhelming question that preoccupied the Cabinet. The answer, it decided, was not force – which against five million trained fighting men could scarcely be effective – but ideas. If the soldiers succumbed to the propaganda of the Bolsheviks there was nothing that could be done to save the social order. If, on the other hand, their minds could be filled with what (from the government's point of view) were the 'right' ideas, they would not turn their bayonets against the state. The Cabinet believed that the key was to persuade the servicemen that the Britain to which they were returning would not be the same as it had been in the 'bad old days', but would be a 'land fit for heroes' in which a bright future awaited them without any need for recourse to revolution. Accordingly, the months after the Armistice saw the government promising a wide-ranging programme of social reform and at its heart was the pledge of a great house-building campaign. The cost to the Exchequer would be enormous, but, as the Chancellor said, in face of the danger facing the state, money was no object. Parliament agreed: the housing campaign was the necessary insurance against revolution.

To show the troops and the public how much better life was going to be, the new houses had, as one MP put it, to be 'on quite different lines' from those of the past.[2] The physical model was provided by the garden city movement; the industrial patrons of the movement had, after all, originated the belief now held by the government – that by a dramatic improvement in housing conditions the population would be reconciled to a status quo that was, in other respects, unchanged. The physical products of the garden city movement – cottages with trees and gardens in semi-rural surroundings – were unmistakably different from the housing to which most of the working class had been accustomed before the war. The state undertook to provide 500 000 houses of this sort, built to standards unprecedented in municipal housing, with bathrooms, parlours, and other 'luxuries': in short, 'middle-class houses' providing visible evidence of the great improvement in the conditions of life.[3] The detailed specifications for these houses were set out in the Tudor Walters Report and, so long as the goal of the housing programme remained unchanged, it was houses of this quality that were built (see Figure 36).

In mounting the housing campaign, the state had the benefit of the experience in emergency house-building gained at the Ministry of Munitions during the war. It was from the munitions programme that the 1919 campaign derived its subsidy system, its chief administrators and architects, and its doctrines on housing design. These were

Figure 36   Hammersmith Borough Council's Wormholt estate, London: a typical high quality housing scheme begun in 1919, designed by the then President of the Royal Institute of British Architects, H. T. Hare, and others

essentially the same as the principles and techniques of low-density layout and house design developed by the garden city movement before the war but in one significant respect the garden city legacy was amended. The architecture of the garden city movement had been, generally, romantic and individualistic; but a considerable body of architectural opinion had grown up before the war against this picturesque tradition, which was regarded as particularly inappropriate for a mass housing programme. For the design of the new state houses 'simplification and standardisation', the catch-phrase of the industrial standards movement, provided an alternative architectural doctrine. Simplification and standardisation, as Unwin had argued before the war, was economical and, dressed in neo-Georgian garb, it appealed to architects as an idiom in keeping both with the established canons of taste and with the social and technical realities of the day. Above all, the slogan offered the prospect of ruthlessly efficient mass-production that would 'solve' the housing problem (with all that that meant in political terms) as effectively as Henry Ford had 'solved' the problem of mass-producing motorcars.

The housing programme of 1919 was an insurance against revolution: its purpose was to ensure the survival of the status quo. Behind the smoke-screen of a 'land fit for heroes', the old social order remained intact, ruled as before by the interests of finance and industry. The attitude of industry to the housing programme was ambivalent: on the one hand firms (in York, for instance, Rowntree's and the NER) wanted housing for their employees; but on the other, they did not want resources that they themselves needed for the expansion or maintenance of their own premises transferred to house-building. The financial world was hostile to the housing programme and did all it could to obstruct it. The result was that the resources needed for house-building were not made available and that, with demand for labour, materials and capital far outrunning supply, the rate of house-building was extremely slow and the cost extremely high. While the Treasury complained about the cost, the Cabinet – so long as it hoped to use the housing programme to win what it called the 'battle of opinion' – had to do something about the rate of completions. All sorts of expedients were attempted, including new methods of building, the use of the Office of Works, direct labour, and government pressure on building workers to accept the introduction of additional labour. These were, essentially, attempts to conjure up labour and materials for housing without withdrawing them from other areas of building. As such they were a way of building the houses without causing damage to the dominant economic interests, and thereby of resolving the contradiction between the postwar world presented by official propaganda and the postwar world as it was in reality.

In 1921 the government put an end to the contradiction between propaganda and reality by abandoning the image presented by its own slogans. The rapid change in the economy from boom to slump in the winter of 1920/1 transformed the balance of political forces, undermined the power of labour and eliminated the danger against which the housing programme had been an insurance. With, as Halévy noted, the employers instead of labour on the offensive, the premium on the insurance was regarded as an unnecessary expense and the housing programme was axed. At the same time, and for the same reason, the high standards adopted in 1918–19 were jettisoned; for any houses still to be built under the 1919 Act the ministry demanded a reversion to the type of houses built before the war, with higher densities and with the parlours and the other amenities of 1918–19 omitted. With the change in the political climate, the housing programme that in 1918–19 had appeared to offer the best hope of social salvation assumed, for some people, the appearance of inexplicable extravagance.

Although it was prematurely brought to a halt, the 'homes fit for heroes' campaign had important lasting consequences for public housing in Britain. In terms of both the scale and the quality of municipal housing, it created a precedent to which subsequent reformers could refer and, to some extent, a standard from which departures had to be justified. Never again could the idea of local authorities providing housing on a large scale for the general needs of the population be labelled an unprecedented innovation. Nor could it be alleged that local authority housing was, by definition, something reserved only for those unable to obtain anything better, for all over the country there were municipal estates that were of a far higher standard than anything provided for the working class by private enterprise. Moreover, in the years 1918–21 the notion of high quality public housing, particularly as set out by the Tudor Walters Report, acquired an authority that subsequent attacks and smears could not entirely obliterate: however much the ministry's advice after 1921 might contravene its particular recommendations, it was a bold Minister of Health who would dare to openly discount the Tudor Walters Report as a whole. Accordingly, in the years after 1921, while housing standards (particularly in terms of space and equipment) were driven down, the general concept of municipal garden suburbs remained intact.

For, as Mond predicted at the time, the decision to bring the 'homes fit for heroes' campaign to a halt did not mean the end of state intervention in housing. In the critical period after the Armistice, the government had done everything in its power to persuade the country that the housing campaign was the proof of the legitimacy of the state and of the irrelevance of revolution. After July 1921 the Cabinet was no longer prepared to finance the housing campaign, but it found that, having been accorded this unique status, housing could not be simply ignored or treated as though the promises and claims of 1918 and 1919 had never been made. With the basic material problem unchanged – a severe shortage of houses which private enterprise, expecting a future fall in costs, was not prepared to meet – the government found itself caught up in the momentum of the legitimatory process that it had itself set in motion. In the year or so following the decision to axe the housing campaign, the government, thanks to the time-lag involved in building operations, was still able to point to the large number of municipal houses becoming available for occupation (67000 in the twelve months up to March 1922); but as building programmes commenced before July 1921 came to an end and the supply of houses began to dry up, the government came under increasing pressure to introduce new measures. In response, the Conservative government announced a new initiative in March 1923, designed primarily to stimulate the activities of private builders. When the first Labour government took office the following year, a further Housing Act was introduced which, in keeping with the traditional demands of organised labour for decent housing, consolidated and extended the innovations made in 1919. The result was that the 1920s as a whole became a decade in which local authorities built housing on garden city lines, often using the sites originally purchased under the 1919 Act. Even if it did not match up to the standards of 1919–21, this council housing built in the remainder of the 1920s was nonetheless of a reasonable quality – particularly in comparison to the minimum-standard slum clearance projects that dominated the 1930s.

In recent years there has been a marked renewal of interest in urban questions, not least in housing and housing policy. Starting with the pioneering work of Manuel Castells and others, this has led to the appearance of a formidable body of literature which, even if it has not always lived up to its early promise, has, overall, transformed our understanding of urban phenomena. It would be inappropriate at this stage to enter into the specific questions and issues with which this new school has been concerned; readers familiar with its main themes will already have recognised the points at which my narrative has dealt with questions debated in this literature. In conclusion, nonetheless, it is worth mentioning one or two points of a general nature arising from 'homes fit for heroes', which suggest a rather different way of looking at urban questions from that which has prevailed in this recent work.

In *The Urban Question* Castells introduced a method of analysis that concentrated on the material or economic level, using in particular the concept of 'collective consumption' (referring to such things as education, health care, housing, and other urban amenities) and defining 'the urban in terms of collective reproduction of labour power and . . . the city in terms of a unit of this process of reproduction'.[4] The effect, if not the intention, has been that urban questions, including housing, have been seen by followers of Castells in predominantly material terms. Thus housing has been defined as 'a crucial element in the reproduction of labour power'[5] and state intervention as a response to 'the inability of the private economy to meet the minimum needs in housing'.[6] Ironically, this is not unlike the old liberal view of housing policy as a more or less direct response to perceived housing problems: what Marian Bowley would have called 'problems of overcrowding and housing shortage' reappear under the new guise of 'contradictions in the reproduction of labour power', and in each case their role is the same – to explain state intervention.[7] But the evidence of 'homes fit for heroes' shows that the attempt to locate the determinants of housing policy solely at the material level does not work. If it had been difficulties in the reproduction of labour power that led to state intervention, we would expect employers and employers' organisations (such as the Federation of British Industries) to have taken the lead in urging the new policy onto the state. But this was not the case; in fact, the pressure from business interests was rather the opposite – towards freeing resources for the open market regardless of the consequences for housing. The idea of a massive housing campaign arose not in the industrial but in the political domain (in Whitehall and Westminster); and its function, as members of both Cabinet and House of Commons said, was to influence people's ideas about the state and society. This is not to deny that in practice state housing also served the function of reproducing labour power: but it is clear that both the motive for, and the primary determinant of, state intervention in 1918–19 came from the political and ideological levels rather than the economic. The implication must be that if we are to understand how state policy works in practice, we must give rather more attention to political and ideological factors than recent theoretical writings have suggested.

A further general point that emerges from 'homes fit for heroes' concerns the relationship of ideology and design. As Castells and Merrett have noted, the whole question of architecture and design has been almost entirely overlooked in the recent urban literature.[8] Equally, in a neatly complimentary manner, the ideological aspects of design have been largely ignored by historians of architecture and design, including those who, over the last few years, have sought new approaches to the subject.[9] One of the reasons for this is that for designers at the drawing-board, the suggestion that design is an ideological process is largely incomprehensible since it seems unconnected with their own daily experience. Yet the evidence of 'homes fit for heroes' suggests that design can perform this ideological function. Here too those responsible for designing the schemes were concerned with questions of aesthetics and practicality and not at all with questions of ideology and revolution. But this does not alter the fact that ideology provided the raison d'etre of the housing campaign and that it was through design that the ideological function was to be performed: as MPs said – repeatedly – the design of the houses was to prove to the people that revolution was unnecessary.

With 'homes fit for heroes', we see ideology operating through design: it was through the design of buildings that the state hoped to instil into the population ideas favourable to the continuing existence of the status quo. Even if we do not accept the view that the survival of capitalist societies in general has depended on ideology, 'homes fit for heroes' suggests, at the least, that the conventional phrase 'the social function of design' involves a good deal more than is usually allowed. For the inference from 'homes fit for heroes' is, first, that design is not, as it is usually presented, a self-contained affair that those interested in 'society' can leave to the design specialists; and, secondly, that the processes of ideology are not confined to those channels dealing explicitly with ideas (education, the press, television, etc.), which have usually been identified as the 'ideological apparatus' of society. On the contrary: it seems that design – the silent testimony of inarticulate objects – is one of the ways in which 'suitable' ideas are propagated and reinforced. 'Homes fit for heroes' provides valuable evidence of this process at work; and it suggests that if we are to come to terms with either ideology or design, then the relationship of the one to the other must be further examined and documented.

References

Abbreviations

HC Bill   House of Commons Bill
HC Deb   House of Commons Debates
HLL   House of Lords Library
JAIA   *Journal of the American Institute of Architects*
LPA   Local and Personal Acts
LCC   London County Council
PGA   Public and General Acts
PP   Parliamentary Papers
PRO   Public Record Office
TPR   *Town Planning Review*

1. The Legacy of the Garden City Movement

1. Quoted in W. Creese, *The Search for Environment. The Garden City: Before and After* (1966) p. 23. For contemporary accounts see P. Abercrombie. 'Modern town planning in England: A comparative review of "garden city" schemes in England', *TPR*, vol. I (1910) pp. 18–38 and 111–28; and E. G. Culpin, *The Garden City Movement Up-to-Date* (1913).
2. E. Cadbury, 'Scientific management', *Sociological Review*, vol. VII no. 2 (1914) p. 106.
3. Quoted in *The Garden City*, New Series (NS) vol. III no. 28 (May–June 1908) pp. 80–81.
4. W. L. George, *Labour and Housing at Port Sunlight* (1909) p. 62.
5. Quoted in J. Cornes, *Modern Housing in Town and Country* (1905) p. 71.
6. W. Alexander Harvey, *The Model Village and its Cottages: Bournville* (1906) p. 4.
7. C. B. Purdom, *The Garden City* (1913) p. 26.
8. E. Howard, *Garden Cities of Tomorrow* (Faber 1965) p. 142.
9. C. B. Purdom, *The Building of Satellite Towns* (1949) pp. 82–4.
10. Culpin, *The Garden City Movement Up-to-Date* p. 9.
11. *The Garden City*, vol. I no. 4 (July 1905) p. 65; *Municipal Journal*, vol. XV (13 April 1906) pp. 399–401.
12. *Housing Journal*, vol. LXIX (April 1907) p. 3. For the statement on housing and 'ordinary labourers' (made by The Garden City Tenants) see *The Garden City*, NS vol. I no. 9 (October 1906) p. 196.
13. *The Garden City*, NS vol. IV no. 32 (February 1909) p. 182.
14. R. Unwin, *Town Planning in Practice* (1909) p. 11.
15. PRO HLG 29/106 (Memorandum on Byelaws May 1912). For pre-bylaw residential development, see F. Engels, *The Condition of the Working Class in England* (Panther 1969) p. 88.
16. *Municipal Journal*, vol. XV (1 June 1906) p. 595.
17. R. Unwin, *Nothing Gained by Overcrowding! How the Garden City Type of Development may Benefit both Owner and Occupier* (1912) p. 7.

18. Unwin, *Town Planning in Practice*, p. 302; LPA 6 Edw VII c. cxcii, Hampstead Garden Suburb Act 1906.
19. PP 1918 Cd 9213 vii, 'Report of the Departmental Committee on Building Bye-Laws'.
20. PP 1918 Cd 9191 vii, 'Report of the Committee appointed by the President of the Local Government Board and the Secretary for Scotland to consider questions of building construction in connection with the provision of dwellings for the working classes in England and Wales, and Scotland, and report upon methods of securing economy and despatch in the provision of such dwellings' (The Tudor Walters Report), paragraph 58.
21. Cd 9191 (Tudor Walters Report), paragraph 66.
22. Unwin, *Town Planning in Practice*, p. 363.
23. C. Sitte, *Der Städtebau* (1895); English translation by G. R. Collins and C. C. Collins as *City Planning according to Artistic Principles* (1965).
24. Unwin, *Town Planning in Practice*, p. 138.
25. Unwin, *Town Planning in Practice*, p. 140: see also R. Unwin. 'Town planning at Hampstead', *Garden Cities and Town Planning*, NS vol. 1 no. 1 (February 1911) pp. 6–12 and NS vol. 1 no. 4 (May 1911) pp. 82–5.
26. Unwin, *Town Planning in Practice*, p. 325; see also H. R. Aldridge, *The National Housing Manual* (1923) pp. 116–18.
27. R. Unwin, *Cottage Plans and Common Sense* (1902) pp. 3 and 5–6.
28. L. E. Waddilove, *One Man's Vision* (1954) p. 24.
29. Unwin, *Cottage Plans and Common Sense*, p. 11.
30. *The Garden City*, NS vol. 1 no. 9 (October 1906) p. 187.
31. *The Garden City*, NS vol. 1 no. 3 (April 1906) p. 55.
32. *The Garden City*, NS vol. 1 no. 3 (April 1906) p. 55; see also NS vol. 1 no. 10 (November 1906) p. 208 and NS vol. 1 no. 11 (December 1906) p. 226.
33. *The Garden City*, NS vol. 1 no. 4 (May 1906) pp. 91–3.
34. R. Unwin, 'Cottage building in Garden City', *The Garden City*, NS vol. 1 no. 5 (June 1906) pp. 107–11; Harvey, *The Model Village and its Cottages*, pp. 5 and 17–19.

2. Housing and the State before 1914

1. Edinburgh Town Council, 'Report by the Sub-Committee of the Lord Provost's Committee as to the sanitary improvement of the city, and minutes of the Lord Provost's Committee and the Town Council thereon', 28 March to 9 April 1866; quoted in P. J. Smith, 'Planning concepts in the improvement schemes of Victorian Edinburgh' (First International Conference on the History of Urban and Regional Planning, London 1977) p. 30.
2. F. Engels, 'The Housing Question', in Marx and Engels, *Selected Works* (Lawrence & Wishart) vol. II pp. 323–4.
3. LCC, *The Housing Question in London, 1855–1900* (1900) pp. 190–210; W. Vere Hole, 'The Housing of the Working Classes in Britain, 1850–1914' (University of London Ph.D thesis 1965) pp. 392–9; see also D. Gregory Jones, 'Some Early Works of the LCC Architect's Department', *Architectural Association Journal* vol. LXX no. 786 (November 1954) pp. 95–105.
4. A. T. Mallier, 'Housing in Coventry. The Development of Municipal Action 1890–1908' (University of Birmingham M.Soc.Sci. thesis 1969) p. 28.
5. City of York, *Annual Report of the Medical Officer of Health for the Year 1913*, pp. 125–30.
6. Mallier, 'Housing in Coventry', p. 72; O. A. Hartley, 'Housing Policy in Four

Lincolnshire Towns, 1919–1959' (University of Oxford D.Phil thesis 1969) pp. 155–60; D. Englander, 'The Workmen's National Housing Council, 1898–1914' (University of Warwick MA thesis 1973) p. 11 *et seq.*

7. S. Martin Gaskell, 'Sheffield City Council and the development of suburban areas prior to World War One', in S. Pollard and C. Holmes (eds), *Essays in the Economic and Social History of South Yorkshire* (1976) pp. 187–202.

8. See LCC, *Housing of the Working Classes in London* (1913); Vere Hole, 'The Housing of the Working Classes', pp. 412–20; Englander, 'The Workmen's National Housing Council', pp. 239–60.

9. PRO HLG 29/106 (figures on housing 1912).

10. PP 1914 Cd 7610 xxxviii, '43rd Annual Report of the LGB 1913–1914. Part II. Housing and Town Planning', p. xxxviii.

11. F. Knee and R. Williams, *The Labourer and his Cottage* (1905) p. 76; *The Garden City*, vol. 1 no. 4 (July 1905) pp. 49–51.

12. National Unionist Association of Conservative and Liberal Unionist Organisations, *The History of Housing Reform* (with a foreword by Rt Hon. A. Bonar Law MP) (1913) p. 20; see also Land Enquiry Committee, *The Land. Vol. 1. Rural* (1913).

13. *The Times*, 3 May 1908; PGA 9 Edw VII c. 44, Housing, Town Planning etc. Act 1909; see also *The Times*, 28 April 1906 and HC Bill 1906 [9], Housing of the Working Classes Amendment Bill.

14. B. R. Mitchell and P. Deane, *Abstract of British Historical Statistics* (CUP 1962) pp. 240 and 344–5; D. K. Sheppard *The Growth and Role of UK Financial Institutions* (Methuen 1971) p. 170.

15. PRO HLG 29/96 (Asquith to Burns, 28 February 1907); see also PP 1906 HC 376 ix, 'Report and Special Report from the Select Committee on the Housing of the Working Classes Amendment Bill', p. 29.

16. PRO HLG 29/96 (Adrian to Provis, 7 November 1907 and Draft of Bill 207–1, 16 March 1907).

17. PRO HLG 29/96 (Provis to Thring, 11 December 1907).

18. PRO HLG 29/96 (Draft of a Town Planning Bill February 1907).

19. *Municipal Journal* vol. xx (23 December 1911) pp. 1207–8; HC Bill 1911 [385], A Bill to provide for the better application and enforcement of the Housing of the Working Classes Act.

20. 59 HC Deb, 20 March 1914 col 2391. As reintroduced in 1913, the Bill divided the £1 million grant equally between rural and urban areas, but the urban grant was available only for action under Parts I and II, not under Part III. See PRO HLG 29/107 (LGB Memorandum on the Housing of the Working Classes Bill 1913).

21. 35 HC Deb, 15 March 1912, col. 1416; see also *The History of Housing Reform*, p. 32.

22. PRO CAB 37/120 no. 72 (Asquith speech, 9 December 1913); see also H. V. Emy, 'The land campaign', in A. J. P. Taylor (ed.), *Lloyd George: Twelve Essays* (1971) pp. 35–68; and B. B. Gilbert, 'David Lloyd George: The reform of British land-holding and the budget of 1914', *Historical Journal*, vol. xxi no. 1 (1978) pp. 117–41.

23. 62 HC Deb, 4 May 1914, cols 56–94 (Lloyd George).

24. HLL Samuel Papers A44 (speech at Sheffield, 14 May 1914).

25. Cornes, *Modern Housing in Town and Country*, p. 7.

26. *Municipal Journal*, vol. xxiii (24 April 1914) pp. 499–500.

27. W. Thompson, *The Housing Handbook* (1903) p. 193; Cornes, *Modern Housing in Town and Country*, pp. 91–5; J. N. Tarn, *Five Per Cent Philanthropy* (CUP 1973) pp. 56–9.

28. *Journal of the Royal Institute of British Architects* vol. xvi 3rd series (1909) p. 420.

29. LCC, Minutes of Proceedings, 18 May 1909.
30. *The Builder*, vol. cv no. 3691 (31 October 1913) pp. 451–2; for a discussion of Old Oak, see M. Swenarton, 'London's housing history', *The Architects' Journal*, vol. CLXXII no. 33 (13 August 1980), pp. 299–300.
31. The Housing of the Working Classes Acts 1890 to 1909, *Memorandum with respect to the Provision and Arrangement of Houses for the Working Classes* (1913).
32. *The Times*, 3 May 1908; see also PP 1914 Cd 7610 xxxviii, p. lxix; and J. S. Nettlefold, *Practical Housing* (1908).
33. Thompson, *Housing Handbook*, p. 128.
34. *Municipal Journal*, vol. XXIII (24 April 1914) pp. 499–500.
35. Land Enquiry Committee, *The Land. Vol. 11. Urban* (1914) p. 209.
36. PRO CAB 37/116 no. 58 ('Rural land' by W. Runciman, September 1913).
37. 59 HC Deb, 20 March 1914, col. 2458 (H. Samuel).
38. See HLL Lloyd George Papers C 2/1–4/– and Seebohm Rowntree Papers (University of York) LEC 22.
39. PRO CAB 41/34 no. 11 (27 March 1913).
40. PP 1913 Cd 6708 xv, 'Report of the Departmental Committee appointed by the President of the Board of Agriculture and Fisheries to inquire into and report as to Buildings for Small Holdings in England and Wales, together with Abstract of the Evidence, Appendices, and a series of Plans and Specifications', paragraph 14; see also B. Parker and R. Unwin. 'The cheap cottage: What is really needed', *The Garden City*, vol. 1 no. 4, (July 1905) pp. 55–8.
41. PP 1914 Cd 7328 xi, 'Annual Report of Proceedings under the Small Holdings and Allotments Acts 1908 and 1910 ... for the year 1913. Part I. Small Holdings', p. 8; Advisory Committee on Rural Cottages, *Report of the Committee Appointed by the President of the Board of Agriculture and Fisheries to Consider and Advise the Board on Plans, Models, Specifications and Methods of Construction for Rural Cottages and Outbuildings* (1915).
42. P. Wilding. 'Towards Exchequer subsidies for housing 1906–1914', *Social and Economic Administration*, vol. VI (1972) p. 3.
43. PRO T1/11838/25107. I am much indebted to Meta Zimmeck for this reference.
44. *The Times*, 16 February 1910 and 29 March 1910. For Unwin's engagement by the Admiralty see PRO T1/11838/25107 no. 4444.
45. PRO CAB 37/120 no. 67 (Admiralty memorandum on housing of government employees).
46. PRO T1/11838/25107 no. 16506 (Bradbury to Masterman, 24 April 1914).
47. PRO T1/11838/25107 no. 7665 (Admiralty to Treasury, 8 April 1914).
48. PRO T1/11838/25107 no. 16506 (Bradbury to Masterman, 24 April 1914).
49. PRO T1/11838/25107 no. 7665 (Admiralty to Treasury, 8 April 1914).
50. PRO T1/11838/25107 no. 7665 (Runciman to Churchill, 10 March 1914).
51. PRO CAB 37/120 no. 65 ('Housing of Government Employees', 26 May 1914).
52. HC Bill 1914 [315], Housing Bill.
53. 65 HC Deb, 20 July 1914, col. 13 (Runciman); PGA 4 & 5, Geo V c. 31, Housing Act 1914.

3. *The Wartime Housing Programme*

1. PGA 4 & 5, Geo V c. 52, Housing (no. 2) Act 1914; 65 HC Deb, 8 August 1914, col. 2211 (H. Samuel).
2. *Housing Journal*, vol. XCIX (February 1915) pp. 7–8.

3. Reprinted in *Municipal Journal*, vol. xxiii (28 August 1914) p. 1029.
4. *Housing Journal*, vol. xcix (February 1915) pp. 7–8.
5. *Kentish Independent*, 25 June 1915.
6. PRO T161/68 s5222/1 (War Office to LGB, 30 December 1914). For the facts and figures, see *Official History of the Ministry of Munitions* (12 vols; 1922) vol. 5 part 5, 'Provision for the Housing of Munitions Workers' (hereafter *Official History*), p. 2.
7. C. Addison, *Politics from Within* (1922) pp. 211–12.
8. PRO T132 (Treasury to Ministry of Munitions, 15 June 1915).
9. See the correspondence on this point between the Treasury and the War Office in July–August 1915: PRO T161/68 s5222/2.
10. E. G. Culpin. 'The remarkable application of town-planning principles to the war-time necessities of England', *JAIA*, vol. v no. 4 (1917) p. 157; and 'The community sense', *Garden Cities and Town Planning*, vol. v no. 10 (1915) p. 198. For a fuller treatment, see S. Pepper and M. Swenarton, 'Home front: Garden suburbs for munitions workers 1915 to 1918', *Architectural Review*, vol. clxiii no. 976 (June 1978) pp. 366–75.
11. PRO T161/68 s5222/1 (War Office to LGB, 30 December 1914). This file contains the Woolwich material from December 1914 and January 1915 quoted in this and the following paragraphs.
12. F. Baines, 'A government housing scheme', *Municipal Journal*, vol. xxvi (28 September 1917) p. 947; *Official History*, p. 83.
13. F. Baines. 'The Well Hall housing scheme', *The Builder*, vol. cxviii no. 4037 (18 June 1920) p. 727.
14. *Municipal Journal*, vol. xxiii (11 December 1914) p. 1343. Unwin succeeded Thomas Adams, who had been appointed to the Canadian Conservation Commission.
15. PRO T161/68 s5222/1 (Office of Works to the Treasury, 22 January 1915); *Municipal Journal*, vol. xxvi (28 September 1917) pp. 947 and 956; *Official History*, pp. 83–4; G. Allen, *The Cheap Cottage and Small House* (sixth edn, 1919) p. 19.
16. *Municipal Journal*, vol. xxvii (26 January 1918) p. 448 and vol. xxvi (28 September 1917) p. 947; *Official History*, p. 83. For Roe Green, see PRO T161/191 s17955; *The Builder*, vol. cxiv no. 3909 (4 January 1918) pp. 5–8; *Municipal Journal*, vol. xxvi (23 May 1917) p. 511.
17. C. Sitte, *City Planning According to Artistic Principles* (translated by G. R. Collins and C. C. Collins; 1965) p. 61.
18. PRO Works 22/10/1 ('Sir Frank Baines').
19. PRO MUN 2/2 (Ministry of Munitions Secret Weekly Report, 18 December 1915); 'Eastriggs, an industrial town built by the British Government'. *JAIA*, vol. v no. 10 (1917) pp. 499–514; Addison, *Politics from Within*, p. 153; *Official History*, pp. 68–9; PRO MUN 5/158 (Note on visit to Gretna by G. H. Duckworth, 10 February 1916); MUN 5/96 346.2/1 ('Housing operations in 1915: Report on explosives section' by R. Unwin, 17 December 1915).
20. C. Addison. *Four-and-a-Half Years* (2 vols, 1933–4) pp. 210 and 214.
21. *JAIA*, vol. v no. 10 (1917) p. 502.
22. *JAIA*, vol. v no. 10 (1917) pp. 499–514. See also *Report of the Advisory Committee on Rural Cottages* (1915) pp. 54–5 and 62–3.
23. *Official History*, pp. 73–75.
24. Allen, *The Cheap Cottage and Small House* (1919) p. 70; PRO Reco 1/631 WH 70 ('Gretna Green and Eastriggs' by Mrs Alwyn Lloyd).
25. *JAIA*, vol. v no. 4 (1917) pp. 158–9.

26. C. R. Ashbee, *A Book of Cottages and Little Houses* (1906) pp. 111–13; see also Unwin, *Cottage Plans and Common Sense* (1902).

27. C. H. Reilly. 'The city of the future', *TPR*, vol. I (1910) pp. 193–4. For a detailed examination of the views of the Liverpool group and of the Dormanstown scheme, see S. Pepper and M. Swenarton. 'Neo-Georgian maison-type: The Liverpool School and the architecture of mass housing', *Architectural Review*, vol. CLXVII no. 1002 (August 1980) pp. 87–92.

28. P. Abercrombie, 'The Square House', *TPR*, vol. IV (1913) pp. 35–43; S. C. Ramsey, 'The small house of a hundred years ago', *TPR*, vol. VI (1916) pp. 222–5; L. B. Budden. 'The standardisation of elements of design in domestic architecture', *TPR*, vol. VI (1916) pp. 238–43; S. D. Adshead, 'The standard cottage', *TPR*, vol. VI (1916) pp. 244–9.

29. *TPR*, vol. VI (1916) p. 245.

30. 114 HC Deb, 7 April 1919, col. 1791 (N. Billing), see also F. H. Heath and A. L. Hetherington, *Industrial Research and Development in the UK: a Survey* (1946); and British Standards Association, *50 Years of British Standards* (1951).

31. *The Builder*, vol. CXIV no. 3909 (4 January 1918) p. 5. See also *Municipal Journal*, vol. XXVII (26 April 1918) p. 448.

4. *The Drift of Policy 1916–19*

1. PP 1918 Cd 9087 xxvi, 'Housing in England and Wales. Memorandum by the Housing Advisory Panel of the Ministry of Reconstruction', p. 4.

2. 'LGB Memorandum on Housing and the War', 29 June 1916; quoted in P. B. Johnson, *Land Fit for Heroes. The Planning of British Reconstruction 1916–1919* (University of Chicago Press 1968) pp. 20–21, who gives the reference as [PRO Reco] Box 40 RC27.

3. *Municipal Journal* vol. XXVI (11 May 1917) pp. 447–8.

4. M. I. Cole (ed.) *Beatrice Webb's Diaries 1912–1924* (1952) p. 82; see also K. Middlemas (ed.), *Thomas Jones. Whitehall Diary*, vol. I (OUP 1969) pp. 23–6; and Johnson, *Land Fit for Heroes*, pp. 36–67.

5. PRO Reco I/477 no. 2737 ('Housing in England and Wales' by B. S. Rowntree, May 1917); see also Johnson, *Land fit for Heroes*, p. 65.

6. PRO CAB 24/19 GT 1058 (14 June 1917); see also *Municipal Journal*, vol. XXVI (11 May 1917) pp. 447–8; vol. XXVI (18 May 1917) p. 469; vol. XXVI (25 May 1917) pp. 495–6; and *Housing Journal*, vol. CX (August 1917) pp. 1–5.

7. PRO CAB 23/3 WC 190 (19 July 1917); see also C. J. Wrigley, 'Lloyd George and the Labour Movement' (University of London Ph.D thesis 1973) pp. 295–305.

8. PP 1917–18 Cd 8696 xv 'Summary of the Reports of the Commission of Enquiry into Industrial Unrest by the Rt Hon. G. N. Barnes', p. 6. For the reports see PP 1917–18 Cd 8662–Cd 8669 xv.

9. Cd 8696, pp. 6–7.

10. Reprinted in *Housing Journal*, vol. CX (August 1917) p. 8.

11. *Municipal Journal*, vol. XXVI (3 August 1917) p. 737.

12. PRO T128 (Treasury to LGB, 16 November 1917).

13. *Thomas Jones Diary*, p. 43; see also J. Hinton. *The First Shop Stewards Movement* (George Allen & Unwin 1973) p. 243 *et seq.*

14. Quoted in P. R. Wilding, 'Government and Housing: A Study in the Development of Social Policy 1906–1939' (University of Manchester D.Phil thesis 1970) p. 69, who gives the reference as PRO Reco I/30 part I (letter from LGB to J. T. Davies, November 1917).

15. PRO T128 (Treasury to LGB, 5 January 1918).
16. PRO CAB 24/42 GT 3617 (memorandum on Housing of the Working Classes after the War by Hayes Fisher, February 1918).
17. *The Times*, 1 February 1918; quoted in Hinton, *First Shop Stewards Movement*, p. 261.
18. PRO CAB 24/44 GT 3814 (Committee on Civil Disturbance, 5 March 1918).
19. PRO CAB 24/42 GT 3693 (memorandum by Barnes).
20. PRO CAB 23/5 WC 364 (12 March 1918).
21. *Municipal Journal*, vol. XXVII (22 March 1918) pp. 317 and 319.
22. Addison, *Four-and-a-Half Years*, p. 424.
23. Addison, *Four-and-a-Half Years*, p. 414.
24. PRO CAB 24/44 GT 3803 (memorandum by Addison).
25. *Municipal Journal*, vol. XXVII (27 September 1918) p. 969.
26. PRO CAB 24/71 GT 6497 (memorandum by Geddes, 17 December 1918); see also *Municipal Journal*, vol. XXVII (20 September 1918) pp. 947–8.
27. *Municipal Journal*, vol. XXVII (4 October 1918) p. 991.
28. PRO LAB 2/555/F (DR) 103 (Ministry of Labour memorandum, 22 February 1919).
29. PRO CAB 24/70 GT 6425 (2 December 1918).
30. HLL Lloyd George Papers F/30/3/13 (30 January 1919); quoted in Wrigley, 'Lloyd George and the Labour Movement', p. 383.
31. PRO CAB 23/9 WC 523 (31 January 1919) and WC 527 (6 February 1919).
32. PRO CAB 27/59 (Industrial Unrest Committee); CAB 23/9 WC 525 (4 February 1919).
33. HLL Lloyd George Papers F/30/3/32 (20 March 1919); quoted in Wrigley, 'Lloyd George and the Labour Movement' pp. 413–14.
34. PRO CAB 23/9 WC 520 (28 January 1919); see also CAB 23/9 WC 519 (27 January 1919).
35. PRO CAB 24/111 CP 1830 (2 September 1920); quoted in S. R. Ward. 'Intelligence surveillance of British ex-servicemen 1918–20', *Historical Journal*, vol. XVI no. 1 (1973) p. 179.
36. HLL Lloyd George Papers F/30/3/32 (20 March 1919); quoted in Wrigley, 'Lloyd George and the Labour Movement', pp. 413–14.
37. PRO CAB 23/9 WC 539 (3 March 1919).
38. 114 HC Deb, 8 April 1919, col. 1956 (W. Astor).
39. *The Times*, 13 November 1918; quoted in B. B. Gilbert, *British Social Policy 1914–1939* (Batsford 1970) p. 19.
40. *Municipal Journal*, vol. XXVII (29 November 1918) p. 1165.
41. PP 1919 Cmd 413 xxiv, pp. 173–4 and p. 80.
42. PRO CAB 24/71 GT 6497.
43. PRO HLG 29/122 (Note for Mr Heseltine by W. Wallace).
44. PRO HLG 29/122 (Treasury memorandum on revised LGB proposals).
45. PP 1919 Cmd 413 xxiv, pp. 175–9.
46. PRO CAB 23/9 WC 539 (3 March 1919).
47. PRO CAB 23/9 WC 539 (3 March 1919) and WC 541 (4 March 1919).
48. PRO CAB 27/56 (Housing Bill Committee, 5 March 1919).
49. PRO HLG 29/117 (Press Release, 19 March 1919); *The Times*, 2 April 1919.
50. PRO HLG 29/117 (Notes by Sir A. Symonds for the Second Reading); CAB 27/56 (Housing Bill Committee, 5 March 1919).
51. *The Times* 9 July 1919; see also PP 1919 Cmd 125 xli, 'Housing, Town Planning etc. Bill: Estimate of Probable Expenditure'.

52. PRO HLG 29/117 (Notes by Sir A. Symonds for the Second Reading).
53. Cmd 125.
54. 114 HC Deb, 7 April 1919, col. 1714 (Addison). For slum clearance policy, see *The Times*, 5 February 1919; and PRO HLG 29/116 and HLG 29/122.
55. 114 HC Deb, 8 April 1919, col. 1922 (Sir P. Pilditch).
56. PRO HLG 29/122 (Treasury memorandum on revised LGB proposals); see also HLG 29/117 (Financial Resolution of 14 April 1919); *Housing Journal*, vol. cxvii (1919) p. 9; Reco 1/641 (Draft Report by the Federation of British Industries).
57. PRO HLG 29/122 ('Land Agents Society. Report of Parliamentary Committee on Housing, Town Planning etc. Bill').
58. PRO HLG 29/122 (Land Agents Society Report).
59. PRO HLG 29/117 (Standing Committee A, 1–15 May 1919, New Clauses); see also HLG 29/116 (Committee on Simplification of Town Planning Procedure February 1919).
60. 114 HC Deb, 8 April 1919, col. 1947 (Astor).
61. 114 HC Deb, 7 April 1919, col. 1785 (N. Billing).
62. 114 HC Deb, 7 April 1919, col. 1799 (Captain Ormsby Gore).
63. 114 HC Deb, 7 April 1919, cols 1740 and 1743 (Sir D. Maclean).
64. 114 HC Deb, 7 April 1919, col. 1762 (J. Gilbert).
65. 114 HC Deb, 7 April 1919, col. 1810 (Sir J. Bethell).
66. 114 HC Deb, 7 April 1919, col. 1773 (Pretyman).
67. 114 HC Deb, 7 April 1919, col. 1763 (Gilbert).

5. A New Standard for State Housing

1. PRO Reco 1/624 (LGB observations on Interim Report of Women's Sub-committee, 27 August 1918).
2. The Housing of the Working Classes Acts, 1890 to 1909. *Memorandum with respect to the Provision and Arrangement of Houses for the Working Classes.* 1913; *Memorandum for the use of Local Authorities with respect to the Provision and Arrangement of Houses for the Working Classes* (1917).
3. *TPR*, vol. v (1918–19) pp. 13–20.
4. *The Builder*, vol. cxiv no. 3922 (5 April 1918) p. 207. The conditions for the competition are in PRO Reco 1/634; see also T128/2 (Treasury to LGB, 29 August 1917); Reco 1/624 (LGB to Ministry of Reconstruction, 27 June 1918); Royal Institute of British Architects, *Housing of the Working Classes in England and Wales: Cottage Designs* (1918).
5. *Housing Journal*, vol. ci (August 1915) p. 3.
6. *Housing Journal*, vol. cx (August 1917) p. 2. The Labour Party was relatively slow in taking up housing standards: see Joint Committee on Labour Problems after the War, *A Million New Houses after the War* (1917).
7. Record of First Meeting of Panel Four; quoted in Johnson, *Land Fit for Heroes*, pp. 59–60, who gives the reference as [PRO Reco] Box 40.
8. Minute of Rowntree to Addison (14 September 1917), quoted in Johnson, *Land Fit for Heroes*, p. 90, who gives the reference as PRO Reco/ H69 Box 32.
9. PRO Reco 1/624 ('Interim Report of the Women's Housing Sub-Committee', pp. 16 and 41).
10. PRO Reco 1/624 (Note by the Secretary of the Sub-Committee, 30 August 1918); see also PP 1918 Cd 9166 x, 'Ministry of Reconstruction Advisory Council. Women's Housing Sub-Committee. First Interim Report'.
11. PP 1918 Cd 9191 vii, 'Report of the Committee appointed by the President of the

Local Government Board and the Secretary for Scotland to consider questions of building construction in connection with the provision of dwellings for the working classes in England and Wales, and Scotland, and report upon methods of securing economy and despatch in the provision of such dwellings' (The Tudor Walters Report).

12. *Municipal Journal*, vol. xxvii (15 November 1918) pp. 1119–20; see also vol. xxvii (9 August 1918) p. 817 and PRO Reco 1/624 (LGB Observations 27 August 1918).

13. *Municipal Journal*, vol. xxvii (15 November 1918) pp. 1119–20.

14. PRO Reco 1/631 WH 93 ('Interview with Mr. R. Unwin', 29 July 1918).

15. PRO Reco 1/630 (Women's Housing Sub-Committee, 17 and 18 July 1918, evidence of B. S. Rowntree).

16. Speech of Lloyd George to Liberals at 10 Downing Street, 12 November 1918; reported in *The Times*, 13 November 1918; and quoted in Gilbert, *British Social Policy*, p. 19.

17. PP 1919 Cmd 413 xxiv, '48th Annual Report of the LGB for 1918–1919', p. 174 (Circular of 14 November 1918).

18. PRO CAB 24/71 GT 6497 (memorandum by Geddes, 17 December 1918).

19. 114 HC Deb, 8 April 1919, col. 1895 (LtCol. Royds). Addison acknowledged his debt to the Tudor Walters Report: 114 HC Deb, 7 April 1919, col. 1736.

20. 114 HC Deb, 7 April 1919, cols 1762 (Gilbert) and 1784 (Billing); 114 HC Deb, 8 April 1919, col. 1900 (Tudor Walters); 114 HC Deb, 7 April 1919, col. 1791 (Billing).

21. PRO MH 78/64 (Staff for Housing Department).

22. Local Government Board, *Manual on the Preparation of State-Aided Housing Schemes* (1919) p. 30.

23. S. Pollard, *The Development of the British Economy. Second Edition. 1914–1967* (1969) p. 90.

24. Addison, *Four-and-a-Half Years*, p. 427.

6. *The Cabinet and the Housing Campaign*

1. PP 1918 Cd 9197 vii, 'Report of the Committee appointed by the Minister of Reconstruction to consider the position of the Building Industry after the War'.

2. PRO CAB 27/42 DC 32 (memorandum by Lord Weir, December 1918); see also Johnson, *Land Fit for Heroes*, pp. 249–337.

3. 110 HC Deb, 15 November 1918, col. 3145 (Addison).

4. A. J. P. Taylor, *English History 1914–1945* (Penguin Books 1970) pp. 113–14.

5. PRO CAB 27/42 DC 29 (memorandum by Addison, 3 December 1918).

6. PRO CAB 27/49 (2nd minutes of Demobilisation Committee, 20 December 1918).

7. PRO CAB 27/49 (2nd minutes, 20 December 1918).

8. See PRO HLG 52/61 (Local Authority Contracts).

9. PRO CAB 23/18 c 7 (19) (14 November 1919).

10. PRO CAB 24/89 GT 8272 (memorandum by Horne, 6 October 1919).

11. PRO CAB 24/90 GT 8354 (memorandum by Chamberlain, 16 October 1919).

12. PRO CAB 27/66 CHC FSC 1 (17 November 1919).

13. Addison, *Betrayal of the Slums*, p. 25; PGA 9 & 10 Geo V c. 99, Housing (Additional Powers) Act 1919.

14. HC Bill 1920 [215] and HC Bill 1921 [54].

15. PRO CAB 24/75 GT 6887 (25 February 1919); see also P. K. Clyne. 'Reopening the case of the Lloyd George coalition and the post-war economic transition', *Journal of British Studies*, vol. x no. 1 (1970) pp. 162–75; and S. Howson. 'The

origins of "dear money", 1919–20', *Economic History Review*, second series, vol. XXVII (1974) pp. 88–107.

16. PP 1918 Cd 9182 vii, 'First Interim Report of the Committee on Currency and Foreign Exchanges after the War', paragraphs 16 and 17.

17. 123 HC Deb, 15 December 1919, cols 43–5 (Chamberlain). See also P. J. Grigg, *Prejudice and Judgement* (1948) p. 62.

18. PRO T 154/1 (Treasury to Ministry of Health, 25 July 1919).

19. PRO CAB 27/66 CP 94 (memorandum by Addison, 11 November 1919).

20. PRO CAB 27/66 CHC 2 (15 November 1919).

21. PRO CAB 27/66 CHC FSC 1 (17 November 1919).

22. PRO CAB 23/18 c 8 (19) (20 November 1919).

23. PP 1919 Cmd 444 xxii, 'Interim Report of the Treasury Committee on Housing Finance'.

24. Cmd 444, p. 5.

25. *Municipal Journal*, vol. XXIX (20 February 1920) p. 188.

26. PRO CAB 24/97 CP 545 (memorandum by Addison, 28 January 1920).

27. PRO CAB 24/104 CP 1183 (memorandum by Addison, 29 April 1920).

28. S. Marriner, 'Cash and concrete. Liquidity problems in the mass production of "homes for heroes"', *Business History*, vol. XVIII no. 2 (1976) p. 155.

29. PRO CAB 23/37 (Conference 30, 30 April 1920); *Municipal Journal*, vol. XXIX (20 August 1920) p. 802 and vol. XXIX (19 November 1920) p. 1066.

30. PRO HLG 48/698 (Report of the Housing Finance Advisory Committee 26 April 1921); Howson, 'Origins of dear money', p. 89.

31. PRO HLG 52/881 (3rd meeting, 20 January 1920).

32. PRO CAB 24/119 CP 2532 (memorandum by Addison, 2 February 1921).

33. Figures on completions from PP 1921 Cmd 1446 xiii, p. 58 and PP 1922 Cmd 1713 viii, p. 41; and on costs from PP 1919 Cmd 125 xli and *Municipal Journal*, vol. XXX (1 July 1921) p. 499.

34. PRO CAB 24/92 CP 3 (memorandum by Addison, 27 October 1919).

35. The grant was later increased by £100 and the time-limit extended: *Municipal Journal*, vol. XXIX (14 May 1920) p. 496; PGA 11 & 12 Geo V c. 19, Housing Act 1921.

36. Ministry of Health, *Housing*, vol. 1 (24 November 1919) p. 129.

37. PRO CAB 24/92 CP 3 (memorandum by Addison, 27 October 1919).

38. PRO HLG 52/881 (6th meeting, 10 February 1920).

39. PRO CAB 24/92 CP 73 (memorandum by Chamberlain, 7 November 1919); CAB 23/18 c 8 (19) (20 November 1919).

40. See PRO HLG 52/880 (5th meeting, 25 October 1920) and PP 1921 Cmd 1175 xxviii.

41. Ministry of Health, *Housing*, vol. 1 (10 November 1919) p. 117; PRO HLG 52/881 (Astor Committee, 4th meeting, 26 January 1920).

42. PRO CAB 23/18 c 7 (19) (14 November 1919); *Municipal Journal* vol. XXVIII (19 December 1919) p. 1275 and vol. XXIX (20 February 1920) p. 189; 126 HC Deb, 10 March 1920, col. 1265 (Addison).

43. PRO CAB 27/89 CP 1593 (Report by Chairman of the Housing Committee, 14 July 1920).

44. PRO CAB 27/89 CP 1593.

45. PRO CAB 24/115 CP 2145 (Second Interim Report of the Cabinet Committee on Unemployment, 25 November 1920); *Housing*, vol. II (11 October 1920) pp. 88 and 92; PRO CAB 24/119 CP 2536 (Reply of the NFBTO, 4 February 1921).

46. PRO HLG 52/881 (5th meeting, 3 February 1920).
47. PRO HLG 31/1 (Memorandum to Housing Commissioners no. 34, 21 August 1919); HLG 52/881 (17th meeting, 11 May 1920); *Municipal Journal*, vol. xxix (17 September 1920) p. 879; vol. xxix (29 October 1920) p. 1007; vol. xxix (26 November 1920) p. 1085; vol. xxix (10 December 1920) p. 1125.
48. *Municipal Journal*, vol. xxix (6 February 1920) p. 123; vol. xxix (11 June 1920) p. 579; vol. xxx (7 January 1921) pp. 13–15; vol. xxx (25 February 1921) p. 157.
49. PRO CAB 24/107 CP 1455 (memorandum by Mond, 14 June 1920).
50. *Municipal Journal*, vol. xxix (17 September 1920) p. 875.
51. PP 1921 Cmd 1447 xiii pp. 45–9; PRO HLG 49/5 (memorandum on special methods of construction, 4 May 1921).
52. Bowley, *Housing and the State*, p. 23.
53. Sources of figures: Cmd 1447, p. 44; PRO CAB 24/119 CP 2532; PP 1921 Cmd 1446 xiii, p. 58; PP 1922 Cmd 1713 viii, p. 41.
54. PRO T 161/132 (Notes by A. W. Hurst, 27 June and 8 July 1921).
55. PRO CAB 24/90 GT 8354 (memorandum by Chamberlain, 16 October 1919).
56. PRO CAB 24/106 CP 1330 (memorandum by Chamberlain, 20 May 1920).
57. PRO HLG 68/29 (minute by A. W. Robinson, 30 June 1920).
58. PRO CAB 27/89 (1st Conclusions of Housing Committee, 17 June 1920).
59. PRO CAB 23/38 (Conference 70, 15 December 1920); see also G. D. H. Cole, *A Short History of the British Working Class Movement 1789–1947* (1960) pp. 396–8.
60. S. R. Ward, 'Intelligence surveillance of British ex-servicemen 1918–20', *Historical Journal*, vol. xvi no. 1 (1973) p. 187.
61. PRO CAB 23/22 c 49 (20) (17 August 1920).
62. PRO CAB 23/25 c 23 (21) (18 April 1921).
63. PRO CAB 27/71 FC 52 (note by Chamberlain, 20 November 1920) and CAB 27/71 (28th Conclusions, 29 November 1920).
64. PRO CAB 27/71 FC 66 (memorandum by Addison, 25 January 1921).
65. PRO HLG 68/29 (memorandum to Housing Commissioners no. 85a, 22 February 1921).
66. PRO HLG 68/29 (Chamberlain to Addison, 9 March 1921; Addison to Chamberlain, 11 March 1921); *Municipal Journal*, vol. xxx (20 May 1921) p. 365.
67. HLL Lloyd George Papers F7/4/6, quoted by P. Rowland, *Lloyd George* (1975) p. 538.
68. PRO CAB 23/26 c 55 (21) (29 June 1921).
69. PRO CAB 24/123 CP 2919 (memorandum by Horne, 9 May 1921) and CAB 23/25 c 38 (21) (11 May 1921).
70. PRO CAB 24/125 CP 3067 (memorandum by Mond, 22 June 1921).
71. PRO T 161/132 (Note by Hurst, 27 June 1921).
72. PRO CAB 27/71 (35th Conclusions, 30 June 1921). Gilbert (*British Social Policy*, p. 152) erroneously gives the date of this meeting as 30 January 1921.
73. PRO CAB 23/26 c 58 (21) (11 July 1921).
74. PRO CAB 24/126 CP 3111 (memorandum by Mond, 7 July 1921).
75. PRO CAB 24/126 CP 3133 (Amended Draft Statement of the Minister of Health). 144 HC Deb, 14 July 1921, cols 1483–5 (Mond).

7. *The Ministry and the Housing Campaign*

1. PRO CAB 24/71 GT 6497 (memorandum by Geddes, 17 December 1918).
2. A. Sayle, *The Houses of the Workers* (1924) p. 82.

3. Ministry of Health, *Standard Specification for Cottages* (D82) (August 1919).
4. *Municipal Journal*, vol. XVIII (2 May 1919) p. 431.
5. PRO HLG 31/1 (Memoranda to Housing Commissioners no. 21, 4 July 1919, and no. 76, 16 December 1919).
6. PRO CAB 24/93 (memorandum by Mond, 11 November 1919).
7. Local Government Board, *Manual on the Preparation of State-Aided Housing Schemes* (1919) (hereafter *Manual*) p. 4.
8. *Housing*, vol. I (27 September 1919) p. 84.
9. *Municipal Journal*, vol. XXX (5 August 1921) p. 585; PP 1922 Cmd 1713 viii, 'Third Annual Report of the Ministry of Health', pp. xi and 46.
10. *Manual*, p. 4.
11. *Manual*, p. 21; see also PP 1921 Cmd 1447 xiii, 'Report of the Departmental Committee on the High Cost of Building Working Class Dwellings', p. 9; *Housing*, vol. I (8 December 1919) pp. 146–7 and vol. I (22 December 1919) pp. 162–3.
12. R. Unwin, 'The Town Extension Plan', *Manchester University Lectures* no. 14 (1912); *Manual*, p. 5; *Housing*, vol. I (12 April 1920) pp. 267 and 269.
13. *Housing*, vol. II (30 August 1920) pp. 43 and 56.
14. *Housing*, vol. II (30 August 1920) pp. 42–43.
15. *Housing*, vol. I (19 July 1919) p. 6.
16. *Housing*, vol. I (19 July 1919) p. 6.
17. *Housing*, vol. I (10 November 1919) p. 122.
18. *Housing*, vol. I (24 May 1920) p. 303; see also vol. I (8 December 1919) p. 145.
19. *Housing*, vol. I (24 May 1920) p. 303.
20. PRO HLG 68/29 (Memorandum to Housing Commissioners no. 85a, 22 February 1921); see also HLG 68/29 (Note on Discussion, 9 December 1920).
21. PRO HLG 52/880 (23rd meeting, 18 April 1921).
22. *Municipal Journal* vol. XXX (9 September 1921) p. 684 and vol. XXX (7 October 1921) p. 734.
23. PRO HLG 29/116 (G 235 memorandum by Addison, February 1919, Appendix B).
24. PRO HLG 31/1 (memorandum to Housing Commissioners no. 15, 5 June 1919).
25. PP 1919 Cmd 125 xli; PP 1921 Cmd 1447 xiii, p. 44.
26. PRO HLG 31/1 (memorandum to Housing Commissioners no. 28, 30 July 1919).
27. Cmd 1447, p. 7.
28. PRO CAB 27/66 CP 94 (memorandum by Addison, 11 November 1919).
29. PRO HLG 52/870 (2nd meeting, 26 November 1919); HLG 52/881 (3rd meeting, 20 January 1920; 9th meeting, 24 February 1920; 14th meeting, 30 March 1920); Ministry of Health, *Type Plans and Elevations of Houses designed by the Ministry of Health in connection with State-Aided Housing Schemes* (1920).
30. *Municipal Journal*, vol. XXIX (7 May 1920) p. 474.
31. PRO HLG 31/1 (memorandum to Housing Commissioners no. 21, 4 July 1919).
32. *Type Plans and Elevations*, p. 1.
33. The ledger, kept by S. Pointon Taylor, is in the possession of S. Pepper. Contracts for 115 307 houses were entered into by local authorities between 31 March 1920 and 31 March 1921: Cmd 1446, p. 58.
34. *Housing*, vol. II (14 February 1921) p. 229; see also PRO HLG 31/2 (memorandum to Housing Commissioners no. 136, 25 June 1921).
35. City of York, Housing Committee Minutes, 19 December 1921; *Municipal Journal*, vol. XXX (13 May 1921) p. 355.
36. *Municipal Journal*, vol. XXX (19 August 1921) p. 617; vol. XXX (7 October 1921) p. 734; vol. XXX (2 December 1921) p. 908; vol. XXXII (19 January 1923) p. 37.
37. *Municipal Journal*, vol. XXXI (7 July 1922) p. 487.

8. House-building in London and York

1. B. S. Rowntree, *Portrait of a City's Housing* (edited with an introduction and comments by R. L. Reiss; 1945) p. 9.

   The accounts in this chapter are largely drawn from the official records of the LCC and the York City Council, which are not cited individually. For London the principal sources are: LCC Minutes of Proceedings, 1907–1922; Housing of the Working Classes Committee, 1918–1919; Housing Committee, 1919–1923; Building and Development Sub-Committee, 1919–1922; collection of LCC house plans and estate layouts (all at Greater London Council County Hall). Also LCC, *Housing: with Particular Reference to Post-war Housing Schemes* (1928) and PRO HLG 29/112. For York the principal sources are: York City Council Minutes, 1914–1924; Health Committee Minutes, 1914–1920; Housing Committee Minutes, 1920–1923; Annual Reports of the Medical Officer of Health and of the City Engineer and Surveyor, 1912–1923; collection of house plans and layouts (all in the City Archives, York City Library).

2. See M. Swenarton, 'Having a bath. English domestic bathrooms c. 1890–1940', in Design Council, *Leisure in the Twentieth Century. History of Design* (1977) pp. 92–9.

3. *Municipal Journal*, vol. XXIX (5 March 1920) p. 241. See also Ministry of Health, General Housing Memorandum no. 8 'Financial Assistance to Local Authorities', October 1919.

4. *Municipal Journal*, vol. XXVIII (7 November 1919) p. 104; *Annual Report of the York and District Trades and Labour Council for the year 1920*, pp. 1 and 3.

5. See *Housing*, vol. 1 (24 November 1919) p. 133 and vol. 1 (29 March 1920) p. 255; *Garden Cities and Town Planning*, vol. XI (1921) pp. 63–6 and 234–6; *Country Life*, vol. LVIII (31 October 1925) pp. 680–1; Waddilove, *One Man's Vision*, pp. 17–18 and 25–6.

6. B. S. Rowntree, *Poverty and Progress* (1941) pp. 231–2.

7. A. Sayle, *The Houses of the Workers* (1924) p. 140.

Conclusion

1. E. Halévy, *The Era of Tyrannies. Essays on Socialism and War* (translated by R. K. Webb; 1967) p. 151.

2. 114 HC Deb, 7 April 1919, col. 1762 (Gilbert).

3. Chairman of Housing Sub-Committee of Grimsby Town Council, April 1919; quoted in O. A. Hartley, 'Housing Policy in Four Lincolnshire Towns 1919–1959' (University of Oxford D.Phil thesis 1969) p. 103.

4. M. Castells, *The Urban Question. A Marxist Approach* (Edward Arnold 1976; French original 1972) p. 439.

5. A. Hooper, 'The political economy of housing in Britain', *International Journal of Urban and Regional Research*, vol. II no. 1 (1978) p. 182.

6. Castells, *The Urban Question*, p. 158.

7. M. Bowley, *Housing and the State 1919–1944* (1945); C. G. Pickvance, 'Housing: Reproduction of capital and reproduction of labour power: Some recent French work', *Antipode* vol. VIII no. 1 (1976) pp. 58–68.

8. Castells, *The Urban Question*, p. 468; S. Merrett, *State Housing in Britain* (Routledge & Kegan Paul 1979) p. 101.

9. A. Forty, 'Lorenzo of the underground', *London Journal*, vol. V no. 1 (1979) pp. 113–19; M. Swenarton, 'Should we stop exhibiting design?', *London Journal*, vol. VI no. 1 (1980) pp. 111–15.

Index

For Product Safety Concerns and Information please contact our EU
representative GPSR@taylorandfrancis.com
Taylor & Francis Verlag GmbH, Kaufingerstraße 24, 80331 München, Germany

www.ingramcontent.com/pod-product-compliance
Lightning Source LLC
Chambersburg PA
CBHW070410270326
41926CB00014B/2774